SOMETHING I SAID

A Collection of Columns

Susie Berta

Boll Weevil Press

2023

Something I Said ©2023 by Susie Berta
All rights reserved.

Published by Boll Weevil Press, bollweevilpress.com

Library of Congress CIP data
Berta, Susie
Something I Said / Susie Berta.
1. Essays
814 — dc22

   ISBN: 978-1-7334670-7-0

Also available from Boll Weevil Press
   The Veterinarian's Wife, Susie Berta
   Another Farewell to the Theatre, Marc Honea
   Lichtenbergianism: procrastination as a creative strategy, Dale Lyles
   Flies at the Well: The Trial of the Killer John Wallace, Jim Halliday / W. Jeff
      Bishop
   Personality Matters, Mr. Personality

Something I Said was designed by Dale Lyles. Front cover design by Susie Berta.

Dedicated to Rick and our sweet family. Always.

"I know you do."

Rick and Susie
"The Queen and the Maytag Man"
The last Halloween to have fun before Covid

I'm an author/writer from a small town. While I'm not syndicated, or famous, or among NYT best sellers or prize winners (yet) I've published my memoir, written lots of columns, and now I've published another book, this one.

This book is a compilation of newspaper columns I wrote over the last couple of years for my local newspaper, The Newnan Times Herald, in the lovely southern town of Newnan, Georgia.

Starting out as a food and garden columnist in 2020, I was promoted to weekly Opinion columnist in 2022. I thought of it as a huge vote of confidence by the publishers Clay Neely and Beth Neely, and since it meant I could write whatever my heart desired, I was thrilled with the possibilities.

Actually, they had already let me write anything as a food and garden columnist, and I had turned those columns into a hybrid food, garden, and opinion column. Clay said the food columns I was cranking out had raised the bar for normal, run of the mill newspaper food columns. Then, I guessed, on the strength of the columns I was already writing, I was asked to consider writing for the Opinion page. They needed a strong, female voice, he said, and he asked me if I would consider it. I couldn't say yes fast enough. Let me go whole hog and write about anything and everything and how I felt about all of it? Yes, please! And so they did. And so I did. And I am forever grateful.

As a result, the columns in this book cover a wide range of topics, from my food column days in 2020 right into my Opinion columns, all the way to August, 2023. Some are funny. Some dead serious. All, ahem, are entertaining in my book (see what I did there?).

A few of my columns contain excerpts from my memoir, *The Veterinarian's Wife* published earlier by Boll Weevil Press in January, 2022. I took the chance to shamelessly publicize my own book a time or two in my newspaper columns, and I'm not sorry. I got great responses, and book sales, too. Maybe, you, too, will consider buying it once you've read this book of columns. Everywhere books are sold, by the way.

I am a very happy fish swimming in a small literary pond, and I'm having a great time. I have swum around and around for several years in these waters, now, and I hope you'll share my enthusiasm for the columns you are about to read in this book.

Come on in. The water's fine.
Cannonball!
Susie Berta
Summer, 2023

Contents

Cooking Essentials and How to Cook a Roast 3
Eureka Moment in the Garden 7
The Martha Effect: Baked Brie with Raspberries & Almonds 12
Umami State of Mind, Not Your Mama's Irish Stew 16
Blessings, Banes, Good Books, Tasty Bites, and Carpe Diem 20
Love and Holidays in the Time of Covid 30
Happy Anew Year 39
Thirty Years 43
When Life Gives You Lemons 47
Beauty and the Beast 52
A Culinary Koan 59
Beat the Summer Heat 63
Peachy Keen Road Trip 72
Waiting for Cobbler 76
Still Falling For Fall 81
Adventures with Chicken Skin 84
For the Love of a Southern February 89
Rupert Brooke, My Mother, and Me 92
For Better or Worse 96
The Torch is Passed, Over and Over Again 100
Just a Suggestion 104
Truths, Lies, and Crosswords 108
Things We Keep, Things We Don't 112
Perspective 116
Bright Lights, Dark Skies 120
It's That Time of Year 125
What is Love? 129
Past, Present, Future 133
Old 136
What Fresh Hell is This? 141
Making It Work 146
A Man and A Woman 151
Mayday! 155
Orly And Other Ghosts, A Two Part Series 160
Last Stand 166
App-solution or App-rehension? 170
Who's On First in the Garden? 173
Words Sting 176
Sshh! 179
Summer Lament 182
Positivities 185

The Nerve!	188
What's Up With That?	191
The Myth of Mayberry	194
Solace in Sacred Spaces	198
Nostalgia, an Old Timer's Curse	201
Ads Infinitum!	204
You Are Here	207
Something Good: The Three A's	211
Loneliness is a mugger. Choice is the answer	214
Be Like Boyd	217
Grown-Up	220
The Things We Tell Ourselves	223
The Season	226
Remembering Nola	229
Letting Go	232
Alchemy and Insight	235
Words	238
The Holidays	241
Christmas, 1962	243
Happy New Year. Oh Frabjous Day!	246
Telling the Truth and Getting Real	249
Clutter	252
Becoming	255
Worth Something	259
Simple Gifts	262
Lessons on the long trip home	265
Roads and Razors	268
Open the Pod Bay Doors HAL	271
Too Soon	274
Thoughts	278
Into the Woods	281
Daylilies and Cherry Trees	283
Decisions Take You Forward	286
Being Here, There, and Everywhere	289
New Resolve	292
Random Thoughts	294
Me and Chat GPT	297
Spring Lament	300
Thoughts on Love and Mothers Day	302
What Century Is This?	305
One Man's Dream is Another Man's Worst Nightmare	308
Who Are You?	312
52 Years	315

Whodunnit?	318
Swiftly Flow the Years	321
Rumi's Notion	325
The Joys of Travel	329
Sunday Lessons	333
Scary	336
Car 54 Where You At	339
You Could Be What?	342

FOOD & GARDEN COLUMNS

2 — Something I Said

Cooking Essentials and How to Cook a Roast
8-26-2020

You can tell a lot about a woman by the way she handles 3 things: microwaves, hormones, and water retention; also by her answer to the question, "Name the 3 things you can't live without when you cook?"

If your list starts with Hamburger Helper, then bless your heart.

Here's my list: Kitchen Bouquet, Jane's Krazy Salt, and good quality meat. OK, throw in lemon juice. Add a sharp knife (do not throw the knife). So that's five. Microwaves are good but not essential, unless I'm reheating a meal saved in the refrigerator, or preparing Mac n Cheese in those little ready to nuke cups for my kindergarten grandson, or reheating my coffee that went cold before I could finish it because I was fixing Mac n Cheese for my grandson. Ok, I take it back. Make microwaves number 6, and while I'm thinking about it, a properly calibrated oven for roasting and baking. We're up to 7 now, you say. Fine so be it. Wait. A reliable, oven-safe digital meat thermometer!

That is my list and I'll stand by it: **My ~~Three Five Six Seven~~ Eight Essentials for Cooking**. If I decide to throw another one or two in, (I'm sorely tempted. Pots and pans? Equipment? Utensils? Where does it stop?) I'll let you know, and I'll stand by that list, too.

Meanwhile, here's my recipe for how to cook a roast, proven over decades of Christmas dinners and special occasions. You can ask my dinner guests, especially my brother who, I swear, travels all the way from DC every Christmas just so he can steal the first piece of deliciously unctuous, crispy crackling off the roast before Christmas dinner. I've even been known to give the recipe, tied with a bow onto a new roasting pan, as wedding gifts.

This is the best roast ever. Your efforts will be rewarded. And you can do this for any special occasion, not just holidays. Say, my birthday. Or yours. Tell me what time you're serving, and I'll be there. (Also, if we're still social distancing, I can sit on your porch outside if necessary, and vice versa).

HOW TO COOK A (STANDING RIB) ROAST

- 1 bodacious prime beef "standing rib" roast: An expensive cut of meat. They do go on sale. And they freeze. Yes, there are other cuts of beef for roasts, and they are swell for certain things, but this one is our family's traditional, dee-luxe, holiday/special occasion roast.
- Tell the butcher you want him to cut you a fresh standing rib roast. To make carving easier, tell him to cut the chine bone and he will wrap it back up for you with string like new, in a nice package for roasting. Get it at least 3 ribs thick or else why bother? You want leftovers for sandwiches. You know the dogs will want the bones. Take note of the weight of your roast.
- Kitchen Bouquet Browning & Seasoning Sauce (look for it in a 4 oz brown bottle where you find the A-1). No substitutes. Please, I beg you.
- Original Mixed-Up Salt from Jane's Krazy Mixed Up Seasonings (look for it in the herbs and spices aisle). Again, it's a proprietary ingredient. No substitutes or I won't be responsible for the outcome).
- Garlic powder or garlic salt, your choice

- Parsley flakes (fresh it makes you feel better, but dried is fine. Seriously, dried parsley is so déclassé, I know, but it works. Plus, at Christmas, good luck marching out to the parsley bed and finding anything worth using. Publix is always an option.)

INSTRUCTIONS:
1. Preheat oven to 450° (yes 450. I'll explain in a minute).
2. Let the roast sit out on the counter for 15-20 minutes to get the chill off. Roasting time will be more accurate this way. Just be sure the big dogs aren't around.
3. Unwrap the roast and give it a rinse under the faucet. Dry it off and put the roast, FAT SIDE UP on a rack sprayed with Pam in a roasting pan sprayed with same.
4. Slather Kitchen Bouquet all over top, bottom, and sides of the roast with your hands. Messy but totally important. This will seal in the juices. You will have to wash your hands and the bottle of Kitchen Bouquet when you're done, but trust me, it's worth the mess.
5. Sprinkle the Krazy Salt liberally all over the roast and by liberally, I mean more than you would expect to be appropriate. Cover all the surfaces well.
6. Sprinkle the garlic powder or garlic salt the same way.
7. Sprinkle the parsley flakes, using a lighter hand. Still, don't skimp.
8. Pat that roast all over with your hands to get all the sprinkled goodness well-stuck (not an official culinary term). Messy again, so you'll need to wash your hands again.
9. Put about ¼–½ cup water in the bottom of the pan just to keep the pan from smoking til you get fat drippings going.
10. Put the whole thing in your preheated 450° oven. This high temp will help seal in the juices, but you must leave it at this high setting only briefly or you'll have smoking, expensive black coal for dinner. DON'T LEAVE. JUST STAND THERE AND HAVE A SIP (OR TWO) OF WINE. TURN THE HEAT

DOWN TO 350° AFTER 5 MINUTES!

11. Cook beef at 350° for 15–20 minutes per pound for a beautiful medium-rare prime rib (internal temp 140°). Always estimate cooking time on the early side if you don't have an oven-safe meat thermometer. You can use your analog thermometer to check periodically, and sometimes you might need another few minutes. Watch it like a hawk.
12. For the love of Elvis, don't overcook it. That would be a mortal sin.

NOTE: In emergencies, you can actually cook a roast like this from a frozen state. I don't recommend it, but it can be done. Just add some cooking time. You will certainly want to use the meat thermometer later on as it cooks. Be prepared to possibly double the cooking time. Still, 140° internal temp is your goal. Guessing can be difficult, and the anxiety just isn't any fun.

When the roast is done, remove it from the oven and let it sit on the rack for at least 10–15 minutes before messing with it. This is called "letting the meat rest." I think it's good for the cook to rest during this time, too, if possible. Time for another glass of wine and one last bite of hors d'oeuvres. You will also want to stand near the roast to guard it from marauders who are after their first greedy pull of crackling off your masterpiece.

Then, remove the roast to a carving board, carve some thick, juicy slices, and enjoy.

GRILLING: This can be done on a grill if you don't want to heat up your kitchen in the summer. Make sure the grill has a heat calibration system, and controllable heat areas. You'll do everything the same in a pan on a rack except cook it over the "cool" side of the grill (it's not actually cool, it just means it's the side that isn't over the grill's direct flame).

ALSO: Pork Roast can be done exactly the same, except sprinkle and rub lots of Dill Weed into the roast in addition. Cook pork for 30 minutes per pound. Use your meat thermometer, too.

Eureka Moment in the Garden
9-12-2020

It was once a lovely, shady spot in our backyard: two small dogwood trees, surrounded by lush green ivy ground cover, neatly kept within a curving bed line at the grassy sod on one side, and at the rock wall that borders the woodland path on the other side. For years it was this way. I grew accustomed. Comfortable. Familiar. Another plus? Low maintenance!

Then things started changing. The dogwoods got sick and spindly; their branches produced fewer leaves, and those that remained were yellowing and falling. We pulled all the ivy underneath, hoping to clear the roots of any competition for food and water. We mulched. We fed them with tree spikes. All to no avail. The dogwoods continued to struggle and die.

So we made plans. The dogwoods came down, leaving behind a glaring, bare slash of shadeless ground that was once tranquil and lush. The sudden starkness and a shocking unfamiliarity put me off-kilter. What to do? We dreamed of a lovely patio pad, a place to put chairs and a fire pit in the fall and spring. In summer, we would lay out our grandson's inflatable kiddie pool there. I was envisioning the plantings around our patio addition, which would provide what I call the all-important "nestle factor." (nestle factor: not an official landscaping term but coined by me as my personal landscaping criteria.) We could do this ourselves, we decided with confidence, and so we eagerly got string and wood and started staking off the spot.

Enter reality. The slope of the land was steeper than we had realized, and the area needed significant leveling if we were to relax someday on a patio here; enough leveling to require major digging, substantial footings, and more manpower than we were willing or, let's face it, able, to dedicate. This dream was no longer a quick DIY weekend project. We called a landscaper to bid on the project. When the bid came in at triple our max budget, our vision slid straight into the dumper. We could not afford our dream.

When I am forced to take a philosophical approach—when I don't get what I want—I am given two options:

1. Pout, fume, abandon all hope, take my ball, and go home.

2. Pout and fume–or not (always a choice) and/or hang on and move on, opening my mind to exploring other options.

Defeat? Hopelessness? Nope. I chose Door Number 2, which might not produce ideas right away. But giving myself permission to accept that an idea will come, whenever it comes, opens up the channels. Being closed off, angry, and inflexible creates nothing but an impossible void surrounded by impenetrable walls, where creativity is neither welcome nor possible.

I decided to "be with it" for a while. I had no idea what to do with our bare spot, the spot that made me itch with discomfort and squint from the glare. But I let the old heart and brain perk while giving myself permission to embrace the change forced upon me. I was "ready to receive." Several weeks passed as I called on my patience yet again and studied that spot. Each time I came up with nothing, I reminded myself this would be a process, and it would take what it takes. I had to trust in the process.

Then, after the emerald lawn smelled of fresh grass clippings, the backyard was clean, and the day crystal blue, I took my place on the sunny bench across the yard from "the spot." This time something shifted in my brain, dropping a piece of a puzzle into place.

As though for the first time, I noticed the familiar stones that had been serving as single-file border stones on the grassy edge. I walked over and starting chucking the rocks into the center of the bed. I wasn't sure why yet, but I knew I didn't want that stone border anymore. Dismantling the barrier of stones was transformational, clearing a place in my mind for the next step. How this one simple act could invigorate me in an instant astonished me. I hadn't realized I had been holding my breath all this time, waiting for an all-encompassing answer, when what I needed was the just first step. Nothing more. Chucking those rocks opened up room to breathe and see. I initially considered the pile of discarded stones sitting in the center to be a temporary repository. Then the next step came to me; another puzzle piece fell into place in my brain. A cairn? Really? Yep. That's it. A cairn.

I approached the pile of stones, examining each one, stacking and carefully balancing them like a totem. It became the funkiest sculpture, and it was merely the most mind-bending, satisfying, Zen-like artistic endeavor I had undertaken in recent memory.

This was the ticket. So I created a spot where nothing is forever; nothing is constant, and everything is changing; a place that invites, even requires, interaction. This describes what gardeners do, anyway. Nothing we plant is forever. We interact, move plants, and create spaces. So I guess this space is no different in that way. But coming to this solution with this space became a new, revelatory process, most likely because it involves not only input from me as creator-gardener but also from anyone who visits my garden.

Rarely—ok, never—have I ever created a bed with the thought that any old soul passing by had permission to dismantle it and create their own vision. No, this spot is unique. The simple cairn I built will stand until someone—anyone—walks by and makes their own version with the stones available there. Or until the wind blows it down, or a squirrel dislodges a rock, and it all tumbles into a heap. Whatever happens, it's interactive, meditative, ever-changing fun, destined for change, an opportunity waiting to happen, a lesson in letting go, expecting and embracing transformation in ways I cannot predict by starting over, re-building, finding balance.

Cairns have an ancient history, existing for diverse reasons. Cairns mark burial places; stand as markers to travelers, pointing the way to safety or home; represent symbols of friendship and hope; serve as metaphors for spiritual beings. These rock formations,

sculptures, if you will, stand balanced, without benefit of cement, and exist everywhere, from Scotland to Sedona. And now, in my backyard.

I installed small starter plantings that will grow and nestle around the bed and into the sunny landscape, and I have my first cairn as the seed from which more ideas will germinate. Oh look, here's one: lay stones as a hardscape ground cover around the cairn, serving as an anchor and a bridge between stone and natural plant materials. If I've learned anything from this experience, decisions take you forward, and they don't always have to be all-encompassing. Just one decision will knock down a roadblock, and you're on your way past it, one decision at a time.

I recently re-watched my DVD of one of my favorite musical productions, *Sunday in the Park with George*, based on the painter,

Seurat, and his revolutionary painting, "La Grande Jatte." It's no coincidence the music and lyrics from that show resonated within me during this whole adventure, reminding me of the elements to consider: Order. Design. Tension. Color. Balance. Light. An artist and a gardener must find their own way. It starts with the willingness. So, I am moving on. I am exploring the light. I am getting through, and it is something new and different of my own. One decision at a time.

Thanks be to the universe. Eureka. I'm on my way.

The Martha Effect: Baked Brie with Raspberries & Almonds
9-23-2020

    I don't know about you, but I get genuine pleasure in surprising guests with a fabulous, upscale appetizer that looks and tastes like you worked a lot harder than you did. Baked brie with raspberries and almonds is one of those recipes that has what I call "The Martha Effect." It looks every bit like Martha Stewart's skillful, professional handiwork, and tastes top-notch, so much so that Martha herself could've executed it and brought it to the party. Except it was just lil' ol' you in your non-state-of-the-art kitchen without a single overpriced Le Creuset pot or shiny All-Clad pan to your name, and it was easy peasy. While you won't rake in royalties from a tv show, and you have no cookbook deals, you will get praise and admiration from your family and friends.

    If you have a perverse need to over-gild the lily, consider the flour trick. Flick a bit of flour on your apron, which you will remove with a flair the moment people walk in. *"Oh, Quelle Surprise!"* you'll demur, letting them get a glimpse of the evidence on your apron. They'll see how hard you have worked to give them the best in culinary artistry! *Why, yes, I ground the wheat and stomped the grapes myself, but, oh pshaw, it was worth all the trouble to entertain you!* Or you can relax and be yourself, confident that this hors d'oeuvre will do all the bragging for you.

People will swoon. It's as beautiful as it is delicious. Guests will flatter you and tell you in sincere wonderment that they couldn't possibly make this grand, mysterious thing. Well, I'm here to tell you it ain't that hard. Yes, they can. And so can you. If you really are Martha Stewart quality, then good for you. But, like most of us, if you aren't anywhere close to Martha's level, people will think you are every bit her equal. Rejoice and be glad for the Martha Effect! You are smart enough to make a simple, delicious recipe and present it like a queen. So for your next hen party at your friend's house (someday, sans pandemic), volunteer to bring a baked brie. If the party's at your home (someday, sans pandemic), sprinkle some flour and bake a brie!

- ½ cup raspberry preserves — In my dotage, I prefer seedless... less dental hoopla without all those pesky seeds. But you can certainly use the real thing if you don't have seed issues. And then, while you're at it, you can throw in a couple of fresh or frozen raspberries with the preserves. Have fun!
- A handful of sliced almonds — Toasted lightly in a small pan with butter is nice. Be aware they toast fast, so don't walk away. Keep them stirred and remove when lightly browned. Don't over-brown them, or they'll taste bitter and worse, burnt. Toasting the almonds is totally optional, however. I skip the toasting all the time if I'm in a hurry. Or I am feeling lazy. Either of which is often.
- 1 frozen puff pastry sheet - NOT phyllo, or pie crust, or puff pastry shells. PUFF PASTRY SHEETS, people, *sheets*! I use Pepperidge Farm. In a long box. 2/box. Freezer section.
- 1 round Brie cheese - I like Ile de France, and I get the larger one, about 13 oz and approximately 6" or so in diameter. Note: Please resist the temptation to purchase anybody's grocery store, ready-to-go, pre-packaged Baked Brie... um, not EVEN in the ballpark. You'll lose Martha points, too, guaranteed.

Seriously, stick with the plan—worth the effort.
- 1 large egg, beaten well, in a small cup or bowl (for glaze)
- Crackers (I like Wheat Thins!), or baguette slices
- Fruit as garnish: grapes - seedless red and green, washed, dried, and clipped into small sections for your guests' convenience. Also, thin apple wedges are nice. Fan them out amongst the grapes. And whole strawberries are lovely for color, flavor, and texture, too.

Preheat oven to 400°.

1. Thaw the frozen puff pastry sheet on the counter for about 30 minutes or until it unfolds easily without breaking at the seams. Then unfold it onto a baking sheet. If you just happen to have a fancy, round dish made especially for baking brie, good for you. Use that! If not, the baking sheet is swell. (You can roll the pastry sheet out into a 12" square, but I don't always mess with all that. Comes out great as is (unrolled) IMHO. Your preference, of course.)
2. Place brie in the center of the pastry. (You can slice off the top of the brie's white rind or leave it as is. Again, your preference. I've done it both ways. Lately, I've opted for the NOT. See "in a hurry" or "feeling lazy" above.)
3. Spoon the raspberry preserves (and fresh berries if you opted for seeds) all over the top of the brie.
4. Sprinkle almonds on top of the preserves.
5. Fold the pastry up and over cheese, carefully pulling to stretch a little if necessary, overlapping edges on top and sides so everything is sealed up in an excellent small package.
6. Brush the egg glaze all over the top and sides of the pastry. The egg glaze helps seal the edges. Just don't leave any holes or open places, or you'll have a godforsaken melted mess of brie all over your baking sheet instead of inside your pastry. Not optimal. Don't stress over the way the pastry looks on top after you've folded it all together. It will all bake out, and

nobody will care. For extra Martha points, though, save a little piece of the pastry aside. Cut something clever out of it, free-style or with a cookie-cutter, like a leaf or a heart - or your alma mater's logo (Kidding, not kidding. Football down south is everything. There's always the Super Bowl, too – sans pandemic) and glue it on the top using your egg glaze. Again, I'm over that step. But it does make an impressive presentation if you're feeling the need for extra points and can't help yourself. The first step is accepting you have a problem.
7. Pop the baking sheet and your soon to be golden prize into the oven.
8. Bake in the oven until the pastry is deep golden brown (about 30 minutes).
9. Let it cool on the counter 20 minutes.
10. Using a super-wide spatula, carefully remove your pastry from the baking sheet and place your golden masterpiece on a serving platter or cheese board.
11. Arrange your fruit on the platter or board, being sure to leave a little room for the cheese to goosh out. Don't forget a small hors d'oeuvre knife or two.
12. Pour some nice Prosecco or Champagne or Sparkling Juice or any wine in a pretty wine glass.
13. Bask in the splendor.
14. You're welcome. You can do this!

Soooo, maybe YOU can bring the Baked Brie to the party next time?

Umami State of Mind. Not Your Mama's Irish Stew

10-8-2020

If you haven't heard the word or had the pleasure of experiencing "umami" (pronounced oo-mah-mee) then you are missing out. Actually, you may have already experienced it and not even known it, so consider yourself blessed. Umami is an elusive culinary term that describes the near-indescribable, a "fifth taste" beyond the four we all know so well, "salty, sweet, sour, and bitter." The best we have in our language to describe it is the translation from Japanese, meaning "savory, pleasant taste." Umami evokes a delicious sensation that coats the tongue in mouthwatering and long-lasting flavor. It's almost a state of mind.

Turns out we all possess certain taste receptors on our tongues that respond to the "umami" in all kinds of foods like savory broths, meats, mushrooms, tomatoes, fermented cheeses, soups, stews, and more. There's an official "Umami Information Center" (umamiinfo.com). There's even an "Umami International Symposium." The first one in Hawaii explained umami in scientific terms. They tacked on a bunch of multi-syllable fancy-pants chemistry words to define it, just one or two of which I recognize and none of which I fully understand, (not now or have I ever), like peptides, and amino acids. I know I could count on my smart friend, Gina Watkiss, a chemistry teacher, to decipher all the chemical terms for me. But frankly, I will thank her anyway and save her the trouble because I am hopeless. I pretty much don't care about all the four and five syllable, over-my-head scientific details. I just care about the results: rich, mysterious, earthy depth of flavor that knocks your socks off. How's that for plain English? And oh, sweet Elvis and Umami. Have I got a recipe for you.

We made this Irish Stew last St. Patrick's Day, and it is an all-out umami-fest. But you need not wait for March to roll around. I have featured it here and now because it's fall, and a hearty stew is perfect for right now. And I contend that in addition, we could all stand to partake of something—anything—amazing while we schlep around at home in our slippers and yoga pants, wishing for normalcy. Covid-19 has been such a party-pooper, but it will not ruin this party in your mouth.

You can cook it traditionally on the stovetop all the way, or you can start it on the stove and transfer it to a crock pot for no-fuss, non-pot-watching expediency. The recipe serves 6, so if it's just the two of you, fill your bowl and then enjoy the leftovers. That umami flavor is just as good re-heated the second and third time as it was the first. Freeze it, too. But just do it. You're welcome.

- 6 oz bacon, diced
- 2 pounds beef chuck roast, cut into 1-inch pieces. Sprinkle with salt, pepper, flour, and toss to coat the pieces. Set aside.
- 3 tablespoons all-purpose flour
- 2 medium-large yellow onions, chopped
- 3 cloves garlic, minced
- 4 medium firm, Yukon Gold potatoes, cut in 1-inch piece
- 2 large carrots, chopped in ½-inch pieces
- 2 stalks celery, chopped in ½-inch pieces
- 1 large parsnip chopped into ½-inch pieces
- 1 bottle (1 pint/16 oz) Guinness Extra Stout—True story: I sent my husband to the store with the shopping list and he

came back with a 6-pack of Guinness, saying "Well, they didn't sell single bottles, so, darn it, I had to buy six." Right. Fair warning: Prepare for this. It will happen. Man deserves a reward. Don't sweat the small stuff, I say.

- 1 cup strong beef broth
- 2 tablespoons Worcestershire sauce
- ¼ cup tomato paste
- 1 tablespoon dried and ground porcini mushrooms—Please. I just buy the plastic package of dried Porcini mushrooms at Publix (the one on Bullsboro only in Newnan), and I don't bother with any chopping or grinding foolishness. Just reconstitute them in some hot broth for a few minutes first before adding them to your recipe.
- 1 teaspoon dried thyme
- 1 teaspoon dried rosemary (I have a rosemary bush, so I cut two stalks and lay them on top of the stew before I put the lid on the crock pot.)
- 1-½ teaspoon salt (I'm a nut for Himalayan pink salt, lately, whole crystals in a salt grinder. But I don't make it a thing. Use whatever you have.)
- ¼ teaspoon freshly ground black pepper
- 2 bay leaves

INSTRUCTIONS:

Tip: Prep *all* your ingredients in advance, and I mean they should be sliced, diced, measured, and laid out on your counter for easy selection when it's time to grab each one. Nothing more annoying than time-consuming interruptions to the cooking process while you chop carrots or mince garlic and your onions are burning.

1. Fry the bacon in a Dutch oven or heavy pot (I use a big 14" flat pan with high sides). When it's done, remove it with a slotted spoon, leaving all those luscious bacon drippings in the pan.
2. Brown the beef on all sides in the bacon drippings. Work in batches; don't overcrowd the pieces or you'll end up

just boiling them rather than giving them that caramelized lusciousness on the surface.
3. Remove batches of meat to a plate and repeat batches til all is browned.
4. Add onions to the pan and fry them until lightly browned, about 10 minutes.
5. Add vegetables and cook for another 5 minutes.
6. Add the bottle of Guinness (while your husband is swigging the other 5) and bring to rapid boil for 2 minutes, de-glazing the pan by scraping up all the tasty browned bits on the bottom. Pure gold.
7. Return the beef and bacon to the pan along with all the remaining ingredients and stir to combine.
8. At this point you can transfer everything to your slow cooker if you prefer. (Put a liner in your slow cooker unless you just like scrubbing for days). I use a big ladle to make the transfer. Follow the remaining steps and then cook on LOW for 6-8 hrs. or HIGH for 3-4 hours.
9. If opting for the stove-top, leave it all in the pan and bring to a boil. Reduce the heat to low, cover and simmer for 2 hours.

Be sure you have some crusty loaves of warm bread and real butter to serve with your hearty, delicious, umami-infused stew.

Blessings. Banes. Good Books. Tasty Bites. and Carpe Diem
11-18-2020

Meetings and gatherings these days are a challenge. One word: "pandemic."

Unlike in pre-internet pandemics, we now have technological options, virtual platforms created to emulate face to face meetings. No longer in use solely by businesses, these platforms have become commonplace for the population at large. Now everybody and their cousin can tune in to see the baby's new tooth. Or read a grandchild a bedtime story. Or "meet for coffee," each in his own kitchen - in pajama bottoms and house slippers – making toasting gestures toward a flat monitor bearing a friend's face. Or say goodbye to a loved one alone in the hospital.

Do these virtual gatherings ease the pain of separation? Do they contribute to actual well-being? Maybe. But at best they serve as pale substitutes for reality.

We have Facetime on iPhones and whatever Android phones have, and lots of others, like the ever-vigilant Amazon robot with the hair trigger, and now has a video screen, whose name starts with an "A" and ends in "lexa" which I hardly dare utter aloud or in print. If she hears even a close facsimile of her name she perks up, glows green, and starts talking. Especially frustrating when I'm already in a Zoom meeting trying to help a fellow Zoomer unmute themselves.

So take Zoom. Please, take Zoom! (If your age is under, oh, "ancient," Google Henny Youngman's wife joke. You'll get the reference. Maybe you had to be there.) Zoom's a blessing and a bane in hard times. There's a learning curve, and if you Zoom, who hasn't heard or uttered the words, "Unmute yourself!" or "Mute yourself, the dogs are barking!" or "Can you see me now? Why can't you see me?" or received/sent a text that says, "How do I log on to Zoom? It's not letting me in! Help!" For all its trouble and pallor, though, it may well be the best virtual blessing we have at the moment. We must cultivate gratitude where we can. Before March 2020 I had never heard of Zoom. Now it's part of our everyday language. I predict here and now that sooner than later the Oxford English Dictionary will initiate "Zoom" as a brand-new word – a proper noun - into their official lexicon. Watch for it. Bet my annual Zoom subscription on it.

All that to say, connections and conversations are vital to humans. Pandemics throw a huge wrench in our spokes. Our familiar customs and forward motion lurch to a sudden stop. We make do, though, because we must. Clubs and churches and businesses are having to figure things out. I'm a member of a small Book Club. It has become a favorite pastime over the years. We still meet in person as we are very small, but we don't touch each other, and we keep our distance. I miss hugging. And we get to enjoy someone else's cooking. Try eating over Zoom. Nobody serves you anything on Zoom; it's DIY all the way. There's no crying in baseball and there are no culinary surprises in Zoom.

That said, I am also in a writing group of talented women writers who meet bi-weekly via Zoom, and as a one-time surprise, our lovely Chargé D'affaires, Meredith Wilson, made her famous, delectable shortbread, wrapped it lovingly in papers and boxes tied with ribbons, and mailed one package to each of us so we could all break shortbread "together" during our next Zoom. What an incredible gift. It was a wonderful surprise. But unsustainable. The postage alone…

My book club, *Carpe Diem!* (exclamation mark intentional, like *Jeopardy!*) is a small and discerning once-a-month group of 5 ladies with eclectic backgrounds and tastes. Glenda Davis, retired AP English teacher; Gina Watkiss, chemistry teacher; Lauren Jones, current member of the Carnegie Library Board and Carol Burke, retired member; and me, well, whatever I am. I will not resort to ageism jokes here, but we are a mature, feisty, fun, opinionated gaggle.

We choose books we think will entertain but also might edify or inspire. We've read everything from Terry Kay to Shakespeare. Some of our research metrics before choosing a book include the NY Times and Wall Street Journal book lists, literary prizes and awards, Amazon and other reviews, oldies but goodies, and word of mouth. Some of our book selections have been the latest best sellers, and some have been classics we all say we read in school but didn't - or did and want to revisit.

I have learned so much from these ladies and the books we read. Forty-two books, thus far.

Some of our selections even turn up occasionally as answers to *Jeopardy!* questions (RIP, Alex). Thanks to my book club, I've come up with correct responses multiple times sitting in my den watching *Jeopardy!* because we've read E.M. Forester's *A Passage to India*, Wilkie Collins' *The Moonstone*, Ruth Rendell's *Tree of Hands*, and *Suite Française* by Irene Nemirovsky.

Sometimes book reviews let us down, and we end up choosing a stinker. Sometimes our views are divided. I'm usually the one who suggests the loser book. But I've made some really great suggestions, too. If you haven't read *An Odyssey, A Father, A Son, and an Epic* by Daniel Mendelsohn you're missing out on a winner. Also *The Dutch House* by Ann Patchett, and *Eleanor Oliphant is Completely Fine* by Gail Honeyman are at the top of our favorites list.

So here we are, at the refreshments portion of our in-person, socially distanced, Book Club scenario, and the other focus of this column.

We serve some fabulous food!

Nota Bene: Book Clubs, especially in the south, can be competitions: who can outdo whom? Florist centerpieces. Elaborate table settings. Expensive eats.

We're different. We're easy, and we are all great cooks. We offer refreshments that are uncomplicated and are delectable. We like flowers from Kroger as well as the florist. We drink wine but not fancy stuff. We're not stodgy, but neither do we want to be that group that focuses on the party and "maybe a book club will break out if there's time."

We like to put the emphasis on the book and then serve up something delightfully smart and tasty without breaking a sweat on our demure, southern foreheads. Actually, we do have one New Englander in our midst, but we don't hold that against Gina, nor does she, us.

So, since I've already shared some of our reading exploits, the ladies and I are sharing a few of our snacks as evidence of really wonderful things you, too, can serve without feeling the least bit intimidated. Oh, and one little entertaining tip: we often squeeze in a store-bought goodie or two with our homemade eats. Nothing wrong with that! Starbucks' Cranberry Bliss cake (you can purchase a whole frozen loaf if you inquire at the counter) is an absolute winner. They only carry it at holiday time. Fresh Market's candy bins bear lovely little lagniappes that don't break the bank, like gold-leafed chocolate balls. And the carrot cake from the Publix bakery is extraordinary.

Happy Reading. Happy Zooming. Happy Social Distancing. Be smart. Be careful. And whatever you do, have good friends, read good books, and make good, delicious things. These are blessings. Food for the mind. Food for the body. Food for the soul. Get together safely however you can and share yourself and your gifts with others. We all need nourishing right now, in so very many ways.

Carpe Diem, y'all!

CARPE DIEM! RECIPES:

Gina's Recipes
SALISBURY STREET FUDGE

Serves 16

Refrigerate: at least 4 hours

INGREDIENTS

- 2 3-oz packages cream cheese
- 4 cups confectioners sugar (sift or don't, your choice)
- 4 oz unsweetened chocolate, melted
- 2 ½ teaspoons vanilla extract
- 1 cup chopped walnut meats

1. In a bowl cream the cheese.
2. Slowly (Gina emphasizes slow-w-w-w-w-ly!) blend in sugar and chocolate.
3. Blend in vanilla and nuts.
4. Press into well-greased 8x8 inch pan.
5. Refrigerate for at least 4 hours.
6. Cut into squares.

BAKED APPETIZER PIE

Gina says in New England they eat this in the mornings. In the south, Glenda says they eat it for dinner or supper. In the south, there's a difference, you know.

Serves 8

Bake 20 minutes at 350°

INGREDIENTS

- 8-oz package cream cheese, softened
- 2 tablespoons milk
- 2-½ ounce package sliced dried beef, finely chopped. Gina's came in a 4.5 oz jar. From Armour.
- 3 tablespoons minced onion
- 2 tablespoons chopped green pepper

- ⅛ teaspoon pepper
- ½ cup sour cream
- ¼ cup coarsely chopped walnuts

1. Blend cheese with milk. Stir in beef, onion, green pepper, and pepper.
2. Mix well.
3. Stir in sour cream.
4. Spoon mixture into shallow baking dish and sprinkle top with walnuts.
5. Bake at 350° for 20 minutes until bubbly.
6. Serve hot with assorted crackers.

Lauren's and Carol's Recipe
CHEESE ROUNDS

Makes about 100
Bake 10–15 minutes at 350°

INGREDIENTS
- 1 stick butter
- 2 cups grated sharp cheese (Cracker Barrel or Wisconsin)
- 1 cup flour
- 1 teaspoon salt
- Tabasco or red pepper to taste

1. Blend ingredients together. Divide mixture into 2 balls, then work each ball into long roll about one-inch thick.
2. Wrap in wax paper and chill.
3. Slice very thin.
4. Put whole pecan half on top of each.
5. Place on un-greased baking sheet and bake at 350 for 10–15 minutes.

GLENDA'S POUND CAKE

Talking about southern traditions, (that have absolutely nothing to do with pound cake) Glenda shared her family's southern ham tradition with us. When she was in her teens and learning to cook, every time her mother cooked a ham, she always cut off what she called "the nub end" and saved it to make soup stock. So Glenda learned to always cut off the nub end because her mother did. She asked her mother once why she did that, and her mother said it was because her grandmother did. So Glenda asked her grandmother why she always cut off the nub end of the ham. And she replied, laughing, that during the war the government took up everybody's aluminum and metal cookware for the war effort. She said because she had five children to cook for, she kept back one pan, but a whole ham wouldn't fit in it. So she cut off the nub end to make it fit the pan. And so the tradition was born and will continue as testament and homage to the women cooks in Glenda's southern family.

Now, on to the pound cake, another southern delight.

INGREDIENTS
- 3 cups sugar
- 2 sticks salted butter
- 6 eggs, separated
- 3 cups all-purpose flour
- ¼ teaspoon baking soda
- 8 oz sour cream
- 1 teaspoon pure vanilla

1. Combine sugar and butter. Beat til fluffy.
2. Then add egg yolks to batter one at a time while mixing.
3. Beat egg whites in separate bowl until stiff and set aside.
4. Sift flour and baking soda together.
5. Alternate adding flour and sour cream to batter, beginning and ending with flour.
6. Add vanilla to batter.
7. Mix well.

8. Fold in beaten egg whites.
9. Bake in well-greased tube pan for 75 minutes at 325°. Cool for 30 minutes and remove from pan.

THE SECRET: Leave eggs and butter out overnight to come to room temperature. Beat the sugar and butter until it cries for mercy and use Mexican vanilla.

Susie's Recipes
<u>**COOKIE TRUFFLES**</u>
   INGREDIENTS
- 11 9-oz package chocolate sandwich cookies with white filling (Oreos, ok?) finely crushed
- 8-oz package cream cheese, softened
- 1 pound white or dark baking chocolate, coarsely chopped
- Line a large baking sheet with parchment, waxed paper, or foil, and set aside.

1. In a large bowl combine crushed cookies and cream cheese.
2. Beat with an electric mixer on low speed until well mixed.
3. Shape mixture into 1-inch balls and chill or freeze until firm.
4. In a large saucepan, cook and stir chocolate over low heat until melted. (You can also melt chocolate in the microwave but do not heat it longer than 30 seconds at a time. After each 30 seconds, remove the bowl and stir, then replace in microwave for another 30 seconds. Repeat until melted)
5. Cool slightly.
6. Dip each ball into melted chocolate; let excess drip back into pan.
7. Place dipped truffles on prepared baking sheet.
8. Chill truffles about 1 hour or until firm.

Store covered, in the refrigerator up to 1 week, or freeze up to 1 month.

*Extra added touch. To serve, I insert a toothpick on top of each truffle, and onto the toothpick I stick a Bing cherry. Not maraschino, cherries, but Bings, the deep, dark red ones. Get them on the cherries aisle and look for "Bada Bing Cherries."

MARINATED CHEESE & OLIVES APPETIZER

8 Servings

Dress up store-bought cheese like this.

INGREDIENTS

- 3 oz cheddar cheese, cubed
- 3 oz Havarti, cubed
- 3 oz New Zealander or Parmentino, cubed – NOTE: If you can't find this exact cheese, no worries. Just substitute with any semi firm cheese. Browse the grocery cheese section. Because we were reading a book about a Scottish family, I got a little pack of Scottish cheeses. (The book was *Shuggie Bain* by Douglas Stuart. One of those super-highly recommended books on all kinds of awards lists that was full of Scottish sadness, family dysfunction, and stark poverty and nobody liked it but Gina and me.)
- ¼ cup green olives, pitted or stuffed with pimiento
- ¼ cup black olives
- 1 tablespoon olive oil
- 1 tablespoon vinegar
- ½ teaspoon dried Italian herbs (I used an Italian parmesan herb mix for bread dipping, and it was fab!)

1. Add the cheeses and olives to a medium bowl.
2. In a small bowl, whisk together the oil, vinegar, and seasoning. Pour over cheese.
3. Cover and refrigerate for at least one hour before serving.
4. Serve in a decorative bowl on a wooden platter alongside some summer sausages and crackers.

Be sure to have a nice little container of toothpicks, too.

PIEDMONT DRIVING CLUB'S BUTTERED SALTINES

Makes 48 crackers

Get one benefit from Piedmont Driving Club's menu without paying the membership fee. I saw this recipe in an article in the newspaper awhile back and believe it or not it has become a well-publicized phenomenon. The chef created a flyer after so many requests, and it's available upon request. Apparently, they were created by another chef in 1972 at the Capital City Club when he ran out of oyster crackers and had to punt. So he baked some saltines in butter and a star was born. These things are deceptively simple, but rich in buttery flavor and add a touch of class to plain Saltines.

INGREDIENTS
- ½ pound butter
- 48 square Nabisco saltine crackers (no substitutes. Other brands don't stay crisp)

1. Preheat oven to 400°. Have a rimmed baking sheet ready.
2. In a small saucepan, make clarified butter by melting butter and skimming off white foam. Keep skimming until butter is clear and golden. This should yield about ¾ cup clarified butter.
3. In a large bowl, combine crackers with clarified butter.
4. Toss gently to coat crackers.
5. Transfer crackers to prepared baking sheet, laying crackers flat, side by side.
6. Bake 3 minutes or until golden brown.

Serve warm.

Love and Holidays in the Time of Covid
12-9-2020

Dear Diary:

Things are really weird this year. The Holidays are here, and we're still in the throes of a worldwide pandemic. We had a very small but fine Thanksgiving, immediate family members only. I had fun setting the table as I always do, with my customary artsy fall centerpiece, placemats, cloth napkins, chargers, china, candles, and sterling flatware. I trotted out my collection of ceramic pilgrim salt and pepper shakers from Publix, the adults and the children, a sizeable collection of which I am both sentimentally proud and loath to admit. Our elder adult son, Scotty and his better half, Val cooked the whole meal, and it was fabulous. Really fabulous, starting with morning Mimosas, a charcuterie board worthy of a magazine spread, and our traditional cheese ring, an appetizer that has reached epic holiday status in our family.

I thought it was the perfect arrangement: they offered to cook everything while we would provide a clean house (at least the parts you can see) and a lovely holiday atmosphere. Deal!

Meanwhile, I had forgotten one thing about our deal of the day: cleaning house is a lot of work. I only do it once a year at holiday time, whether it needs it or not (totally kidding, sort of).

By the time they stepped foot in our house, I had already had the carpets and furniture cleaned, moved everything back into place, mopped, dusted, vacuumed, cleaned the bathrooms, polished silver, rummaged through the basement for stored holiday décor and schlepped it all upstairs, searched the storage closets for all the stuff I needed to decorate and to serve, eat, and drink everything. Then, I executed all last-minute things in a final flurry, with precious little time to shower and exchange my sweaty work-pajamas for presentable holiday-wear, all without benefit of Cinderella's helpful birds and mice. Funny how the mind forgets all the exhausting details when idealizing the big, finished picture.

I think my house gets bigger every year. And I get older every year, too. My energy has limits. But I am not complaining. I am reveling in it all.

While the body was already flagging, the spirit was still willing. And joyous. And when, at 9:30am on Thanksgiving Day, they lugged in bag after bag and box after box of supplies and food items I was awed. Clearly, they had gone to the utmost effort, with great love, and it showed.

A turkey went into the oven while a ham was baking at their house across town, which Scotty monitored constantly with a high-tech, remote oven thermometer. Gee, and I actually thought of giving him a little dinky, digital meat thermometer for Christmas like the one I have. Silly me. This thing he's got looks like a NASA space shuttle control panel. He's a pro now, with pro toys. I am no longer the mother of rookie cooks with much to learn. Mea culpa.

And thanks be to God and Elvis. I take my place now behind my adult boys, both fine cooks. Scotty's younger brother, Nick, actually chose cooking as his profession and is now a fine executive chef at a huge country club for expats in far-away Hong Kong. I am immensely proud of them both. And Scotty's better half, Val, is his perfect culinary complement, an absolute ace in the kitchen.

I plopped down at our kitchen island and watched amazed, as stuff kept coming through the door in a seemingly endless loop like Mickey's mops and water buckets. Once the parade finally ended, my kitchen now knee deep and piled high with potential, they got to work.

Magic ensued. I was handed a Mimosa while a charcuterie board appeared, and Scotty explained each item after dropping the coup de grace in the center of the board, a small comb of sweet honey. Classy! There were big fat Greek olives in a luxurious, oily mix, razor thin velvety slices of Smoking Goose Culatello in white wine, shaved Manchego cheese, and Horseradish Cheese Spread, all from Ace Growlers on the square in Newnan; perfect cubes of Boar's Head Truffle Goat Cheese and Kerrygold Reserve Cheddar, creamy slices of French Brie; spicy rounds of Pepper-Coated Salami and Volpy Pepperoni Nuggets, Bagel Chips, Firehook sea salt crackers, and that all-impressive honeycomb (all from Publix, Newnan).

Newnan has so much to offer. It is no longer just "The City of [beautiful] Homes" but also a vibrant, progressive city of wonderful eateries, shops, art galleries, and entrepreneurs, especially around the court square. Some folks don't know our dynamic square exists. I'm here to tell them: it's here. Worth it. Right now, especially, while shop owners are struggling to stay open in the middle of a pandemic, wear a mask, explore the area, and buy local. Cile Smith will serve you with a smile at the Redneck Gourmet; Phyllis Graham will regale you with enrobed chocolate delights at Let Them Eat Toffee. Downtown Olive and Kitchen Supply has THE best dipper seasonings to pair with olive oils to die for. Knife and Stone makes a rich, creamy mushroom soup with crispy little surprise bits of prosciutto, and they'll even do takeout, and deliver it to you in your car. Ace Growlers has expanded from a craft beer purveyor to include beautiful meats, seafood, herbed Banner Butter, and all manner of tasty items.

There are too many more wonders around the square to enumerate. Just know that these businesses on our town square are townspeople who depend on us in the community for their livelihoods. Sure, go to Publix for some stuff. But for the stuff you just can't get just anywhere, and for the friends you make that you can't make elsewhere, the square and its shop owners are unparalleled and essential.

So, back to Thanksgiving morning. After a while, renewed from a brief rest sitting at our island, delighted by the camaraderie, and fortified by hors d'oeuvres and morning adult beverages, I knew my job was only partially done. I had already set a beautiful table while my sweet husband, Rick assembled our annual tradition: turkey cookies. But now it was time to clear the decks and bring on the serving dishes, meat platters, serving spoons, forks. Carving knives. Water pitchers. Bread basket. Gravy boat. Then, there were the pans, pots, and utensils piling up in the sink.

Dishwasher wanted. That would be Rick and me. All hands were on deck now, many hands trying to make light work. Val toiled away making from-scratch dressing and gravy. Hint: prep involved an entire hen and some straight-up alchemy because I swear, the final product was supernatural. I would follow her dressing and gravy anywhere. Scotty assembled the orange crescent rolls, popping them in the oven while running back and forth to the grill outside where he tended to his sweet street corn on the cob, and making a trip back to his house to fetch the ham and then glaze it to a fine, sweet shine at our house.

Once we had it all together, laid out in bountiful buffet style on the kitchen table, we filled our dishes and strode happily down the hall with plates heavy laden, into the dining room, where we held hands around the table, stretched out a little further to reach each other than in past years, bowed our heads in a moment of spoken gratitude, praise, and thanks, and had our fill. I will confess, I wondered how I managed to do this whole thing for so many years when sometimes there were as many as 26 people for dinner.

Christmas this year will most likely be weird, too, just like all of 2020. No huge crowds. Last year I made a humongous dessert platter fit for all our guests, our neighbors, Santa, all his elves, and their elf neighbors. That was a pretty spectacular effort and so much fun: a 3-D homemade gingerbread house cake sprinkled with sugar snow in the center of a platter surrounded by snow-globe cupcakes I made with little trees and gelatin globes on top, all accompanied by an excess of store-bought chocolate Santas and goodies. Nope, that's not happening this year. Things will be pared down, for sure. No visitors from out of town this year. No dear friends or extended family of choice to add to the table. Just immediate family. I hope. And that's ok. Even if it's just Rick and me, I'll be setting a beautiful table and at the very least I'll be cooking my famous roast beef, Rick will be the Ricotta Cookie-making master for neighbor gifts, and we'll still make fun goodies like reindeer in a jar for the kids. But whatever we do, and however we do it, we will put our hearts into it, guaranteed. Because:

Because right now, in these pandemic days, there is joy in the holidays tempered by uncertainty, sadness, and grief for those who are sick, those who worry for them, and those who are not here to sit at our tables. Because the places I set at my Christmas table will be, just like my Thanksgiving table, as beautiful as I can make them, just with fewer places than in years past, but no fewer memories and no less import. Because my food and table preparations aren't just for show. Because putting forth my best effort is an offering meant to honor the occasion and the dear ones who join us at our table along with those who are absent. Because I am not a Wise Man nor a King, I bring what offerings I can. My heart. It's there in Christina Rossetti's (public domain) poem:

> What can I give Him, poor as I am?
> If I were a shepherd, I would bring a lamb.
> If I were a wise man, I would do my part.
> Yet what can I give Him?
> Give Him my heart.

Give my heart. For me, it all comes down to family, love, kindness, and gratitude. Because I am grateful to my toes that I am not waiting in long food lines at the local food pantry. Because I am not, nor is anyone in my family, in the hospital dying of Covid-19. Because my house still stands unharmed by fire or flood or hurricanes or tornadoes or death. Because I pray for all those that have suffered any of these. Because even now we can give of ourselves in kindness and in service to others. Because we have love in this world despite darkness and oppression. Because I observe this holiday and every holiday in my own way, at table, with utmost love and reverence, whether it be with many or few, tired or not, no matter what. Because Love is the alpha, the omega, and the bottom line. Always, always love.

>Love came down at Christmas...
>Love all lovely, Love divine...
>Love was born at Christmas...
>Star and angels gave the sign...
>Love shall be our token...
>Love shall be yours and love be mine.
>
>— Christina Rossetti

THE NOW FAMOUS CHEESE RING

Plucked from obscurity and the pages of the *Tea Time for the Masters Cookbook*, this appetizer has been a famous family favorite for years. I think one year we made at least 6 of them over the span of Thanksgiving and Christmas, during which time Scotty mastered the art. If you ever take it to a party, they will clamor for the recipe:

- 1 pound sharp NY cheddar, grated
- 1 cup pecans, chopped
- ¾ cup mayo
- 1 medium onion, grated

or chopped fine
- 1 clove garlic, pressed
- ½ teaspoon Tabasco
- 1 cup strawberry preserves or Polaner All-Fruit

Combine all ingredients except preserves and mix well. Chill. Mold into ring. Fill center with strawberry preserves. Serve with crackers.

TURKEY COOKIES

- Easy!
- Pecan Sandies and Keebler Fudge Stripe cookies
- Candy corn
- Chocolate bon bons for the body
- Google eyes optional
- melted chocolate for assembly
- Also, sliced almonds or mini marshmallows for "tail feathers"

Place pecan sandy flat. Put a dollop of chocolate on top far side of the cookie and place a Fudge Stripe Cookie on its edge for the "tail" atop the melted chocolate. Wait til it's solidified to continue. You can prop up a whole line of them using a strip of sturdy bent cardboard in an "L" shape against the backs of the "tails."

Place a dollop of melted chocolate on top of sandy cookie just in front of the "tail" and place a bon bon on the chocolate. Again, wait to solidify.

Using candy corn, affix with chocolate on pecan sandy cookie in front of bon bon as "legs." Also place a candy corn as a "beak" on the top front of the bon bon body.

Eyes can be simple tiny dots of chocolate applied with a toothpick dotted on the beak, or separate google eyes purchased on the baking decorating aisle, glued on either side of the beak with melted chocolate. You may leave well enough alone at this point or choose to adorn the "tail" further with thin sliced almonds at the upper edge (affixed with chocolate) or even mini marshmallows.

Serve on a dessert plate, or write names on strips of stiff paper, prop the paper on turkey's feet, and place on small plates or doilies on the table at each place as place cards.

SCOTTY'S SWEET STREET CORN

- Corn on the cob
- 1 can of coconut milk
- 2 tablespoon of brown sugar to start
- 2 bay leaves

You can add a touch of cayenne if you want to add some heat.

1. Coconut milk, brown sugar and bay leaves in a sauce pot and bring up to a very low simmer. Then taste and add more brown sugar to preference. This is not a recipe for structured people. This will never be made the exact same every time. It's the foundation of a recipe and then tweaked every time you make it.
2. Place corn over direct heat on grill. Gas or charcoal is fine. Once corn begins to warm up, begin basting coconut sauce onto the corn. Let them sit a few minutes to let the sauce thicken and stick to the corn and then turn. Re-apply, sit, turn. Repeat until corn has that beautiful brown/black/yellow

mosaic of colors.

You can eat straight off the cob. I like to cook more corn than I need and then cut it off the corn and then use it in my pulled pork and mojo chicken tacos with homemade pickled red onions, but that is a whole other story.

ORANGE CRESCENT ROLLS

- rind of 1 orange, zested or finely grated
- ½ cup sugar
- 3 packages Pillsbury crescent rolls – Note: use the GRANDS Crescent Rolls. Big and fluffy!
- melted butter

1. Combine orange rind and sugar. Let sit hours or overnight.
2. When ready to serve, unroll dough from package but do not separate. Brush liberally with melted butter.
3. Measure 1 teaspoon of orange-sugar mixture for each triangle. Brush mixture over surface, one triangle at a time.
4. Cut apart and roll as directed on package for jelly roll. Place on cookie sheets lined with Reynolds Wrap Release non-stick aluminum foil or on Silpat mat. Optional: brush tops again with butter (do not brush tops with egg white).
5. Bake at 375° for 11–15 minutes. Do not overbake!

Happy Anew Year
1-6-2021

And I do mean anew.

Time to start anew after a sucky 2020 (gone but not ever forgotten). 2021 is where it's at now. But let's just review for a brief moment, shall we?

What last year spelled out for us:

Life is full of dichotomies: life and death, the haves and the have nots, the sick and the well, good and evil, real and imaginary, helpful and not helpful, civilized and savage, Democrats and Republicans. Life and death are not necessarily easy nor are they predictable. And if you ever thought they were, 2020 thoroughly disabused us all of that silly notion. We are not promised tomorrow.

So Carpe damn Diem, children.

That's why on New Year's Day 2021, Rick and I begin anew by fixing our traditional southern New Year's good luck meal, "Rick's Really Good Turnip Green Soup." We watch the GA Bulldogs win in the Peach Bowl against Cincinnati, and oh yes, what's that stuff sitting on the floor by our basement door? Oh, that's just my "go bag" and purse, packed just in case we have to run to the basement because there are tornado warnings all around us today.

Perhaps this might be a good time to talk about the little chameleon who snuck in to my kitchen while the door was open yesterday. Why was the door open? Because I was coming inside and tripped up the steps, quite ungracefully, landing likewise, and the door stayed open until I could get up. That took way longer than it should have.

He must've scooted in and has been hiding out because we didn't discover him until this morning, on our kitchen island among the ingredients for soup! We covered him gently with a box, slid a stiff paper underneath, and Rick took him outside to release him. I still haven't, however, shaken the horrifying idea of a lizard, cute notwithstanding, falling into my soup pot somehow. This is what lids are for. Covered pots are for repelling surprise lizard-guests and protecting pristine soup. See? Nothing is straightforward or congruent or predictable in this life.

Meanwhile we pack away Christmas. I didn't decorate as much this year, and that meant fewer trips up and down the stairs from the basement where every last Christmas thing is stored, which may just be a trend I want to embrace for the future. At this age it's quality not quantity. It's about 10 trips on the staircase this year vs 100 or more (it seems) in years past. This has been the holiday of masks and horrors, especially if you've suffered, or are currently suffering, from Covid, had to care for those who suffered, had to quarantine, were forced to be apart from loved ones, or had to say goodbye to them forever, in absentia via a discomfiting Zoom or Facetime session. But vaccines are beginning to appear, and 2021 looks to be a lot less hopeless than 2020.

Now another dichotomy appears: vaccine takers and vaccine not-takers. See what I mean? Dichotomies R Us.

So we learn that life is not a straight line and we shouldn't expect it to be. That doesn't mean we can't live in hope and help ourselves and others in selfless ways. So we do: contribute what we can to the world with our donations, our votes, our kindness, inclusion, and selfless compassion. Or we don't. Ding, dichotomy again. Rick and I choose the "do." At least we try to. #notperfect. #onlyhuman.

We eat our southern good luck meal on New Year's Day, with greens for the color of money, pork for progress because pigs root forward, goes the story. Don't eat chicken or turkey on New Year's Day because they scratch backwards, and for the love of Elvis don't eat beef because cows stand still, and no one wants any of that. We eat black-eyed peas, too, for good measure. I don't know why, exactly, but I'm pretty sure it has to do with beans swelling, therefore symbolizing growth and prosperity.

I've even heard of some folks throwing a dime in the pot with the black-eyed peas for an extra dose of good luck for the person who gets the dime in their serving. Not so sure that's prosperity or even a semi-great idea since a dime is smaller than a plastic baby hidden in a Marti Gras King Cake, and it's not very lucky, is it, if you swallow a heavy metal and end up in the ER during a pandemic, or anytime for that matter? If you're lucky, you can opt for waiting vigilantly. If you survive. Is there such a thing as dime poisoning? Well, I flat don't like the idea of dimes – or lizards for that matter - flavoring my soup or my black-eyed peas.

Also, this year we opted out of making golden, buttered cornbread or sweet mini corn-bread muffins, an obvious symbol of prosperity, riches, and gold. Duh. We are officially jumping on the diet wagon. Carbs and their evil twin, sugar aren't coming along. Eating better will most certainly not be an easy, straight path, either, but it's a start. That joke about gaining Covid-19 like the Freshman-15 is real. Maybe even a pound or two more, or multiples thereof, if some of us were to be honest.

I hope 2021 brings all of us a very different year than the last one. All we can do, when there is a choice, is choose our dichotomies carefully. When there is no choice, like dying, for example, when we or a loved one would really rather not, I wish us all love and comfort and strength and forward motion through the impossibly difficult.

And a big, hearty bowl of possibilities for those who remain, and are able: Rick's Really Good Turnip Green New Year's Day soup.

RICK'S REALLY GOOD TURNIP GREEN NEW YEAR'S DAY SOUP

After Rick's 2006 pheasant hunting trip to Iowa, he couldn't wait to try this recipe for soup given to him by Mr. Ellis Camp. It's absolutely delicious, and very hearty. It's our southern New Year's Day Soup every year.

- 1 lb sausage (Jimmy Dean), cooked
- 1 16-oz can black-eyed peas
- 1 16-oz can navy beans
- 1 16-oz can northern beans
- 1 16-oz can or box of chicken broth
- 1 27-oz can turnip greens

1. Cook & drain sausage. Mix all together in large pot and cook til heated through. I like to simmer it for an hour, so flavors are really blended.
2. Serve with chopped onion and sour cream for toppings, and a side of golden corn bread or sweet corn muffins.

Thirty Years
(NO RECIPES. JUST FOOD FOR THOUGHT.)
JAN/FEB-2021

I just had a funeral for a close associate I've known for over three decades. RIP my Jenn-Aire cooktop.

That cooktop was pristine and beautiful when it came to our new house thirty-one years ago. We had just purchased our "forever" home in 1989. Because the house had been on the market for a while, and I had aesthetic vision beyond the awful gold shag carpets and heavy gold drapes, and the teeny tiny linoleum-floored kitchen, we got it for a song. That made it possible for us to add on to the entire back half of the house, creating a new, roomy kitchen, laundry room, and main floor bedroom. My knack for seeing the value of the "good bones" of a house, the proceeds from the sale of our starter house on Dixon Street, and a sum of money from our share of the sale of Rick's mom's house in Atlanta the year before made it all possible. I think of her every time I step foot in my kitchen.

How many appliances last for over thirty years? Very few. But this one did. It was a stalwart. And like Rome, all roads in our house lead to the center, the kitchen and the cooktop that sits in the center of the kitchen island, the center of activity. It saw us through decades of family meals, parties, holidays; thirty-one years of boiling tea kettles, baby bottles, and small pots of hard-boiled eggs; big pots of homemade soup, and chili; and large stockpots of boiling water with just a touch of sugar for our summers of Silver Queen corn; heart-shaped Sunday pancakes on the griddle for our children and then our children's children. Around that island where our cooktop sits are the memories of friends and loved ones gathered around it, talking, laughing, crying, fighting, apologizing, confessing, celebrating, busily cooking, drinking and toasting, eating, even singing together, and holding hands to say grace encircling the island and that cooktop. If an inanimate object can capture the "place" of a home, this one did. But nothing lasts forever, and our cooktop didn't, either. It was dead and it was time for it to go.

After its unceremonious removal by the expert technicians, I bowed my head and said farewell to a dear friend as it went out the door, into the back of their truck, and onto the pile of other discarded appliances from the day's work orders. And when they came back through the door, I welcomed the installation of a brand new one in its place.

It was a thing to behold. Different, new, and beautiful. Modern and once again, pristine. I wondered if this new one would last another thirty years, and what it – and the world – would look like if it did. I knew in that moment that I would never know the answer to that question. Sobering thought: I turned 71 this year. Alas, I am too damn old to survive it. But I also know that the old cooktop was beneficent in its retreat. When it gave up the ghost, it did not take with it all the spirits and the memories. It kindly left them all in the room, in the air, in the hearts, in the minds, and in the very fiber of all who were here in our kitchen, around our island.

So what will the next thirty years bring, and how much of it will I get to see? The past thirty-two have certainly been eventful.

By the end of 1989, when I was 39, and my husband 40, the Berlin Wall came down, there was a massacre in Tiananmen Square in Beijing, the World Wide Web was invented, and we bought our "forever" house. Our boys were little.

Last year in 2020, a wall at our southern border was partially up, there were protests in Hong Kong for their lives to matter, we started experiencing a worldwide pandemic and well over one million people died worldwide. For the first time in my life, we experienced lock-downs, quarantines, isolation, and a general disruption of normality; politically things got really messy and polarized; wearing protective face masks became political; people protested in the streets of the U.S. for black lives to matter; it seemed everybody was angry and a wild presidential election in November was the most impactful in my memory.

Spring 2021 is here, and we still live in the same "forever" house, with landscaping and a garden we have tended over the years, a few new furnishings, some new playground equipment, a playhouse for our grandchildren they are quickly outgrowing, and a new cooktop. The house is minus two children who grew up here, but who still visit, one often, the other only periodically. One of our boys is now approaching his mid-forties, and the other is in his late thirties. The one who visits "often" lives in Newnan. The other, our periodic visitor, lives in Hong Kong. We have grandchildren. And my husband and I will celebrate our 50th wedding anniversary in June. We are retired. We are happy. We are in our very early seventies (emphasis on very early for my sake). We worry for our world now and wonder about a future thirty years from now that we won't live to see.

What will the world look like in 2051? It is my fervent hope it will be good, for everyone's sake. *Everyone's*. But I wonder if that's even possible. Will we all find common ground after all our schisms, enough to heal the separation and wounds we all suffer today? *Have we ever?* The human condition is comprised of every second of a man's life, say, from birth, to standing around a kitchen island, to leaving the building forever. Or from birth, to a homeless shelter or a premature visit to the morgue. Austrian neurologist, psychiatrist, and Holocaust survivor, Viktor Frankl, says, "the meaning of life differs from man to man, from day to day and from hour to hour."

Historically, all mankind has never been on the same page, and

I don't know that another thirty years will change it. But what is a goal except something to strive for? Even our goals are different. But I wish, I pray, I hope with all my heart that mankind can find a common decency that is kind, accepting, inclusive, and unselfish. Is that too much to ask?

If you will, in thirty years, come to our house, knock on the door, tell them we sent you. I'll leave that memo telling them to expect you on the island when we go. Please gather 'round the cooktop on the island and hold hands, sing together, and say grace for mankind. That would make me so very happy.

And I'll know, because I'll be in the air, in the room where it happens.

Thanks.

Susie

When Life Gives You Lemons
2-3-2021

Fabulous food doesn't have to be fancy. Famous chef David Chang says, "You can get a Michelin star if you serve the best hamburger in the world." And Thomas Keller believes that "A recipe has no soul. You, as the cook, must bring soul to the recipe." That's what great cooks do: they use ingredients and play with their food and put soul into what they make. But they usually have a firm foundation from which to operate, concepts that are pretty much gospel in the culinary world. Acid, salt, fat, and heat are four of them.

Lemons and/or lemon juice are an absolute necessity in a good cook's kitchen. And so is salt. These two elements (acid and salt) are two of the four pillars of good cooking, the other two being fat and heat. I'm a disciple of all four, actually. I learned this from my mom a long time ago, but there's also a wonderful book by Samin Nosrat, *Salt, Fat, Acid, Heat, Mastering the Elements of Good Cooking*, that backs me up on this. The book has been around since 2017, but I gifted it to myself for Christmas, and also gave one to my son who lives nearby. The other son already has this stuff down pat as a pro chef in a faraway land. Anyway, the four title elements in this book are the Matthew, Mark, Luke, and John of foundational cooking for all time and evermore, Amen. I certainly don't know everything there is to know, of course, which is why books are always good, and this one in particular is awesome. It's part instructional, part inspirational, part historical, part story book, part recipe book, and beautifully illustrated, to boot. A feast for the eyes, the brain, the spirit, and the ol' breadbasket. Yay!

I was fortunate to have a mother who was an excellent cook, who taught me about using acid, salt, fat, and heat. Her culinary mentor was Julia Child, who preached the very same four gospels in her day, with her own inimitable style and flourish. You'll recall her high-pitched "Bon Appetit!" and her signature slug-of-wine TV show sign-off. Julia learned how to cook from the all-time grandaddy of cookbooks, *The Joy of Cooking* and by spending time in culinary school in France. *Mastering the Art of French Cooking Volumes I and II* were two of Saint Julia's most beneficent gifts to humanity, and all three books became my mother's culinary bibles. They gave my mom a firm foundation, and then she reverently passed down to me these cherished tomes along with an oral history and hands-on demonstrations of her knowledge of the four gospels:

<u>Gospel One: Acid</u>. Lemons and other acids (vinegars, other fruits, tomatoes and tomato juice, wine, alcohol, even buttermilk, Parmesan cheese, sour cream, yogurt, and yes, coffee) give food that extra little kick, brightening and balancing flavors.

<u>Gospel Two: Salt</u>. Salt is the golden ticket that opens up and enhances flavors in a way nothing else can.

<u>Gospels Three and Four: Fat and Heat</u>. Fat is flavor and texture and unctuous richness; heat is the magic wand that transmutes food into its ultimate texture and finish. Fat and heat complete the quaternary culinary gospels.

All together, these four things are transformational in cooking, like taking food from flat to vibrant, analog to Hi-def, black and white to Technicolor, quotidian to captivating. The very best, award-winning cooks pledge themselves to the principles of this holy quartet in proper balance, allowing themselves to break free of the surly bonds of static recipes and cans of cream of mushroom soup. These cooks are thus anointed with insight, and inspiration to educate their senses and to use them to make substitutions or additions. They can create food that ascends to the next level, up to and right through the gates of gastronomic paradise. Oh Praise Elvis, squeeze the lemon, pass the salt, keep the fat, and heat the miracle! Follow the gospels, and as a great cook you get a star in your toque and a medal on your chef's jacket!

That's the idea, anyway. I don't claim to be a transcendent, Michelin-star cook and you may not be and don't have to be one, either. But knowing the four pillars is important. And at whatever level we are cooking, be it home cook or professional chef, knowledge and following the gastronomic gospels are power. So if we don't all wear tall white chef hats or chef coats, let's just give ourselves a pat on the back, hold our whisks high, and give a big salute to salt, fat, acid, and heat.

I know, salt is maligned, and in fact, it is verboten for some poor souls. My heart goes out to you who must wander the barren wasteland of bland food. James Beard said, "Where would we be without salt?" He's right, of course, but salt, for some people plays with their blood pressure and can lead to heart attacks and strokes. Granted, there's way too much salt in many ready-to-eat foods. Salt can cause water-retention and edema that makes some folks feel like a sausage bursting in its casing, makes them beg for a larger shoe size, or settle for a pair of fuzzy slippers.

But salt is the ancient preservative. Salt elevates everything, in the proper proportions. Salt is the mother who encourages her shy kid into the spotlight and watches her come alive as a star of the show. I salt and pepper my cantaloupe, making it sweeter and tangy at the same time. Try flaky salt on chocolate chip cookies. I have several salts in my cupboard: table salt (you know the label, with that poor little girl eternally fending off pouring rain with her umbrella), coarse kosher salt, sea salt, flake salt, and a big salt grinder with Himalayan pink salt crystals. Oh, and my favorite mixes of seasoned salt are, of course, Jane's Krazy Mixed-up Salt (do you know me?), Grill Mates Montreal Steak seasoning, and Trader Joe's Lemon Pepper seasoning in its own little grinder which includes salt.

Lemon is another must-have in my kitchen. I squirt it over my cantaloupe before the salt and pepper are added. Salt and acid. Mwah, divine. Fresh lemons, of course, are optimal, but make no mistake. I like economy of scale, too, and a big bottle of fresh lemon juice always has its place. I use it when making my Broiled Chicken and without fail, the combo of acid, salt, fat (chicken skin) and heat are simply marvelous. And it's falling-off-a-log easy. This is fabulous food, and it isn't fancy. Here's how I make it, and you can too!

Bon appetit! And remember enjoy a slug of wine in memory of Julia.

THE VERY BEST BROILED CHICKEN

- Chicken pieces, thigh-leg quarters, or just thighs. Your choice and your choice of amount to cook. You can cook breasts, too if you like. I just prefer thighs and legs for their juiciness.
- Lemon juice
- Jane's Krazy Mixed up Salt, NO substitutes (grocery store, spice/seasoning aisle)
- Paprika

3. Spray slotted broiler pan with cooking spray (and line the underpan with foil for faster cleanup)
4. Arrange chicken pieces, fat side down, on slotted broiler pan.
5. Douse each piece good and proper with a full capful of lemon juice.
6. Shake the Jane's Krazy Mixed up Salt liberally on each piece.
7. Lightly sprinkle each piece evenly with paprika.
8. Pop into oven set on broil at 450° for 15 minutes. Place oven rack about two rungs from the top. Too close and it can burn. Too far away and it just misses the mark, what can I say?
9. After 15 minutes, remove pan from oven, turn chicken over, and apply lemon, salt, and paprika on each piece as before.

10. Return to broiler for 15 more minutes.
11. Pull out a pan of the best broiled chicken ever. Make sure the chicken's internal temp is 165° (160° for white meat).

Your chicken will be juicy, the skin will be luscious, browned and crispy; the whole thing's oh so tasty, and you are so very welcome.

Beauty and the Beast
4-14-2021

On March 26, 2021, in the time it took people to cower and embrace each other in bathtubs, basements, and interior rooms, to breathe in and out in the dark and to pray, the beast came to call just after midnight. It was breathing, too, roaring in fact, blowing out lethal 170 mph breaths, exhaling against everything in its way as it sped across miles of my town, Newnan, GA. It peeled back roofs, shingles, siding, beat windows into shards, walls into splinters, turned order into utter chaos. It sucked up rooted trees, spitting them out on power lines, homes, garages, and schools. For good measure, it blew the trees it didn't ingest into broken, twisted missiles and roadblocks.

When it was finally done the beast lifted itself away and disappeared, indifferent to the turmoil it left in its wake. And when quiet came, the people emerged to behold their places in the world. There was a collective gasp, and then the letting out of heavy, communal breaths of horror and disbelief. Then there were voices calling out in the black night,

"Hey Pat, are you and Pam OK?"

"Yeah, we're alive! How 'bout y'all?"

"We're OK!"

"Help! I smell gas!"

"Oh Miss Connie, your gas line is broken! I'll get my channel locks and turn it off!"

"Thank you!"

"Are you OK in there, Miss Nancy?"

"I am, thank you!"

And so it went, into the first morning light, when the full effects of the beast's rampage were becoming visible. On his rooftop, a young man – our son, Scott - the same one who turned off the gas behind his neighbor's house and checked on his other neighbors - stood and spoke quietly into his phone while making a video, panning across the ugly damage. Broken trees poked their sharp, black silhouettes upward, puncturing the dawning sky. Others lay like splintered Lincoln Logs tossed about everywhere in a suddenly unfamiliar, unnatural landscape. The unwelcome view was painful and harsh, a hideous, open wound, allowing him to see farther than ever before. The once quiet beauty of the place had been swallowed up by the beast and regurgitated, leaving a wretched, hopeless disarray.

And yet, in the quiet, half-light of dawn, as he prepared to speak, there were the sounds of birds.

He spoke for his - and all of - the broken neighborhoods in town when he said, stunned from the ordeal and so eloquent in his quiet assessment, "Any tree that is left standing is going to have to come down, so there are literally no trees left in Hollis Heights. A tree smashed Val's car, and fell all the way through the garage, which is leaning in, so that's gone. All in all, we are incredibly lucky in our specific location. Broken windows, roof damage, siding torn off. We can get stuff out of the garage. We can fix things. We can plant trees. But this is unbelievable."

In a moment of stark realization, the pain obvious on his face, he took a long, deep breath, blew it out, and said, directly to the camera now, "Well, two hours of sleep and the dawn is here. We have to start figuring things out now. Thank you to everyone who has checked in on us. Thank you for all the offers of help. We will call on you when we figure out what we need. But we're ok. Getting power back will be a big bonus. But for now we're gonna start digging out and making sure everyone has what they need around here. Oh, there's my dogwood tree! Wondered where that went. Thank you again for checking on us."

The video was still rolling as he stood looking out, in one more long, pensive moment. Then, he said, his voice catching, emotion on his face and flowing through his words, "But we are the City of Homes, and these homes are still standing."

Indeed. At least some of them. It is the collective spirit of the people that still stands, for sure. We are Newnan strong.

At midnight, on the other side of town, only a mile away, my husband and I were ensconced in our basement, too, after hearing the tornado warning, waiting for the storm to pass, praying it would miss us. We had heavy rain, maybe even hail as best we could determine, tap-tap-tapping on our basement windows. We lost power, internet, and cable. But there was no loud, approaching train blowing over us. We could hear something coming from the south that sounded like a huge white-noise machine. And then it stopped. I called my son.

"Mom, we took a direct hit. We're ok." he said, raw emotion in his voice. "I'm going to look outside now. Oh. My God… There are no trees…"

My husband was already putting on his raincoat and boots. Wild horses couldn't keep him away from rescuing them and the dog. Shortly after midnight, he drove as far as he could toward their house, until the trees and debris prevented him from going any further. He parked and started walking, probably a quarter mile, flashlight in hand. This way and that, right turn, left turn, detouring around debris, through dark gaps in yards and streets, he found himself standing in the dark at what should've been their intersection. It was a foreign land. He questioned if he had come to the right place. A fallen street sign illuminated by his flashlight told him, sadly, that he had, indeed, found it. There were voices, people calling to each other. Shadows wandering through yards looking out for each other and assessing damage.

Four traumatized boys and a dog trekked out of the neighborhood in the pouring rain with GrampaRick, the two parents at their side, reassuring the boys as they found their way to the car. Then their parents returned to secure and assess the damage at their house and their neighbors' houses. By the time the boys and Rick and the dog returned to our house, our power had been restored. Four soaking wet boys and a stinky, wet dog entered our house, traumatized, crying, backpacks soaked through. They needed reassurance, and a safe, dry place with power to unwind and try to sleep.

In Von Trapp fashion, we lined them up at the laundry room. We tossed their wet clothes into the dryer, and wrapped the boys in dry beach towels, blankets, and Rick's warm, just-dried shirts fresh from the dryer. Hot chocolate was some comfort. Hugs were better. They all chose where they wanted to be for the night and bedded down. This small bit of control was all they had left after mother nature had just sent the beast to crush that concept. Choosing one's bed was a small comfort, but it was comfort, nonetheless. It was easily 3am before they were all asleep.

The family joke, later, when jokes were even possible, was that Rick's first priority was rescuing the dog, since he's a veterinarian. Laughter is good medicine. Even if it takes a while to remember laughter is even possible.

In the days following the beast's ugly rampage, the beautiful people of Newnan showed up. They epitomized how goodness survives and thrives, even when things don't. Volunteers with chain saws, equipment, manpower, food, water, and supplies swarmed unbidden, yet oh so welcome, into Newnan's war-torn neighborhoods. Soon piles of debris, 6 feet high and climbing, were forming along the curbs of dusty, dirt-covered streets. Friends drove in from all over to help. They parked in undamaged areas and walked in to the war zone. Folks driving four-wheelers showed up to deliver people who couldn't walk that far but could offer help. The four-wheeler folks also loaded up much needed food, water, and supplies into areas that were inaccessible. Tornado relief groups began to organize and offer their assistance. Food banks and donation centers mobilized, staffed by their own workers and extra volunteers, ordinary citizens answering the call. The county fairgrounds became a central donation location where people could go for items they needed, and showers, laundry, and mental health services. A phone number was established for questions and volunteer opportunities.

Charitable disaster relief organizations like Red Cross arrived. Insurance companies erected tents at various locations and stationed claims centers underneath. Shelters opened. Churches made sandwiches, held clothing drives, walked the neighborhoods handing out water and food, and Easter baskets. Individuals walked the streets pulling coolers, handing out bottled water, sack lunches and snacks. Monetary campaigns were mounted for donations. Newnan was on the news nationwide. Calls and inquiries and volunteers from all over the state and the country poured in to help. Utility workers and linemen worked tirelessly. City and county offices geared up to make recovery as efficient as possible, waiving building permit fees, and discussing policies to help with re-building.

Helpers showed up at the most incredible moments. Rick and I were working to clean up our son's yard, and I noticed the banisters on his front porch were hanging off, nails poking out. I yelled over to Rick, "We need a sledge hammer!" Before he could answer, a woman parked at the curb beside the house opened her truck door and emerged.

"I've got one!" she yelled back, brandishing the long-handled tool like the Olympic torch. "What can I do to help?" And then, this angel proceeded to march right over and knock those banisters off in quick order, happy to help. Then she disappeared to offer her gifts elsewhere. Just. Like. That.

When the official report was released recently by the National Weather Center, it was declared that Newnan had suffered an EF-4 tornado. The beast was a half mile wide, skipping and jumping and barreling its destruction over as many as 39 miles for over an hour. The official, combined preliminary report from Georgia Emergency Management and Homeland Security Agency (GEMA/HS), City of Newnan, and Coweta County assessed the damage at 1744 homes, 120 of which sustained major damage, and 70 of which were completely destroyed.

Officials placed red, yellow, and green stickers on structures to advertise their status, green for "all is well," yellow for "damaged property but habitable," and red for "unsafe and uninhabitable." It is weird seeing them plastered on every house, like some kind of twisted Passover story, all three stickers sometimes appearing in the same block.

All in all, the caring hearts, generosity, support, and love people have displayed has been and continues to be nothing short of mind-boggling, heart-warming, and absolutely beautiful.

And it is by no means over. It will be a long road to recovery. The clean-up and re-building will be a part of Newnan for as long as it takes. Months, years. People are still living in hotel rooms and shelters. Many have lost everything.

In our part of town, only a mile away from our son, we had not one twig out of place. Our azaleas and dogwoods are in full, glorious spring bloom. I feel so fortunate, and I feel guilty. I caught my son standing alone, quiet, and wistful on our back porch at the end of a perfectly beautiful Easter Sunday afternoon last week. Face lifted to the sun, he was studying all our trees, taking in the green, green, green and the outrageous beauty of the blooms; our neatly ordered, partly shaded backyard, clean, and landscaped. I could see the pain on his face, reflecting what had happened on his side of town, and how things would not be same there for a long time, if ever.

That evening, he posted something on facebook that gave me a chill, a jolt of pride, and hope. Being a forester and a charity-minded guy he would think of it, of course. He said, he hoped when it is time to replant that everyone in his neighborhood (and elsewhere) would consider planting cherry trees. He would see if he could get the trees procured and find assistance in the planting.

Think of it! A Newnan Cherry Blossom Festival rising from the dead landscape, resurrecting neighborhoods, binding neighbors, and an entire city, together in solidarity, love, and remembrance. I can think of nothing better to serve as an offering and a living testament to the resilience of a community who rose above the suffering, and planted hope and beauty in the aftermath of a dark, destructive beast. A beast who will not have the last word. #newnanstrong

People taking food to tornado victims are bringing all kinds of wonderful meals. I'll contribute a recipe here, since this is supposed to be a food article. Actually, it's one of my son's favorite side dishes. Just one of the comfort foods along with the love we served up for him and his beautiful family on Easter at our house.

HASH BROWN CASSEROLE

- 2 lb bag frozen hash browns, thawed 30 minutes
- 1 cup diced onion
- 1 can cream of chicken soup
- 1 lb carton sour cream
- 1 stick butter
- 8 oz sharp cheddar, grated
- Salt and pepper

Mix all in bowl. Put in large baking dish. Bake 1 hour at 375°. May make a day ahead. Just refrigerate (or freeze!) and then bake a tad longer. Makes a bunch.

A Culinary Koan
5-19-2021

I learned a new word today. Learning words is one reason I love to read. The word for today is "koan." (Pronounce it KO-ahn.) A koan is essentially a problem or riddle that admits no logical solution. One famous one is, "What is the sound of one hand clapping?" Rooted in Zen, but oft repeated in stand-up comedians' routines and even in the animated move, Kung Fu Panda, it's one of the most famous koans ever. And if one finds a suitable answer to the unanswerable, they are considered enlightened.

I have a koan for you, my very own personal one. "When is a cucumber a zucchini?" While you grapple with that one, allow me to enlighten you with a little story, an excerpt from my book *The Veterinarian's Wife*.

> Rick and I were married in June 1971, and spent that summer in a tiny Athens, GA duplex behind the Gulf station on Park Avenue. Yes, we joked about how he was taking me to Park Avenue. He needed one physics class to graduate and complete Tuskegee Vet School's pre-veterinary requirements. The University of Georgia Veterinary School put him on the waiting list for admission. This meant his chances of getting in

at UGA were not great. Rick decided one physics course would not be too high a hurdle for his chances at gaining admission to Tuskegee, however. He was told they would wait for his transcript before making their decision on his application. Completion of the course didn't guarantee admission, even so. He would have to complete his class, send off his transcript and hope they accepted him.

Rick busied himself with summer school as I tried my newlywed-best to feather our very modest nest and find a job. The kitchen was minuscule; only one person able to squeeze in at a time. I had already demonstrated a complete and utter lack of success at the nearby laundromat, using way too much soap in the washing machine which resulted in just what you might expect: overflowing bubbles, approximating an "I Love Lucy" episode, which I found un-amusing, as did the proprietor who asked that I not return. I was due a successful domestic accomplishment, and as it so happened, I had the potential that same day to have it.

A neighbor had dropped off a sack of fresh-picked vegetables at our door while I was at the laundromat, and I set about to making something special for dinner. In the kitchen I peered in at the long, green vegetables, ripe and still warm from the summer sun. Reaching in, I took them out and laid them on the counter. Four nice big fat zucchinis! I marveled. I had already put two Cornish hens in the oven to roast, basting them with butter every 15 minutes, and they were approaching done. Then, as they were just finishing roasting, showing off a gorgeous golden skin and smelling divine, I retrieved a skillet to begin the vegetables. I washed and sliced the zucchini. Grabbing an onion from the tiny pantry, and butter from the refrigerator, I peeled and sliced the onion, and cut a generous cube of butter from the stick, placing both in a skillet to sizzle. After the onions were soft and smelling fabulous, I placed the zucchini in the skillet to sauté, and just as it was finishing, Rick walked in the door.

"Time for dinner!" I chirped, as a proud new wife and accomplished cook would. He sniffed the air, rich with butter, onions, and Cornish hens.

"Wow," he declared, as he smiled, impressed. "Smells great!"

He sat right down at the table, eager to partake. I served him his plate at our little black, round table on the sun porch off the kitchen. As I sat down with my plate, I saw him looking down at the gorgeous meal I had prepared. I had surprised myself with my new culinary talent. He took a bite of the zucchini.

"Well, there's a first time for everything," he whispered, forcing a smile as he chewed. My eyes wide, I gave him a quizzical look.

"Sweetheart, I have to say," he began, choosing his words, "I have never, ever in my life had sautéed cucumbers." Before I could say a word, he added, "but these are the best sautéed cucumbers I've ever had."

-End of excerpt

So back to our koan du jour. Ready? Here it is: "When is a cucumber a zucchini?" The answer? When you're unenlightened and you think it's one. And even then, it's not one. Not logical? Perfect.

All of this brings me to the recipe du jour. Drum roll – a zucchini recipe. Since those early married days I have learned a lot, and I haven't mistaken a cucumber for a zucchini since. Besides, cooking failures should never be taken as failures, per se. If nothing else, they are opportunities to develop a sense of humor, and learn what not to do the next time. And sweet Elvis, did I learn.

So you can trust me now with one really great zucchini recipe for the summer, especially as it includes tomatoes, and Vidalia onions too. And if you don't know what a zucchini is, you should enlighten yourself. You'll be so glad you did, or you'll have a good laugh telling the story on yourself down the road. If you do know what a zucchini is, you know that a zucchini is not a cucumber, nor is a cucumber a zucchini, no matter what. Om and Namaste, good for you, sing Hallelujah, and praise Elvis. You have arrived.

SUSIE'S ZUCCHINI CASSEROLE

- 6 small to medium zucchini
- 2 medium or 1 large tomato, chopped into large chunks / wedges
- 1 Vidalia onion cut into large wedges
- 1 cup sharp cheddar cheese, cut into small cubes
- ½ cup (or so) sharp cheddar cheese, grated
- ½ cup parmesan cheese
- 2 eggs
- Jane's Krazy Mixed Up Salt sprinkled liberally (do you know me? This spice is essential in my kitchen)

1. Wash zucchini and slice lengthwise into short sticks. Put in microwaveable dish with a little water (¼ cup?) and cover. Microwave on high to parboil for about 5 minutes. Drain.
2. Grease flat Pyrex casserole dish with olive oil or spray. Combine zucchini, tomato, onion, Krazy Salt, parmesan, and cubed cheddar in a bowl and mix well with hands. Place in dish.
3. Beat eggs with 2 tablespoons cold water. Drizzle over vegetables.
4. Distribute grated cheddar on top.
5. Bake uncovered at 350° for 30 minutes.

Beat the Summer Heat
6-23-2021

Ooh, Law it's hot! End of June and it already feels like the middle of July. Apparently, it's hot everywhere in America, though, especially out west in Arizona where people swear their dry heat is not as stifling as our humid, southern heat. Now, they are singing a different tune since their dry heat has ramped up to all new and higher triple digits than ever before. Even they are crying Uncle. We're all sizzling!

It's time to beat the heat with some cooking strategies that don't involve turning on the oven and heating up the kitchen. If you can stand the walk from your door or your pool, to your backyard grill and back without collapsing from heat stroke, you have taken the first step. The only thing we lack at our house is the backyard pool. We shall make do, brave the heat briefly for the grill walk, and enjoy eating in our cool kitchen.

For festive summer gatherings (we can do that now! Yay!) appetizers are nibble-worthy filler-uppers, pairing well with cold refreshing drinks. Fresh-made guacamole with chips, or grilled artichokes, and an ice-cold margarita or Sangria punch are the perfect partners. Texas Caviar is a fine and easy cold dip, made with corn, black beans, onions, and seasonings.

While hamburgers and hot dogs and steaks are pretty standard grilled fare and have their place, how about a simple, light, and lovely grilled salmon fillet with some dill sauce? Go to Costco, BJs, or Sam's and get some nice, thick ones. Or if you're lucky, your freezer still holds some fresh-caught salmon from the last man-trip your husband took to go fishing in Alaska. Or you can order your Alaskan salmon straight from Ed's Kasilof Seafood (https://kasilofseafoods.com/) and just tell everyone you went salmon fishing in Alaska.

If you're not a salmon fan, how about spatch-cocking a chicken on the grill? I mean, you can always prop a whole bird on one of those beer can roasters on the grill, but spatch-cocking is better in my opinion. Because it's flattened out, the chicken actually comes in contact with the grill, and you get nice grill marks and crispy skin. Those beer can roasters are kind of passé now anyway, like Billy the Singing Fish plaques, and mood rings. But whatever floats your boat, it's all good.

There's a frozen, no-cook cranberry ring I make every Christmas. It's good and sweet as a Christmas dessert, and does double duty as a rich, creamy stand-in for homemade ice cream on a hot summer day.

The summer drinks and punches. Oh so many wonderful liquid concoctions exist, and they can be made with alcohol, or without, with a few exceptions. If there's any such thing as a non-alcoholic Margarita, I can't imagine how it could possibly be worth its salted rim. I just don't even want to know. Don't forget the root beer floats for the kids and the grandchildren. I hope our grandchildren will always keep happy memories of us slurping floats through big straws as we sit together on the porch swing in the summertime. We sing, too, between slurps. Silly songs and sea shanties. But that's another article altogether.

Now for the qualifier:

Let us not forget the folks in our town who have neither a pool nor a grill, nor a kitchen, nor even a house after the F-4 tornado disaster blew through on March 26. We are Newnan Strong, and we can all still offer our help in a multitude of ways. Cook a meal for a besieged neighbor or friend. Or help a perfect stranger. Donate. Volunteer. Find folks who need assistance through the various agencies in town whose job it is to help those in need, like local churches, Bridging the Gap, Coweta Community Foundation, One Roof, and others.

GRILLED ARTICHOKES WITH ROASTED GARLIC AND LEMON AIOLI

- Artichokes
- Water to Cover
- 2 lemons, cut in half
- 1 tablespoon black peppercorns
- 1 tablespoon oregano
- ¼ cup olive oil
- 2 bay leaves
- 2 tablespoons kosher salt
- Butter

1. Poach artichokes in the above mixture until bottom leaves easily pull off, about 45 minutes to an hour.
2. Carefully remove from water to cool.
3. Cut artichoke in half lengthwise and remove the choke. When ready to serve, brush with whole butter and finish on grill to reheat.

ROASTED GARLIC AND LEMON AIOLI

- 1 head of roasted garlic (about 8 cloves together in a head) Cut off tops of garlic head, drizzle with olive oil and sprinkle with sea salt and double-wrap garlic head in foil. Place on grill, non-direct heat, close lid and roast for 30-45 minutes
- 1 each lemon (juice & zest)
- 2 cups mayonnaise

Squeeze roasted garlic out into mayo, add lemon and whirl all together in food processor until smooth.

HOMEMADE GUACAMOLE

- 3 Avocados — Find a couple or 3 ripe avocados. If they aren't ripe yet, bring home and place a small paper sack on counter for a day. They will ripen faster that way.
- 2 ripe, Roma tomatoes, chopped – see directions for avocados
- ¼ cup red onion, chopped
- 1 garlic clove, minced
- dash of Tabasco
- Jane's Krazy Salt (Do you know me? Then use this stuff. Makes all the difference)
- ¼ cup cilantro (or not), chopped
- ¼ cup parsley, chopped
- 1 fresh lime (juiced)

1. Slice avocado vertically all the way around and twist halves until they come apart. Remove pit. With spoon scoop avocado into bowl and mix with a fork. Don't mix it to death. Won't hurt to have a few bigger pieces. Your call on whether you want chunkier or smoother guac.
2. Add other ingredients to taste.

If you are like me, you don't do cilantro. But it's your choice.

For leftovers, push guacamole down packing it firmly into a container that has an airtight lid. Gently pour water on top of guac until it's completely covered. Apply lid. Will keep for a couple days without turning brown. To re-serve, pour off water first.

TEXAS CAVIAR

- 2 lbs. frozen corn
- 2 cans black beans
- 1 red onion
- 3 jalapeno peppers (fresh, not canned)
- ½ cup red wine vinegar

- ¼ cup olive oil
- cilantro (⅓ of a bunch?) chopped fine (leave it out if you don't like cilantro)
- salt and pepper

Mix it all together in a bowl. Serve with scoopy corn chips.

MARGARITA - FROM THE HORSE'S MOUTH (BARTENDER) IN CABO SAN LUCAS, MEXICO

Sorry, but I'm a purist with my Margs. I don't do the cruise-ship ones that use mixes and are blended like snow cones or shakes. Nope. I like mine pure and on the rocks. Apparently, the bartender who served me in Mexico felt the same way. I asked him specifically how he made his margaritas. This is what he said, and they are the absolute best.

- 1½ oz tequila
- ½ oz Cointreau
- Juice of one lime
- Ice
- Salted rim if you like that, but I'm a no-salt girl
- Short tub glass

Mix liquors and lime gently, add ice, salt glass rim if you must, and enjoy.

WHITE SANGRIA PUNCH

- 1 cup sliced strawberries
- 1 mango, cubed
- 1 peach, sliced
- ¼ cup granulated sugar
- ¼ cup Grand Marnier
- 1 apple, sliced

- 1 orange, sliced
- 1 lime, sliced
- 1 (750-ml.) bottle dry white wine, chilled (Use white Riesling, Pinot Grigio, Moscato, or Sauvignon Blanc)
- 1 cup club soda, or sprite, or Prosecco

1. In a medium bowl, combine strawberries, mango, peach, sugar, and Grand Marnier. Refrigerate for 1 hour.
2. To a large pitcher, add refrigerated fruit and apple, orange, and lime slices. Pour in white wine and soda, sprite, ginger ale, or Prosecco, and stir to combine. Serve well chilled.

NON-ALCOHOLIC PUNCH FOR A CROWD
Yield 4 gallons

- 4 12-oz cans frozen orange juice concentrate
- 4 12-oz cans frozen lemonade concentrate
- 2 46-oz cans pineapple juice
- 1 cup sugar
- 2 33.8 oz. bottles ginger ale

Dilute frozen concentrates as directed. Add pineapple juice and sugar. Blend well. Add ginger ale just before serving. Best if made a day ahead.

SUMMER ROOT BEER FLOATS

- Crushed ice
- Barq's Root Beer
- Vanilla Ice Cream

Put a little crushed ice in a tall glass. Add root beer. Leave some space at the top. Plop in a scoop of ice cream. Stir. Add large straw. Go sit on the porch swing with a kid and sing.

GRILLED SALMON FILLET

Salmon:
- 4 thick (¾ –1 inch salmon fillets. Do not remove skin on one side if skin is still attached

1. Rub fish with olive oil (or grape-seed oil which has a high smoke point, also)
2. Sprinkle with Montreal seasoning
3. Grill fillets 6-8 minutes on a hot grill (450)° skin-side down so they have nice golden-brown finish.
4. Do not try to move the fish before 6–8 minutes because it will stick at first, and then after time it crisps up and releases, allowing you to carefully flip it
5. Flip ONCE and cook for 1–2 minutes.
6. Internal temp should be about 130° when removed from grill.
7. It should rest for a few minutes until it comes up to 145°.
8. Bring inside and remove skin.

Aioli:
- Sliced cucumber (thin).

Add and mix well:
- ½ cup mayonnaise
- ½ cup sour cream
- 1 green onion chopped
- dill weed, maybe ½ tablespoon
- a little chopped parsley
- lemon juice, several capfuls or ¼ cup
- Krazy Salt
- CRUSHED GARLIC OPTIONAL

Serve salmon fillet on a bed of fresh spinach, top with Cucumber Aioli.

Pairs well with wild and brown rice.

Add cherry tomatoes and fresh parsley for garnish.

GRILLED SPATCH-COCKED CHICKEN

- 1 medium onion, peeled and cut in half
- 1 large garlic clove, peeled
- ⅓ cup packed fresh herbs, such as rosemary, thyme, parsley, and sage leaves
- ¼ cup extra-virgin olive oil
- ½ lemon, zest removed in strips with a peeler
- 1 chicken (3 ½–4 pounds), spatch-cocked (see instructions, below)
- Coarse salt and freshly ground pepper

1. Puree onion, garlic, herbs, oil, and zest in a food processor. Rub some puree under skin of chicken breast. Rub remaining puree over rest of bird. Refrigerate at least 6 hours and up to 8 hours.
2. Let stand at room temperature 30 minutes. Wipe off most of rub, season with salt and pepper.
3. Heat grill to medium-high or set up for indirect heat. Grill chicken, breast side down, covered with vent open, until nicely charred, 10 to 15 minutes.
4. Flip; cook 30 minutes more.
5. Flip again; grill until internal temperature reaches 165° in thickest part of breast, 5 minutes more.
6. Let rest 10 minutes.

To spatch-cock a chicken, cut along each side of the backbone with shears. Remove the backbone. Turn the bird breast side up; flatten it with your palm.

CRANBERRY RING DESSERT

This is like rich ice cream!

- 1 cup fresh cranberries – "blenderized"
- ⅓ cup sugar
- 2 medium oranges
- 1 8-oz package creamed cheese, softened
- 1 teaspoon vanilla
- 1 medium chopped apple
- ½ cup chopped dates
- 1 cup heavy whipping cream

1. Combine cranberries and sugar. Let stand 10 minutes.
2. Peel and section 1 orange. Squeeze and reserve juice. Chop orange fine.
3. Squeeze remaining orange for a total of ⅓ cup juice.
4. In a bowl, put juice, cream cheese and vanilla together and beat till fluffy.
5. Stir in orange sections, cranberries, apples, dates.
6. In a separate bowl, whip cream into peaks. Fold cream into cream cheese mixture.
7. Turn into Bundt pan or angel cake pan or springform pan; or 8x4x2 loaf pan or 8–9 individual molds. Cover with foil.
8. Freeze 3 hours MINIMUM. Overnight is better.
9. When ready to serve, let stand 10–15 minutes and then unmold to a platter or flat cutting board. It will be hard frozen at first, but it will soften quickly.
10. Slice to serve on a plate or in a bowl. Drip chocolate or shave chocolate on top if you like. Also put some cranberries, sugar, and a little Grand Marnier in a small saucepan and simmer til fruit is soft for an adult topping. Let cool before putting on. Serves 8–10

Unmolding tricks:

If it won't unmold after sitting out for 10–15 minutes, set the pan down in a sink or larger pan filled with room temp water (not hot water or you'll melt it!) for a couple of minutes. It may take a couple of tries.

Peachy Keen Road Trip
7-28-2021

I am really keen on peaches, those luscious gifts of summer that can be consumed in so many satisfactory ways. Nothing else quite compares, really, to the flavor, and the sweet, rich juice that runs down your chin when you bite into a whole, ripe peach. If you do that while sitting on a southern porch swing or rocker in the summer with a friend or a loved one at your side, and a dog slumbering at your feet, you might even see Jesus. Or Elvis at a minimum.

We have a favorite place we go at least once every summer to get our fresh, ripe peaches. It's a bit of a road trip, but not far enough to have to pack an overnight bag. The Shed at Fitzgerald Fruit Farms in Woodbury, GA is less than an hour's scenic drive from Newnan, and frankly, I would drive even farther if necessary.

From Newnan, we take Highway 29 south and Alt. Highway 27 south, passing by some terrific sites on the way, Bubba Doo's in Luthersville being a sentimental one for us. Years ago when my husband, Rick, was a practicing large-animal veterinarian running the roads at all hours, he dined at Bubba Doo's often when it was in its heyday. Back then its full name was Bubba Doo's World-Famous Burgers and Oil Filters. Now it is a convenience store and gas station only, rougher around its edges and showing its age, and no longer housing tables or a kitchen serving burgers or any other prepared food. I'm not sure about the oil filters. But it still ranks as a significant memory from years of past travels. It reminds me of a favorite t-shirt I had once that said on the front, "Fred's Fill Dirt and Croissants."

We pass by Moreland Animal Hospital where Rick works (and won Best Veterinary Practice in the most recent Newnan-Coweta Magazine poll). The Lewis Grizzard and Erskine Caldwell Museums are in Moreland, too, if one feels like kicking the brake for some local history and culture. Go ad lib or plan ahead: https://morelandadventure.com/museums.

Once you get to Woodbury, go visit Red Oak Creek Covered Bridge, the oldest and largest wooden covered bridge in Georgia, where else but on Covered Bridge Rd. The historical marker there says it was "built in the 1840s by freed slave and noted bridge builder, Horace King." It's scenic as can be. Walk or drive through the long, dark brown, wood and tin clad, barn-like structure resting on heavy planks and wooden pegs. The bridge spans the creek where the kids can take their shoes off and wade. A picnic table sits beside the creek, a perfect place for a photo and a bite to eat.

But the main event is Fitzgerald Fruit Farms in Woodbury, "the largest first-generation peach operation in the state," according to their website. Read all about them and get directions at https://www.fitzgeraldfruitfarms.com/.

The Shed is their indoor retail space that houses everything from fresh peaches to a wine-tasting room. It's fairly new, this building, since a tornado came through a couple of years ago and wiped their original outdoor fruit stands off the map. This new iteration is air-conditioned and has rockers sitting on their front porch under ceiling fans. You'll have to bring your own dog if you want one of those at your feet while you enjoy your ice cream and rock awhile.

Every day they make fresh, homemade peach and strawberry ice cream. On weekdays they produce about three gallons per day, but on busy weekends they will crank out fifteen or twenty gallons a day to hungry visitors jonesing for a sweet trip to heaven in a cup or cone, the recipe for which is top secret. Trust me, I tried. They are not giving it up.

I highly recommend a trip to The Shed at Fitzgerald's Fruit Farms, 3355 Imlac Rd, Woodbury, GA 30293. Get you some peaches and some ice cream. Eat the ice cream right there and bring a bushel of peaches home. Make sure you get enough that you can eat them fresh, freeze some, and make some wonderful pies, cobblers, and beehives with them. What's a beehive? Since you asked, I'll tell you (see recipe).

And whatever you do, enjoy your peachy keen road trip. Worth it!

PEACH BEEHIVE

- Absolutely perfect peaches, soft but not mushy – 1 per person

Pastry Mix:
- 1⅓ cup flour, unsifted
- ½ cup Crisco
- ¾ teaspoon salt

1. Wash peaches, removing any part of stem remaining. While still wet, roll peaches in bowl of sugar (it won't stick evenly). DO NOT PEEL!
2. Make pastry by blending/pulsing pastry mix ingredients in food processor and then put in mixing bowl.
3. Make a well in dough and add enough water to make a ball (4-5 tablespoon ice water).
4. Press dough into mixing bowl to get most of crumbs into ball. Don't overwork dough.
5. Then transfer to prep board coated with flour and roll into a ¼" – ½" thick rectangle. With sharp knife, cut into ½" strips.
6. Place peach stem-down in palm of hand.
7. Starting at the top, wrap strips around the peach, overlapping strips like a beehive, being sure to cover every inch of peach so juices don't escape while baking.
8. Keep peach in hand while wrapping. Your hand's heat helps

to seal dough.
9. When finished, pat to seal.
10. May be wrapped in Saran in fridge overnight.
11. To bake, place peaches in shallow pan. Coat each with egg white.
12. Bake 375° for about 40 minutes or until slightly brown. Serve warm with homemade vanilla ice cream!

Waiting for Cobbler
9-15-2021

It seems we are living in an era of interminable waiting. Waiting to finish what we start. Waiting for things to change. Seasons, pandemics, minds, hearts. Mail delivery.

I'm waiting. Waiting to sit outside and eat dinner on our porch. I'm also waiting for our new porch chairs to be delivered, which feels a lot like waiting for Godot. Not gonna happen unless somebody changes the script and straightens out the cosmic mystery of the black hole in Austell where packages go to die these days.

Rick and I have worked hard to re-hab our covered back porch so it will be in shape for cooler weather; for sitting outside on a pressure-washed, freshly painted porch under string lights on a clear, nippy night; for enjoying outdoor meals and tailgating as we watch SEC football on a spare TV, newly installed in a gorgeous, $100 miracle-flea-market-find armoire on the porch. Gorgeous notwithstanding, this thing is a behemoth requiring many hard-won steps to fruition.

There was the matter of fetching it, preparing it to protect it from the outside elements, and rehabbing the space it would inhabit. This whole project was a family affair, requiring help from our son, Scott and his lovely partner, Val, who gamely met us in Atlanta and helped lug it onto his flatbed trailer and then into our garage. This thing is impossibly heavy. They all ate their spinach that day, for sure.

I painted the piece with a coat of Marine varnish while Rick removed some brick steps that were impeding the spot where we wanted to place the armoire. First, he tried chipping away with a hammer and small chisel—dink-dink-dink. It would be the twelfth of never before that worked. Then he wised up and went with the big guns, renting a big cement saw. Eureka! He then poured a new cement slab where the useless steps once sat in the way. With a revisit from our son we lugged our behemoth baby up the back steps and into its final resting place at the back of the porch. Perfect fit! It's marvelous! Someone call Good Housekeeping! Bring on the tailgate!

Rick likes to joke about how this $100 miracle find got more expensive by the day. I say it wasn't that much more and it was entirely worth it. Our porch is spiffed up now, so we feel like we're actually visiting some really nice place we've never been before when we go out there. Consider it a pandemic travel strategy. Soon we'll be sipping adult beverages, tailgating, and roasting chocolate-filled marshmallows (at Kroger, you're welcome) in the chiminea with the grandchildren.

We all wait. We wait to live better while life around us is chaotic and disparate, even dangerous. Pretending things aren't that way is no solution. Dealing with things as they actually are, shows promise. Who's to say how, and at what cost? Will we ever agree, or just keep kicking the conundrum can down the road and wait some more? We wait.

I'm waiting for my Editor to deliver her high developmental edit of my book, *The Veterinarian's Wife*, before it goes to the final edit and then the publisher. It's agony, this waiting. My Editor tortured and delighted me with her initial email after receiving my manuscript:

"Hi, Susie, I'm letting you know that I'm getting into your book! Goodness, I love your sass and the way your smart sentence structure prompts me to smile and also continue reading!"

I'll be honest. My first thought was, "Oh wow! Awesome! Now, this is probably a fluke, so when you get past paragraph one, tell me what you really think. I'll try not to despair over the bad news."

I'm not a fatalist as much as I am just overtly insecure and self-deprecating. I'm waiting.

So we are all waiting these days. Waiting on some level for answers, inspiration, hope, and/or resolution. Waiting for good things to happen, or for an unnamed sadness to leave us. I just learned of another person I know who died of Covid. I am waiting for the shock, grief, and anger to subside. It's gotten very old. Everyone can relate right now.

We can all do ourselves a favor, though. Engage. Do something while we wait. Something good. Read or write a book. Rehab your porch. Send a handwritten love note. Make a cobbler. Garden. Wear a mask. Get vaccinations. Volunteer. Smile. Donate some stuff. Yes, you know you have too much stuff. Give it away to someone who needs it. Be kind. Cultivate gratitude. Say so.

Do not engage in comparisons; glide past social media posts that bring you down. You know the ones. Angry posts, perfection photos, and vacation brags that invite us to sit at our pity tables and drink that Kool-Aid made from red dye #2 and the salty tears of toxic envy.

Here's a thought: adjust your response. Choose outright, vicarious pleasure from others who are having more fun than you are right now, and pray they survive it. Cheer them on. Then redefine "fun" or "productive" or "engaged" and go make your own brand of it. Make it positive. And safe. Choose empathy for others if you're the one with it all. Frankly, no one has it all, anyway. Everything's relative. If you are sick, or grieving, or alone, try to remember the people who love you and let it give you comfort.

Recently, we waited for the final shoe to drop in a spectacular mashup of those two venerated canons, Superstition, and Immutable Fact: "Bad news/things come in threes," and "No good deed goes unpunished."

ONE: Working on our porch improvement task two weeks ago, Rick dropped a granite slab on his big toe. Sweet Mother of Bob Vila, that hurt. He's okay. Miraculously nothing was broken (his toe or the granite) and he's walking, but his toe may look like a catcher's mitt for a good, long time.

TWO: Yesterday, billows of smoke filled the house and set off the fire alarm as Rick was "seasoning" an oiled cast iron pot in the oven at 400° for what turned out to be just a tad too long.

THREE: Also yesterday, Rick was helping our grandson and boy scout, Harper, make "camp out cobbler" in the newly seasoned cast iron pot of recent fire-drill calamity. See number two above. This entailed the first use of an outdoor, metal cooking stove Harper had proudly created in his welding class at boy scout camp this summer. Which in turn involved red-hot coals and fire inside said gizmo, the pot sitting on top, and more red-hot coals piled on the lid of the pot, heating the cast iron pot and the cobbler ingredients clear through, top to bottom.

Then, it was time for the big reveal: perfect peach cobbler! Little did they know Bad Thing Number Three was waiting in the wings for just the right moment to pounce. With long tongs Rick grasped the handle of the red-hot lid to safely lift it off the pot. Cue Number Three! Aaaand Action! The cast iron lid full of hot coals and ash tipped to one side, dropping its volcanic load directly into that pot full of beautiful, outdoor-oven-baked boy scout cobbler. Yep. Stunned silence. A few expletives. And the joke: "Care for a plate of hot coal-ash with a soupçon of cobbler?" This whole endeavor had become a sad country music song, just without a pickup truck, or dog dyin' the day mama got outta prison. No, this was just a simple cuss it and cry in yer beer song (root beer for the kids). BUT WAIT. There's that "wait," again.

If bad news comes in threes, so can good news:

ONE: Rick dug underneath the inedible, hot mess and found one tiny pocket of pristine cobbler deep down inside.

TWO: Harper judged it delicious.

THREE: This was only a trial run. We have more ingredients, and more coal, along with a cleaned pot, and Harper's welded gizmo. The campout is this weekend, where Harper will shine. Lessons were learned. And the three bad things are fulfilled and over. (Until next time. Shhh. Don't jinx it.)

So while we wait, we live; we can become sick of the vicissitudes of life, and all the waiting, waiting, waiting, or we do something, if we can, to make life better. Not just for ourselves, but for others, too. And if we can't make a life better, if it's not in the cards, we say "thanks be" for it, bow our heads in reverence, and we bless it just the same.

Make some cobbler. You've waited long enough for the recipe. Here it is, our version anyway.

And guess what!! My chairs just arrived!! There IS a Godot!

CAMPOUT COBBLER

- 1 box of yellow cake mix
- (2) 30 oz cans of peaches, or fruit of choice. Drained.
- 1 can of Sprite
- 1 stick of butter

Tip: Use a foil Dutch oven liner (try finding one at camp-supply stores) for easier clean up.

1. Spread fruit in the bottom of a lined Dutch oven and then sprinkle cake mix over the top. We used some of our frozen peaches from Fitzgerald Fruit Farms. Stellar!
2. Pour can of Sprite over the peaches and cake mix and stir until all powder is moist.
3. Cut butter into small pats and drop them evenly over the top. This will give the cobbler a nice, golden brown.
4. Cover with lid, place pot on the heat using hot coals on the bottom and apply more hot coals on the lid of the Dutch oven. Cook for about 45 minutes (or if you aren't doing this outside with charcoals, just bake in a 350° oven for 45 minutes.)
5. Serve warm with ice cream or whipped cream.

Celebrate!

Still Falling For Fall
11-3-2021

Whee, Halloween's over. Let's talk Christmas! Yelp. Kidding! Let's not and say we did.

It's not even Thanksgiving yet, people. It's just fall right now. Period.

Poor fall gets a little shortchanged once big holidays steal the show. Yes, there's the end of summer excitement over the autumn leaf shows, and apples, and trips to Helen and the mountains, pumpkin patches, and mums. But at the first mention of pumpkins, Starbuck loses its mind and Halloween hogs the stage. Thanksgiving and Christmas are waiting impatiently in the wings. Must we be so holiday-centric, or can we give fall a little more time to shine on her own merits?

In deference to my beautiful, chilly, messy friend, fall, whose leaves are still beautiful right now, I am here to give her a bit more solo attention in the spotlight before she exits stage left. She will age soon enough and drop her leaves in large numbers on my grass, requiring a ton of yard work. So right now while I still love her, she deserves some well-earned applause of her very own without having to share the stage with holiday scene stealers. Not that there's anything wrong with major holidays. They just need to chill (see what I did there?) and be respectful of mother nature and the season from whence they come.

Soup. Yep. Just good old soup. You can class it up, as in Vichyssoise and Lobster Bisque, but by and large soup is not sexy. You can't hang ornaments and lights on it, or carve it at the dinner table, or fry it up in your hot oil fryer out on the back deck. But how much do we love and adore hot, steamy, soul-warming soup in the chilly fall? All kinds of heaven in a mug or a bowl.

Speaking of spotlights, here's a recipe for a soup I just made that is so yummy it could come from a fine, Michelin star restaurant kitchen, but didn't. I've highly rated it as my own home-cooking brand of Michelin star: the "Culinary DIY Worth a Trip from Anywhere" Star.

I discovered Kasey Trenum's recipe when my husband and I decided recently to take off some extra avoirdupois and embarked on the Keto diet (yay fat and protein, boo carbs and sugar). Seriously, you really would never know. It's just delicious no matter what.

Three CDIYWTA Stars go to: Keto Tuscan Soup. The best part is that actually this soup will work during any season. But as an introduction to fall, it has no peer!

The rakes and blowers are cued and warming up, just in front of those stage hams, Thanksgiving and Christmas. Enjoy fall, y'all, while you can.

KETO TUSCAN SOUP

Prep Time 15 minutes
Cook Time 50 minutes
Serves 8

- 1 lb Italian sausage
- 3 tablespoons butter
- ½ onion
- 2 garlic cloves
- 8 oz chopped radishes peeled and chopped (optional. I hate radishes.)
- ¼ cup chopped tomatoes
- 8 oz mushrooms sliced

- 5 cup chicken broth
- 2 cup heavy whipping cream
- 1 teaspoon basil
- 1 teaspoon parsley
- 1 teaspoon salt
- ½ teaspoon pepper
- ¾ cup sharp cheese
- 4 oz baby spinach
- ½ cup crumbled, cooked bacon
- ½ fresh cauliflower florets

1. In a dutch oven, brown Italian sausage in larger chunks than drain and set aside.
2. In the same dutch oven, add 3 tablespoons butter, garlic, onion, mushrooms, tomatoes, and (if you insist) radishes. Sauté for 7 minutes.
3. Add about ¼ cup of the chicken broth to the pot, then deglaze using a wooden spoon to scrape brown bits from the bottom. All the bits that are stuck to the bottom of your pot are flavorful, so don't discard these.
4. Add the rest of the chicken broth and seasoning, then bring to a boil.
5. Reduce to medium heat and cook for 20–30 minutes with the lid on, or until the radishes are tender. Stoves cook differently, so you may need to adjust your cooking time.
6. Add sausage, heavy whipping cream, and spinach to your pot and simmer on low with the lid on for approximately 10 minutes.
7. Add cheese, cauliflower, and crumbled bacon. Stir until cheese melts.
8. Serve hot. (duh!)

Soup can be frozen for up to 6 weeks in a tightly sealed container.

Adventures with Chicken Skin
12-11-2021

"Meat department. How may I help you?"

"Well, I'm calling because I was wondering if your store carries—or can order for me—chicken skin?"

"Chicken skin? Just the skin? Ma'am, we don't have just skin. That's not even a thing."

"Au contraire, my dear boy, chicken skin is, indeed, a thing, and I aim to get me some."

"So why don't you just buy a bunch of chicken, tear off the skin, and use that?"

"Because I like my chicken broiled with its skin on. I have this whole routine with lemon juice, seasoned salt, and paprika, 30 minutes under the broiler. Can't do better than that. But I also want to fry or bake some chicken skins without having to render the chicken I already have bare-nekkid."

"Really, ma'am? Why do you want to cook just chicken skins, anyway?"

"Because I'm telling you, fried chicken skins are a thing! And because if you haven't had 'em don't knock 'em. I recently had some as a delicious, hot, appetizer at a high-end restaurant on Hilton Head Island. Cut into small bites, cooked up golden and served with a tasty dipping sauce of sump'n-sump'n on the side, they were crunchy, warm, salty little bites of 'dear-lord-these-are-fabulous.' The pink shirt, plaid slacks, golfing resort crowd loved them. Not to mention the retired, coat-and-tie execs and their petite wives wearing classic St John boucle knit suits sitting near us. The millennials gobbled 'em up as they drank and drank. And the casual in-betweens, like my hubby and me? We just tried not to draw too much attention as we savored and slurped one bite after another. Are you familiar with pork rinds, sir?"

"Sure."

"Well fried or baked chicken skins will turn your head away from those cold swine chips, and make you a clucking chicken-skin convert."

"I'm curious, ma'am. Even if the store could order some chicken skins, which we can't, how much skin are we talkin'?"

"Oh, maybe a couple pounds. I'm not trying to open a chicken-skin food truck. Just enough for an appetizer, you know? And enough to reserve a couple pounds in my freezer for future "partays," as the young crowd says. Like what I did there, son?"

"Ha, yes ma'am. Well, ma'am, I guess the best we can do for you is if you buy a bunch of whole chickens then we'll process 'em here at the store for you by removing the skins, but that still leaves you with skins and, um, a lot of nekkid chicken, as you say."

"I suppose I could use that nekkid chicken to make soups, casseroles, and oh yes, chicken salad—breast meat only, of course. I'm sure you are aware there are strict rules in the south about proper chicken salad etiquette."

"Oh, yes ma'am, if you say so. Now will there be anything else I can help you with?"

"I'll think about it. I may take you up on your kind processing offer or maybe I'll just buy some whole chickens and skin them myself. Or, I might just grab my hubby and take a little road trip, but not to the store. I want to go about 3 hours south and visit White Oak Pastures in Bluffton, Georgia. I've checked them out online. They have chicken skins, my dear, just so you know. And a butcher shop, and a general store. And farm tours. And a restaurant. And cabins. They are devoted to animal welfare, land regeneration, and rural revival. Their website says the renovation of the historic building housing their retail business in downtown Bluffton is 'A Bold Return to Giving A Damn.' Oh my, don't they sound sassy? And doesn't that sound like a great adventure!? I mean, nothin' against your grocery store, but…"

"Seems like some pretty expensive chicken skins after all that, ma'am. But sounds like fun, too. You seem very interesting."

"Yes, sir, who knew one could make a whole experience from a chicken-skin quest? Expanding one's knowledge through travel and experiences is a priceless endeavor, whether to the south of France or south Georgia to a working, sustainable, 5,000 acre farm near a little burg, population 100. That settles it. Adventure awaits. Thanks for talking this out with me, young man."

"Uh, my pleasure, ma'am. Sorry I couldn't be of more help."

"Ha, you've been very helpful! I'll bring you a yummy, crispy warm chicken skin when we get back. Would you prefer baked or fried? Flour or flourless? You and your store will become fans, for sure. I just know it."

"Well, okay then, ma'am. It doesn't matter which kind you bring. I sure look forward to that. Maybe after I taste your chicken skin I'll eat my words, too! Oh, and when you come, ask for Darryl."

"My pleasure, Darryl. I'll be sure to do that. Bye-bye."

"Bye, ma'am. You have a great trip. You remind me a lot of my granny. She was great."

"No better compliment, Darryl. None better. Thank you. See you soon."

WEEKLY COLUMNS 2022- 23

For the Love of a Southern February
2-6-2022

I love February.

It's the month of my birthday, my husband's birthday, and Valentine's Day.

I love standing at my kitchen sink, sipping coffee, looking out my big kitchen window in February. No matter my mood, and no matter the weather, I see February miracles out that window that lift me and bestow hope.

Our cherry tree at the back edge of the grass bears the faintest drifts of pale pink buds along bare limbs. Every day they will open a little more, and I get to watch it happen.

Along each side of the woodland garden path, beyond the rose arbor laden with thorny winter-brown canes, the Lenten roses raise their sweet, blooming faces to the sky. Over many Februarys they have spread themselves with abandon, from the path's borders far into the woods, as an ever-expanding ground-cover full of fertile grace. More babies drop and grow every year onto the path, too. When it's warmer, I re-plant them where they are safe so they will grow up and flourish amongst their mamas and siblings.

Daffodils are emerging and if we're lucky, they burst open into bloom at some point during February. Historically, we've had some crazy snows down south in February. Still, the daffodils insist on surviving, poking their green spears above cold, white blankets daring them to freeze or suffocate. The daffodils might slow down a bit, but they ultimately survive, loud and proud and full of promise. I love them for that. My mama always had a vase filled tight with fresh, bright daffodils on our kitchen table every year on my birthday. I try to do the same on our kitchen island now, and if the daffodils are a little late, missing the exact day, it's OK. Close enough. I have faith. Sometimes when I feel helpless, or scared, or lost in a blizzard of emotional snow, it's a good and joyful thing to remember the inevitability of spring and those daffodils. To me, daffodils always mean it's my birthday, spring is coming, someone loves me, and all's right with the world.

February feeds me in so many ways. Our kitchen is the heart of our home, where I can look out the window at the ever-changing landscape; inside my husband and I often sit at the kitchen island to eat, pay bills, cook, chat, welcome family and friends. And in February, we celebrate our birthdays and Valentine's Day. It's where we cook food, congregate, and create memories.

Making Valentine sweets, writing cards, and engaging in little acts of love and kindness all begin in our kitchen. When our boys were little, on Valentine's morning I set their places at the island with big doilies as place mats, red plates, and wine glasses filled with heart-shaped red hots and Hershey kisses. I pressed I Love You into their toast with a little plastic bread-press. Red strawberries adorned their cereal if I could manage to convince them to eat fruit, or they ate some now-forgotten brand of festive, awful sugary cereal made with red dye #2, maybe Trix. Their drinks were "Roy Rogers" served in fancy glasses, usually orange juice with a touch of ginger ale, a splash of red grenadine, and topped with a maraschino cherry. Last but not least, I always folded a paper valentine heart around a white paper napkin. Ah the memories.

But wait. There's more! I must add why I particularly love this February. Way to bury the lede, right? Could be I'm just trying to be cool and not reveal that I am beside myself with unbridled excitement. Too late now. I've said it, so here it is.

My book, *The Veterinarian's Wife, a Memoir by Susie Berta* is out just in time for Valentine's Day! You can go to Amazon and order it right now (paperback only. Kindle available later!). Talk about February love. This thing has been a huge labor of love that I've been cooking up for several years (yes at my computer in my kitchen), and now I get to release it to the world for Valentine's Day. How appropriate, I say. Hope you love it. And if not, wait until after Valentine's Day to tell me, OK?

Love to you all, and enjoy everything February and Valentine's Day have to offer!

Rupert Brooke, My Mother, and Me
2-12-2022

The Literature Clock is a website that displays a literary quote which includes the exact time you're visiting. Here's what I got at 2:50 PM recently:

"…Stands the Church clock at ten to three? And is there honey still for tea?..."

- Last lines of the poem, "The Old Vicarage, Grantchester," by Rupert Brooke

Those who have read my new book, *The Veterinarian's Wife, A Memoir* (on Amazon, wink, wink) may recall that I wrote about the impact one particular Rupert Brooke poem had on my mother and me at a pivotal juncture in our lives. Brooke was my mother's favorite; therefore a sentimental favorite of mine, too. So the coincidental intersection of the Brooke quote I got online and the recent publishing of my book both warms and haunts me.

A celebrated British poet in the early 1900s, Brooke lived in Grantchester, not far from Cambridge, England. If you're not an Anglophile or a traveler, you may not know about this charming village except for the popular fictional PBS mystery series "Grantchester" which is actually filmed there. It features a handsome, crime-solving vicar and plenty of suspense and romance to go along with the gorgeous scenery.

The Rupert Brooke pub is also there, only fourteen miles from Cambridge, or as they happily advertise online, "a scenic 45-minute walk by the river, through the water meadows and up into the village." The renovated pub is "nestled in the beautiful village, a stone's throw from the bustling sights and sounds of Cambridge." Their selling point is "frosty afternoon strolls, warming seasonal food, and cozy fireside evenings." And their namesake, of course, Rupert Brooke. Duh.

I want to go there. Now. Actually I want to go anywhere. Covid is still a cruel party pooper.

Twenty years ago on our one trip abroad together, my husband, Rick and I went to England with his sister, Lisa and her husband, Bob. We visited Cambridge, a "college town" like no other. We were still young enough to enjoy "punting the Cam," which is colloquial for carefully lowering oneself to a seated position onto the bottom of a shallow, tippy, narrow, wooden boat, and floating down the River Cam, while a guide steers the boat with a pole, Venice-style.

We floated past majestic buildings housing old colleges and universities. If you want "old," get out of the United States and travel. "Old" in Britain means buildings from the 1200s in the days of King Henry III and even earlier.

We sailed by the never-ending scenic beauty of sunny riverbanks, glistening green grass, cherry blossoms, and daffodils. Lisa and I were lying back against our spouses, each couple facing the other at opposite ends of the boat. She and Bob looked comfortable. Rick and I settled in, too, and I did my best not to worry about how I would get out of said boat when it was all over. Even so, it was quite the romantic time.

When we disembarked (it wasn't pretty, but I made it) we all trod the Cambridge cobblestones to quaff some ale at a pub and relax. After a refreshing drink, I realized I was about to miss evensong at the famous King's College Chapel. Polling the others at our table and getting zero takers, I ran like a scalded mule from what seemed like one end of Cambridge to the other, making it inside the historic chapel just in time for... how do I describe it? Magic. The building, the service, the music, the choir, the organ, the acoustics, the whole experience was worth every anxious huff, puff, and arthritic protestation from my 53-year-old knees. When the others finally showed up afterward, I emerged to exclaim how four-letter-ing fabulous it was! I have never been one to hold back.

I had no idea about The Rupert Brooke pub in Grantchester back then. I would've included it in our trip. But like so many things, you just can't get everything in. I wanted to visit Wordsworth's house in the Lake District, too, because of his poem and all the daffodils (my spirit flower if you will). Instead we visited the charming, thatch-roofed Cotswolds and then took in a gorgeous garden in the Lake District. It was all good..

There was one little hiccup, though, when we stopped for fuel. It was Bob's turn to jump out and work the fuel pump. Only a few miles down the road, when our re-fueled rental car sputtered and died on the freeway near Lockerbie, Scotland, we realized Bob had accidentally put regular gas into our diesel car. Easy—but eventful—American tourist mistake.

We waited hours for our tow truck to arrive. Finally, in desperation, our men stood guard beside the car on the grassy shoulder to shield us from view of the highway traffic, as we ladies executed—how shall I say this delicately—deep-knee-bend "royal curtsies"—in order to relieve bursting bladders that would not wait. We could not predict the absurd Monty Python moment that was about to ensue.

On the path at the top of the grassy hill, a group of riders on horseback clip-clopped by, getting a full view of our activities. "Cheerio!" shouted everyone, howling and waving.

That would never happen today, only because I've lost the ability to "curtsy." Hooray for old age.

So as I reflect on my serendipity over bumping into Rupert again, I also feel sad for him. He developed septicemia from a mosquito bite, of all things, and died in 1915 at the age of only 27 on a World War I hospital ship off the Greek island of Skyros. He was buried in an olive grove on the island. I guess being buried on a Greek island in an olive grove is a fitting, romantic end for such a poet as Rupert Brooke.

On our next trip, I want to visit Greece and eat the olives and drink Grappa. We will make that happen after we visit Wordsworth's daffodils in England, and that famous pub in Grantchester. We will all hoist a glass to its namesake, Rupert Brooke. And my mother.

For Better or Worse
2-20-2022

No surprise, we have evolved and continue to evolve in so many ways, for better and for worse. The evidence is clear. I haven't seen Fred and Wilma Flintstone pushing a wooden cart through Publix lately, have you? But I haven't been to WalMart in a while, so…

Our holidays have certainly evolved. In ancient times those romantic Roman men showed their love by sacrificing animals and whipping their women with the hides. St. Valentine was brutally executed in the 3rd century AD and became a martyr. Now "Be My Valentine" has a whole different connotation. Chocolates, flowers, and dinner.

Clearly we have moved on.

Our toys have evolved. Straw dolls to Xboxes. Barbie and Ken continue to evade extinction. Together for six decades now, they constantly progress, especially Barbie who has had more personalities than "Sybil."

Barbie's had careers in education, the military, politics, medicine, public service, science, engineering, transportation, the arts, business, sports, journalism, and those that are hard to categorize like beauty queen, beekeeper, and cat burglar. How *does* she do it? She is definitely her own strong, modern woman and continues to choose Ken, who, by the way, now comes in several skin tones, muscular builds, and hair styles. Now if only she would get fat.

We don't wear bustles, or spats anymore, although styles have a way of coming back around again. Fashion is a slippery slope. Just watch the Met Gala every year. Evolution or expensive madness? Your pick. Generally, I try to find timeless looks that stay in style for more than a minute, as long as I have three different sizes to choose from in my closet. And still, there have been times I just didn't fit in with my surroundings.

I wore a bright red car coat to New York City once long ago and felt like a loud, flashing police light in a dark, monochrome sea of mourners. My dear southern friend, Liz, tells a hilarious story about her unfortunate decision to wear a print dress with colorful, oversized flowers to a business meeting in Manhattan years ago. It did not go well, either.

Inventions. What did snorers and the sleep-deprived, sleep apnea-afflicted do in the old days? They snored. There was nothing to do but nudge your partner's arm, pinch your partner's nose shut or open their nostrils with nasal strips. If all else failed, separate bedrooms. Then came C-Pap machines which have now evolved into a little button implanted in your upper chest. Push it and sleep is immediate, and snoring is no more.

That one sounds scary. It would be far too easy for "someone" to push my button before I could order something online or interrupt his jokes.

Robots are here. Boy have we come a long way. Can you imagine Pa Ingalls grounding little Laura because she forgot to plug in the robot?

Recently, my husband and I were lying in bed and we heard a sound in the hallway. Startled and wary, I whispered, "What the hell was that?" and he—the sharp wit, and the one who always talks me off the ledge—said, unfazed, "I don't know but the question is did it jump or was it pushed?"

"Very funny," I whispered back. "Well, we would know the answer to that if we had one of those robots that follows you around your house like a puppy. We could send it out there like a SWAT bot without having to interface with whatever horrible specter occupies our hallway AND HAS NOW MADE ITSELF KNOWN TO US."

Fortunately, I didn't have a little button implanted in my chest.

The next morning we found it: a pen that was slowly sliding off a leaning stack of papers and had finally fallen onto the hardwood floor. Plink! Boo!

We may be evolving, but seriously, as a society, how are we doing?

Back in the 1800s, Wordsworth said, "The World is Too Much With Us." Even then and even now, he is right. Wordsworth is always right. And so are the enduring words of Dylan, Baez, Langston Hughes, Sondheim, Bernstein, and MLK. And now, Mary Oliver, Billy Collins, and youth Poet Laureate Amanda Gorman who all speak their own truths about nature, kindness, oppression, conscience, and struggle.

If we will only listen. And learn.

Our evolving world is getting out of whack. Getting. Spending. Killing. Hating. Judging. Cheating. Lying. Racism. Violence. Resentments. Consumerism. Selfishness. Greed. Man's inhumanity to man. Self-aggrandizement. It's exhausting.

Those really aren't anything new, though, are they? They are as old as the mud in the Mississippi and the ground at Giza. But we are allowing them to dominate us more and more and they are changing our humanity.

Can we take a breath and go a different way? Not backward, either.

If we could evolve and achieve the ultimate best of bests, I think it would be to start believing we can all do better. Then we renounce all those old negatives, and look to the positives: embrace humanity, equal rights, civility, integrity, and compassion. Honor a strong work ethic and have an inclusive commitment to preserving the beneficent human spirit, democracy, peace, and the natural world that surrounds us. That's it. Call it woo-woo if you want but that's my story and I'm sticking to it.

You do you. Don't sweat the small stuff. Go to WalMart. Dress how you like. Keep it legal.

Also, let's allow our fellow humans to go to church or not go to church without judgment. Worship how we like. Be a Christian. Be a Jew. Be a Buddhist. Whittle a stick or play a game online. Get a tattoo, or not. Go to the opera or a rock concert. Or do both. Be gay. Be straight. Go fishin'. Have a conscience. Be conservative. Be liberal. Be undecided.

Just don't be cruel. Don't be exclusionary. Don't be hateful. Don't be a jerk. Don't be stupid. Don't be a criminal. We still need to hold these folks accountable.

Whatever we all do, let's not beat our fellow humans over the head with Flintstone clubs. Or with anything, for that matter. We are—or should be—so much better than that now. Let's find our way forward together and evolve for the better, not for the worse. Cool-headed civility vs hot blooded vengeance. Less schadenfreude, more authentic, collaborative problem-solving. Less murders of the human spirit, more grace.

Let's stop playing angry tug of war using inflammatory language, pulling the rope with malicious energy and intent. Let's drop the rope and come together. Let's remember not to be so busy or solipsistic that we forget what is important, what is vital to the survival of mankind.

Lift up the other guy. Rising tides will only lift boats for those that have boats. So let's build some boats. Bring some kindness into the world each day. Be a good human. Educate yourself. Teach. Speak truth, and speak truth to power for sure, but let's be civil, and commit to finding solutions together. Enjoy the beauty of nature. Nurture and protect it because it's all we have.

Tall order. Let's evolve for the better if we can. Worse is, well, so much worse.

The Torch is Passed. Over and Over Again
2-26-2022

We just finished with the Olympics. It wasn't without extra drama. But it's over now, and I get to watch "This Is Us" on TV again. But this column is not about the Olympics or its famous torch. Not even in the ballpark. Actually, it's about an entirely different ballpark, different drama, different torch.

Years ago I was a paid soloist/staff-singer at a church in Atlanta. One Wednesday night, circa 2001, I was walking down the staircase after a choir rehearsal. Just ahead of me was a dear friend and chorister, and just behind me was his longtime partner, also a dear friend and member of the choir.

It was a couple of years after the horrifying news that broke in 1998 when James Byrd, Jr., a Black man in Texas was murdered by three white supremacists. He had been dragged for two miles by a rope tied to the back of a pickup truck. Of course, he was dead when his body was found on the road. In multiple places. Also that very same year, Matthew Shepard, a gay college student was tortured, stripped naked, tied to a fence one cold Wyoming October, and left to die. Which he most certainly did.

It would take eleven years for our government to pass the official Matthew Shepard and James Byrd, Jr., Hate Crimes Prevention Act of 2009. Progress not perfection. It's a start. But it's not enough.

Because I was such close friends with these two guys on the stairway at church in 2001, I felt comfortable that night asking them uncomfortable, direct questions, questions that revealed my concern and, ultimately, my ignorance and privilege.

I asked one friend, "Phil, can I ask you a dumb question?" Even then, I had an inkling. But I needed to talk to the horse and hear the answer from him.

"Sure, Suze. Anything."

I remember our quiet conversation echoing in the empty stairway, amplified by the acoustics, thinking maybe this was God wanting me not to miss the point.

"Seeing as how you are a Black man, and I'm not, I need to know from you if we have progressed; if 'things' have gotten any better for you after 1998, or if I'm just clueless."

"Well, let me tell you a story," he began in his always soft-spoken, quiet way. "Last week, Ronnie and I went to a Braves game. It had been raining and although the rain stopped, the stadium seats were still wet. When the usher showed us our seats, and he noted which of us would be filing in first, he wiped Ronnie's seat dry and left mine untouched."

"Oh God I'm so sorry," I said, feeling so sad and mad and small and ignorant and clueless all at the same time.

We were at the bottom of the staircase now, standing at the exit door. I turned around to look at Ronnie. His Caucasian face had gone red. Not from rage, but from pain and grief at the memory of the shameful reality.

Two more kind-hearted, wonderful people I have never known. An intelligent, talented, churchgoing, committed couple who sing in the choir, work hard at their jobs, pay taxes, volunteer their time for charities, and call me friend, were sized up by some sad sack at a ballgame and found wanting. This random guy made his judgment based on a superficial yardstick, a red-hot torch of assumptive hate passed down to him, most likely at birth by a racist relative or an entire family.

What he did at that ballgame was pointed, and mean, but not technically punishable by law. No bloodshed. No one died. No trial. No sentence. But people were hurt. He hurt them. Maybe he thought it was a deserved, discourteous jab that would make him feel happily superior and hoped it would make another person feel uncomfortable and denigrated. Mission accomplished.

No one is born with hate and ignorance in their heart. This guy had been carefully taught, anointed, and duly branded. Now he was simply carrying through with his programming. And most likely, he'd be carrying that awful torch to hand down to his own kids after branding them, too.

How many other racist cowboys have carried their torches and seared them like brands into peoples' hearts, souls, and spirits? How many have brought the death of a person's life, and how many times has the world looked the other way, allowing the torches to stay lit?

Clearly, too many.

And here we are. It's February 2022. Thirteen years after the hate crimes law was enacted.

This past week, that law worked. Three white supremacists in a Brunswick court were found guilty of federal hate crimes in addition to the murder convictions they had already received.

During their hate crime trial, the ugly, racial slurs they uttered over and over in texts and emails and comments to others unmasked them even more fully. Free speech means you can say what you want, but what you say has consequences. It should not be lost on us that two of these idiots are father and son. Oh how the torch still glows in its passing down.

One might think "things are better" with the advent of the hate crimes bill and this week's convictions. Yes, thankfully, the case has been rightly tried and justice was served. But too many hate crimes have occurred over the years that have gone unacknowledged, even since the 2009 act was passed. Even one is too many.

The threat of punishment doesn't seem to be a deterrent to those folks. It's been burned into them that they are superior, and above the law. Punishment didn't prevent those three clowns in Brunswick from carrying their torches high, hunting down, and killing a Black human they were convinced was sub-human.

We have the legal mechanism now to try these criminal torchbearers and find them guilty. But what can we do to extinguish their fires altogether? We better find the answer if we care for humanity at all. Changing laws is one thing. Changing a racist population's mindset is a whole different kettle of torches.

I believe it was Einstein who said, "Peace can not be kept by force, it can only be achieved by understanding.

Now, unfortunately, I do not need to ask my dear friends again if "things are any better for them." Hate, prejudice, and discrimination are never-ending, and remain writ large and hot like bright, burning crosses at a Klan rally.

How time flies. And how, sadly, time and hate have stayed the same. The torches still burn.

For shame.

Just a Suggestion
3-6-2022

Did we feast on Fat Tuesday last week? Did we consume buttery, syrupy sweet pancakes at church Pancake Suppers or restaurants or in our own kitchens? Did we don beaded necklaces and feathered masks, and join celebratory parades? Did we drink too many adult beverages to celebrate Mardi Gras? Did we gobble up King Cakes and find the plastic babies?

Did we "laissez les bons temps rouler?"

Indeed, as the Cajuns say, "Oui, Cher!"

To everything there is a season. Now it's time for the parades to roll to a stop. Time for us to digest all those goodies and libations and turn them into food for thought and sober reflection. Time to clean up our acts and make amends.

Not a requirement, of course. Just a suggestion. Do it, or not. But I feel, and am, better when I do. Just sayin'.

For Christians, these days between Shrove Tuesday and Easter Sunday are unique. In many Protestant and Catholic religions around the world the very next day after Shrove Tuesday is Ash Wednesday, the beginning of Lent, a time set aside for atonement and sacrifice. A time to restore, repent, and forgive.

For Jews, this time prepares them for their Passover, celebrating and re-telling the story of their exodus from slavery out of Egypt.

Jews also observe Rosh Hashanah, the Jewish New Year, and Yom Kippur, the Day of Atonement, both in the Fall. The period between Rosh Hashanah and Yom Kippur is known as the "Ten Days of Repentance" and is a time of personal reflection and reverence.

I'm no seminarian or religion expert, but I know as sure as the world isn't flat that there are a lot more holy rites and religious customs out there.

By strict, churchgoing standards I suppose I am a heathen now because I don't attend formal church services much anymore. But I am not detached from God.

I went to church every Sunday and every ecumenical holiday with my children as they grew up in Sunday School classes, singing in children's and youth choirs, participating in youth groups, vacation Bible schools, and going on youth choir tours. I spent many a year in church choir lofts without my children, locally and then miles away, singing with choirs and soloing front and center. I did this mostly without my husband, Rick, a veterinarian, who 9.99 out of 10 Sundays was called away to practice a different brand of ministry for a different kind of flock: emergency veterinary aid to sick or dying large animals.

Now, our children are grown. Rick and I are retired. And we worship God in our own, meaningful way, together. Where two or more are gathered…

I can explain. Quoting from my book, The Veterinarian's Wife, A Memoir:

""Miss Susie," the Amazon Echo smart speaker purrs from my bedside table every Sunday at ten-thirty a.m., "Here's your reminder: Wash your sheets."

"When Echo chimes in softly with that one, it's right after Rick and I have "gone to church." We have just worshipped together at the TV altar of CBS Sunday Morning, in our pajamas while having brunch and coffee. It will have been an hour and a half of blissful enlightenment, sacred affirmation, and spiritual communion—a virtual Eucharist that comforts, feeds, teaches, and at turns, alarms us like a cracking-good sermon.

"Its closing benediction is always masterful with trademark style. It's a spiritually restorative audiovisual montage of sensual blessings: bees buzzing around a pastoral, sunny national park as bison silently graze and kindly breezes blow; a clear brook rushing and burbling over logs and stones as sunlight sparkles on the water; eerie, otherworldly Northern Lights swirling aloft, green and iridescent from horizon out to infinity; a vaulted expanse of black sky studded with endless numbers of twinkling stars, punctuated by the sole sound of chirping crickets.

"These perfect little lagniappes for our souls are the last gifts of peace and hope before the political TV talking heads take over the airways and threaten to extinguish every good vibe in the world.

"All morning, we have been churched, fed by the body of Sunday Morning, and washed in the blood of important, thought-provoking stories, art, music, theater, literature, humor, nature, religion, and humanity. We have been duly reminded of, communed with, and worshipped God, the creator of all things in heaven and on earth.

"Once all of that has happened, and not a minute before, Echo ever so swiftly rips off the ecumenical Band-Aid and kindly harks us back to reality. "Wash your sheets."

"We are dutiful, and penitent. Although, admittedly, we resent—just a tad—Echo's spiritual nirvana-interruptus in favor of menial labor. We accept Echo's virtual, disembodied directive to wash our sheets for the week. And so, we do it. Because we programmed her that way.

"Rick and I work together to strip the sheets off the bed. This is our Sunday, after-church ritual, when we do not rest. We wash away the figurative sins of the world with the soap of bless-ed reality and receive our absolution in clean sheets."

And then we go outside to garden and care for God's amazing gifts.

We volunteer and do good deeds for others when we can and ask forgiveness when we can't.

This Lent, I am giving up chocolate and smoking. Kidding. I don't smoke. It's a mind trick I find helpful. It's easier to give up something when there's already been one victory and I feel like I'm on a roll. Giving up chocolate is a bear. It takes what it takes.

Rick will be giving up an arthritic hip this week at Piedmont Hospital, so he can do physical therapy and puzzle on life's mysteries for 4 to 6 weeks.

But there's more for me, not to give up but to take on. I want to ponder and accept the truth about how I may have contributed to making the world worse, and how I can contribute to make the world better. Not just through thoughts and prayers (which aren't a bad thing) but also through petitioned grace, renewed kindnesses, meaningful action, volunteerism, and humanitarianism. Many others will be doing this, too, impacting—for the better— not just the world, but one nation, one town, one group, one person, one friend, one stranger at a time.

What if we all did that, no matter who, how, when, or where we worship, or what holidays we observe? What if we all made amends without judgment or rancor, followed by thoughtful actions effecting positive change, ad infinitum? That would be one prodigious parade rolling along, wouldn't it? And it would never have to stop.

Oui, Cher!

Not a requirement, of course, but a suggestion. Just sayin'.

Truths, Lies, and Crosswords
3-13-2022

I had a visceral response to a wild crossword puzzle today.
Clue: "Where lab coats get cleaned."
Answer: "P-E-T-S-P-A"
Read it again. I'll wait.
And this one:
Clue: "Place to get a cab."
Answer: "W-I-N-E-R-A-C-K"
Wow.
Now, I ask:

Should groaners like these be celebrated or scorned? Should we be amused or cussing? Or should we congratulate ourselves for even trying to "get the joke?" I believe congratulations are in order.

The creator of these clues was blessed and burdened with a different kind of intelligence. I give them all the credit, as it takes someone very special to come up with punny brain-benders like these. When they were born, Lo the Angel of Linguistic Humor and Crossword Creativity shone round about them and imbued them with droll, exceedingly superior synapses.

Not even if Elvis returned could I come up with PETSPA or WINERACK on my own. I get these answers accidentally, by filling in the letters crossing them. But these crosswords are a fun stretch, which is what makes them so great. They speak the truth in the cleverest of ways, and I totally appreciate the humor.

What's the goal, anyway: to win—which does have its charms—or to learn? Can't we do both? Kurt Vonnegut said he was raised in such an achievement-oriented environment, "so inundated with the Myth of Talent" that he thought it was "only worth doing things if you could WIN at them."

Winning is way fun, but edification is a noble aim and too often underrated. I come from a competitive game-playing family who liked to both win and learn, a Win-Win scenario. But if one didn't win, the learning was still a valuable take-away. That's a Win-Win, too, if you ask me.

Truth is, I never expect to perfectly complete every crossword puzzle I take on, although it happens on occasion, which is satisfying and would be nice if it happened more. But my goal is to try difficult stuff I suck at because it means I often learn patience, experience epiphanies, and discover something new. I welcome and highly recommend that, too.

We should like being introduced to challenges and creative concepts that hone our intellect and reasoning capabilities in puzzles and in life, which, come to think of it, is a pretty good metaphor. Life is a puzzle, isn't it?

Cultivating a curious, open mind, ready to play and learn and think and see outside the box is a very, very good thing

But if these clues and answers were not based in truth, they would be not only worthless and humorless, but a waste of time. That qualifies in my book as criminal. I draw a hard line between clever truths, and specious, malicious falsehoods that are like wolves dressed in military uniforms marching into Ukraine as Putin's "Peacekeeping Parade". What a crock.

Anything that isn't grounded in fact has consequences. Imagine changing the answer for "Where lab coats get cleaned" from P-E-T-S-P-A to, say, "M-A-G-N-E-T-I-C-M-I-C-R-O-C-H-I-P-P-E-D-V-A-C-C-I-N-E-S." Attempting to cram twenty-eight letters into only six boxes in a crossword puzzle is not only idiotic, it literally doesn't fit, no matter who tries to convince you it does.

Taking a deeper dive to discern what really is and isn't fact is not always easy. It takes willingness, effort, and integrity. Confirmation bias is a thing. Sources are skewed. When a person believes a lie, it's near-impossible to disabuse them of it using logic or facts. Too many people eschew critical thinking for an expedient "bandwagon" approach. The roadblocks to the truth are daunting and many. But the truth based on facts must be sussed out and is—without equivocation—vitally and ultimately essential.

Falsehoods are benchmarks of those who do not care to learn anything, whose only goal is to win at any cost and consequence, solely for their own benefit. Lies repeated and reinforced over and over and over are likely to become accepted as fact by those who do not do their homework and rely on sophists and faulty reasoning.

Mr. Putin, for example, is sending his brand of lies out to his country and the world. Many Russian citizens are aware, though, and have bravely protested in the streets, while others listen to one man's propaganda and say, "I believe him because he said it." Danger. Will. Robinson. Trouble ahead.

Best thing we can do isn't just to know there's a difference between fact and fiction but to care about knowing the difference, no matter who is speaking, or who is selling something, or campaigning, or marching into a democratic country to brutally overthrow its government. It's incumbent on all of us to think critically, parse things out, and dig for factual information from reliable sources.

Of course, there is "right and wrong." But for additional perspective, there is also "helpful and not helpful." A good-humored challenge helps the soul. Likewise, education and the arts. Thinking of others and bringing them aid is helpful. The truth is sometimes painful, but ultimately helpful. Lies and mis-information are dismally unhelpful. Every time. If something is not helpful, like war against innocent people, or gaslighting, or telling boldface lies for one's own advancement, or hate, it's wrong AND not helpful.

Let's do the hard work with life's puzzles. Let's discover and tell the truth. Let's be helpful.

One caveat: know when to quit expecting something from someone who doesn't have it to give. At that point, living the factual, helpful truth is all that's left to do.

Things We Keep. Things We Don't
3-20-2022

I overheard him addressing the Amazon Alexa at my desk as I was loading the dishwasher nearby. Was he four, then? Five? He thought he was alone, I suppose. But I was near enough that I could see him standing there and I heard his every precious word. He stood as straight as Christopher Robin talking to Pooh, but with the same little sway in his back as the boy in E. H. White's pen and ink illustrations in A.A. Milne's classic children's book.

"Alexa what are fish tacos made of?"

Alexa replied, "Fish tacos are made of fish, salsa, and tortilla."

"Alexa is an avatar real?"

"Here's something I found on the web. An avatar is not a real image or photo, it is a caricature and can be a bizarre or fantasy figure."

"Alexa what are lamps made of?"

"The outer casings of lamps can be made of brass or tin steel."

"Alexa are you a real person?"

"No I am an A.I."

Alexa what is a A.I.?"

"It means artificial intelligence."

"Alexa I pretty much love you."

"I'm flattered thank you."

My heart could barely stand it, the innocence, the guileless naiveté of a toddler grandson. I'll never forget it.

Visited now with that sudden memory and the familial déjà vu from my parenting days, I recall so many moments of sweetness like this when our sons were little, decades ago. Sans smart speakers then, of course. Their questions to us were similarly charming, pure, and unfettered. They came out of the curious blue, or in response to a book we read together, or something on TV, or from just about anywhere in their sweet, little heads.

Our grandchildren are not grown yet. But already, and too soon, the simplicity of toddler innocence is fading into real life, complex challenges, adolescent strong wills, and teenage angst. I pray I live and love them long enough that by the grace of the god of strong-willed children I will see them mature into productive, happy adults someday, just as our sons are.

Both of our boys are grown men now. No longer innocents, they are the responsible, adult children of older parents. They still ask us questions, though way less often. They will ask until there are no more parents to ask. This absence is not anything parents want to visit on their children. But it is a painful fact of life.

Kids think life goes on forever. They haven't gotten the metaphysical Memo yet, the big picture: life is precious and everything's relative; savor it. Wide-eyed at the starting line the race looks long and endless. They cannot wait to be further down the track, where the race is exciting and they are older and flying free. They think life has repeating finish lines that when crossed they've made it to the next race and the next. They are bulletproof and immortal.

Rick and I are on the side of it where we are getting closer to the finish line. We're not there yet, of course. But we know not when, and we know there are not unlimited races, laps, or time. We wish we, too, could take a couple more laps and have unlimited races so it's not over.

I want to stand on the young toes of children, pin their sneakers down, and whisper, "Don't be in such a hurry! Tempus fugit, yanguns!"

I do fear, too, that when I shuffle off this mortal coil my children will not cherish what I've left behind for them. I more than fear it, I know it. They tease us even now about our basement. They joke about how they are going to back up a truck and summarily sweep it all wholesale into a dumpster. Or worse, hire some stranger to do it. And they are right. Partially. Our basement is full, full of stuff. Some—OK a lot of it—is entirely impersonal and disposable. [Make list here. On second thought, nope. Even my eyes glaze over at the thought.]

But what will they do with "their sacred boxes," those large plastic containers I've stacked in the cupboard into which—for their entire lives—I have reverently placed memories, baby books, first locks of hair, carefully incised newspaper articles of their accomplishments, photos and programs of school plays, letters, and report cards?

Young couples these days don't seem to want silver, china, and crystal from their parents' weddings, or their furniture either.

Rather than things I cherish, I should consider this: what have I given them to cherish that they can tuck away as valuable inner furnishings in their hearts and minds and memories? Did I do enough for them as a mom and was I wise? Was I enough? Will their memories of me be sustained without the need for tactile reminders, stuff they don't need or want? Will their memories bring a smile, or a trip to a therapist's couch?

Recently, I got a text from our son, Nick, our Hong Kong dweller. "Mom," he said, "what's that saying you always use about what folks said during the depression?"

"Oh, you mean 'Use it up, wear it out, make it do?'" I replied. "Got that from your grandmother who lived it!"

"Yes! And what's that movie Dad has talked about for as long as I can remember with the Mountie who dispatches three bad guys at one time?"

"I asked your Dad and he says he remembers the scene vividly but has no idea what movie it was. Sorry. No clue, Bud," I responded.

"I've been wondering what this movie is as long as he's been describing it without ever knowing if it was black & white, technicolor, or otherwise," Nick replied. "I've just imagined possible versions for thirty years. I realized yesterday I never asked. I'm wondering if knowing would only diminish its value. I think the answer is less important than the acknowledgment."

"Yep," I responded, "you never know what you leave with another person do you?"

He ended our conversation with the most incredibly beautiful summation, and suddenly all was made clear to me. Apparently a popular local character and Elvis impersonator named Melvis died recently in Hong Kong.

"Everyone in the city knew who this guy was," Nick told me. "It's been interesting to see the news hit different people each day. Sometimes you see them on the subway, reading an article about his death, or sharing the WhatsApp news that circulated heavily about a week ago. I don't think there were many tears but about eight-million shoulders sagged off the beat; which ain't nothin'."

His words hit me. That's it. The most important thing: to have made a helpful difference no matter how large or small; to have been a positive, loving presence in someone's life; to leave them with good memories, not stuff; to be missed, and for shoulders to sag—whether it be eight-million or eight—on one's passing.

Off the beat works for me, too. And that really ain't nothin'.

It's everything.

Perspective
3-27-2022

Billy Collins is a poet of extraordinary talent. Poet Laureate of the United States from 2001 to 2003, in fact. I was introduced to his work by a fellow writer, and I immediately responded to Collins' poetry with the delight one feels when receiving a surprise gift, the loveliest kind of surprise that hits a soft spot and won't let go.

Collins' dry wit and beautifully crafted poem, "The Lanyard" hit me hard in all my soft places. Speaking to his mother as he remembers the homemade plastic lanyard he gave her as a boy, he compares his modest gift to all the sacrifices she made and the maternal devotion she bestowed on her son over his lifetime. With wry, adult retrospect he finally laments that he actually thought at the time his meager gift made them even. It's a painfully sweet awareness, from a full-grown son's perspective.

Moms can relate to all the camp wallets and woven bracelets and plastic lanyards that come home with their children from camp or school. All the scribbles, crayon drawings, and handmade cards; the lopsided clay bowls and the whittled sticks.

These are moments a mom never forgets, and they are not to be minimized, no matter how trivial they seem to the adult who has outgrown their childhood and looks back smiling in sardonic judgment.

I have received lanyards, and heartache, too, from sons and grandsons alike. So while Collins tenderly acknowledges the irony of his adolescent reasoning, captivating me in the process, I have something to say from a mom's and grandmother's perspective.

I should probably save this subject for a column on Mother's Day weekend. It would be perfect then. But I cannot hold back the overflow in my heart right now. Besides, everybody will be writing about Mother's Day on Mother's Day. Not that that's a bad thing. And if you are a child whose mother or grandmother was or is cold, dysfunctional, ill, or absent, I send you my heart.

As this weekend is the first anniversary of the epic EF-4 Newnan tornado, I imagine many will be writing about it as well. That storm hasn't finished with us even now. There are many local citizens whose long recovery from the damage and destruction is not over yet. My own son is among them. May peace, heart, and resolution be with you all.

Having read Collins' poem, I am a lovesick mess. And frankly, I can't write anything else until I get this out. Trust me, I tried.

I am not, of course, in Billy Collins' literary class. Oh please. But that's ok. He's him. I'm me. We both have value. We both write. He is an author and poet laureate. I'm an author and a columnist. And a mom. He has thoughts. I have thoughts.

Here are mine:

To All My Boys:
Don't you dare judge yourself now, or the worth of you, or the value of what you created for me then, or now. Ever. You have no idea.

So I will tell you.

I put that summer-camp, plastic-laced wallet you wove and so proudly gave me from your heart years ago in the safest place I could think of.

My heart.

Not literally, of course. I carried it in my purse for the longest time. You gifted me with a smile and a warm glow every time I used it.

Oh, I eventually placed it reverently in the box of keepsakes I've been saving since you were born. But things in boxes are not safe. Not really.

Boxes run out of room. Or get misplaced. Or disappear altogether. Things in boxes can decay, fall into ruin.

Houses burn. Buildings crumble. Floods carry things away. Tornadoes blow neighborhoods to shreds.

My heart, however, is safe and secure. Big and boundless. Immutable. Fiercely protective. It stores you, the memories of you, and your treasures forever.

Even when my time comes, which it will, my heart and all that it holds is not emptied or gone.

It is sacred spirit then. Untouchable as breath and air, it lives on around you. And in you forever, as stars and air and love and memory.

Heaven forbid, if God does not choose me first, part of my aching heart will go with you to rest safely upon. You will know the truth then that I am trying to tell you right now.

Willingly, happily, I welcomed you into my heart even before you arrived.

And all you were, and are, and did, and do since then are in it.

Yes, even your colic, smelly diapers, and projectile vomiting.

Your first steps and words. Your tears at the classroom door. Your challenging troubles and angry outbursts. Your stick figure drawings and clay monsters.

Your fevers and fits. Every boo-boo, bad haircut, broken bone, and birthday.

The polka dots you painted on my car. The bone necklace you made for your Boy Scout Native American dance team from a roadkill snake you and your dad bravely boiled in that old pot on the grill.

The three tulip bulbs you bought me with your little allowance when you were six.

"Because," you simply said, "I know how much you love flowers."

Those tulips still bloom each spring. Oh how I adore them. And You.

The cookbook you gave me. You wrote inside it. "You're a great mom," you said. And I cried. Your eyes were moist and we both smiled.

The tacky gnome you chose as a gift for me. I suppose you brushed it off as a prank. Not me. I treasure it. Makes a great doorstop. It has value no decorator could match with any other thing, no matter the cost. I smile every time I pass through the door. And my heart tugs. You are here.

All that and more—and you—have been, and will be, cherished. Secure. Safe.

My heart holds on fiercely to the love and the memories of each and every gift you have ever given me. Including the gift of you, simply you.

I'll have you know, a more precious treasure cannot exist than the ones I keep safe in my heart.

Always. Always. Always.

Bright Lights, Dark Skies
4-2-2022

There are numerous worthwhile ways to contribute to the betterment of society, the environment, and the planet these days. Many groups are well known, both locally and worldwide. The International Dark Sky Association is one I had no idea existed until I read an article about it recently. Google it or just go to darksky.org and prepare to learn about light pollution and what we can all do about it.

According to the website, "The award-winning International Dark Sky Places (IDSP) Program was founded in 2001 to encourage communities, parks and protected areas around the world to preserve and protect dark sites through responsible lighting policies and public education."

I'll be honest. Reading about something called "Dark Sky Parks" worried me. These days it seems we all want our dark paths lighted, especially when we are walking through isolated places at night. Crime, you know, is very much "a thing."

But the idea of responsible lighting policies and public education got my attention. We have choices about the kinds of lights we use, the number of lights we install, and how we choose to use them.

Looking at the US map of officially designated International Dark Sky Places, there's a smattering throughout the country, but the preponderance are out west in NM, AZ, and CO.

Seeing these spots on the map now, I am instantly swept away in time, remembering our trip to Phoenix, Sedona, and the Grand Canyon.

Our travels out west in 2008 took Rick and me to Phoenix, my birthplace, for his veterinary conference. This trip turned out to be quite the sensory delight.

Just outside our hotel room were blooming Oleander shrubs, which took me straight back in a Proustian moment to the high Oleander hedge in our backyard on State Avenue when I was a girl growing up in Phoenix. Separating us from our back-door neighbor, that hedge was more than a geographical boundary. It was a magic hiding place for a six-year-old, full of restful shade and redolent with the distinct smell of organic matter. Mom used to tell us over and over not to ever, under any circumstances, eat the oleander because it was poisonous. I was a good girl and I never ate it. I distinctly recall not wanting to die back there in the magic Oleander hedge and sully its beauty.

When Rick's seminar was over, we zoomed all around and explored. We stayed a few days in Sedona and marveled at the gorgeous red mountains and mesas. We visited one of the many purportedly spiritual "vortices" for which Sedona is well-known. We wanted to test our vortex-woo-woo-meters, but alas, we felt nothing, except a deep appreciation for the landscape.

After all the driving, we decided to take a trip to the Grand Canyon the easy way. We engaged two seats on a group tour van, ably driven by a talkative, lovely hulk of a Native American man wearing denim shirt and jeans and adorned with beautiful turquoise and silver Native American jewelry. A simple wooden flute dangled from the dashboard rear view mirror by a leather beaded cord and a feather.

Leaving Sedona in mid-afternoon we arrived at our destination at the South Rim about an hour before sunset.

The canyon's striated, rusty red rock walls were more than grand.

They were incredible, and the overall scale was overwhelming, beyond spectacular, even a little terrifying.

Pre-iPhone days, I had my Nikon DSLR camera and tripod set up on the unfenced rock ledge reserved for tourists to stand on. Of course I was careful not to position myself too close to the edge, but close enough to make my worried husband hold on to the back of my britches in case the strong winds up there bowled me over into the abyss. It was so crowded, though, I figured if I started to go horizontal, sadly the domino effect would take out the people in front of me before I could ever reach the edge and fall in. Thankfully, our time in that regard with the crowd on the ledge was uneventful.

My photographic skills at the time were underwhelming. I produced no art that evening, just happy snaps of sections of canyon, people, and clouds in blue sky. I'd have done better just to enjoy the moment and leave the artsy photo efforts to professionals' coffee table books and post cards. Lesson learned: the Grand Canyon doth possess its immense beauty and charm, supremely if not impossibly difficult for the average photographer to capture. Like lightning in a jar. Or the universe in one frame.

I had no idea, however, what would be coming our way that was equal to the Grand Canyon or better. Even after all the excitement of seeing this wonder-of-the-world chasm for the first time, my very favorite moment was actually on the ride home in that van.

It was just past sunset when we left the canyon ledge and boarded the van. The views out the windows darkened the further we drove into the uninhabited, open landscape on our way back to Sedona. Finally it was pitch black everywhere. No street lights glowed on this long road through the desert, and there was no traffic, either. We were alone. Folks of a certain age will recall those rock music lyrics that begin, "On a dark desert highway…." I mean to tell you it is the absolute truth. "Dark" doesn't even do it justice out there.

Then the driver announced that since we were, indeed, in the middle of nowhere he would be pulling the van over and we would all be disembarking. Bringing the van to a halt, he invited us all outside.

This stop was not on the itinerary, and I pulsed with sudden anxiety. I had already avoided a grisly death at the windblown canyon precipice earlier. Now I prayed we weren't going to appear in the morning news as victims of an elaborate robbing crew.

That thought was erased the moment I stepped out and looked up.

The view was—and still is—stunning, beyond my ability to adequately describe. I could barely take it all in. I know my jaw dropped and I probably whispered a holy expletive, as I am wont to do when overwhelmed.

Our driver raised his flute and began to play.

Here we were, all of us standing dumbfounded, looking up at the great black sky and sparkling stars, listening to the sounds of one perfect little haunting flute melody. There was magic, breathtaking infinity up there, endless glittering crystals set in an eternal vault of black velvet. I could have spread a blanket on the ground and sat there looking up for hours had it not been for the schedule requiring a timely return to Sedona.

Now that, my friends, was a grand, spiritual moment.

After we all quietly climbed back in the bus, still a little stunned and clearly in an altered state of mind, we were on our way again. The driver told us that this wasn't part of the other tour guides' routines. But speaking reverently and with conviction, he said he felt strongly about acknowledging the dark desert skies and the twinkling stars his Native American people have been appreciating as part of their culture and spiritual beliefs for a very long time. These rare views need to be seen, appreciated, and remembered he said. They need to be treasured and preserved by all people. For all people.

If he was only angling for a generous tip, mission accomplished. But I refuse that notion as his only motivation.

We had all thought we were going on this little adventure solely to look down into a famously grand canyon, deep and wide, full of color and thrilling majesty and then bump our way back home on an uneventful trip down the road in a tourist van.

What we got was very different.

Isolated, standing in the dark in the middle of nowhere in that wide-open desert we had received the miracle. We were given the opportunity to witness an unbroken, cinematic Panavision paradise: the clear, unpolluted black night sky, the full firmament of shining stars, and the Milky Way, from horizon line to horizon line in every direction, and up to infinity and beyond.

So magnificent and yet so elemental, this was a sight we rarely get to fully experience as bustling city-folk in our busy, light-polluted cities and towns.

We live so much of our fast, busy lives face-forward, in bright places, among beautiful lighted buildings and skyscrapers, neon Broadway marquees, Hollywood search beacons, harsh halogen headlamps in heavy traffic, interstate billboards, and soldier-courses of illuminated fixtures on poles along our streets and highways.

In that rare, in-person, scenic moment, our flute-playing driver had duly reminded and instantly re-educated us in the most soul-touching way about the fullness of God's natural gifts above us, and what we would be missing should we light up the planet with too much artificial light.

Perhaps we, as caretakers of Earth, might want to consider ways to lessen light pollution and preserve our night skies where we can. Because light pollution really is "a thing." It affects our wildlife, birds, turtles, our circadian rhythms, our ecosystems.

Visit darksky.com and learn about it and all things we can all do. Replacing harsh outdoor up-lights with fully shielded downward fixtures is just one. Choosing only the places that need illumination is another. And turning off unnecessary lights is a third.

Or if you need more persuasion, go to the middle of nowhere on a dark desert highway between Sedona and the Grand Canyon with a guide who will play his flute, raise your consciousness, and let you experience the miracle for yourself.

It's That Time of Year
4-10-2022

It's spring! It's that time of year! Hooray for "that time of year!"

Gardeners (and parents) will recognize what I am about to say. It's always that time of year. Gardening never ends. All year long there's stuff to do with the care and feeding of living things. Summer, fall, winter, spring, there's never a dull moment. It's always that time of year, for a gardener. The love, commitment, and work never stop.

Kind of like parenting.

There's also the other side of all that "doing" for a gardener. The trick is possessing the fine art of knowing when, what, and how much to do, and when to let something be, at least for the time being.

Kind of like parenting.

A couple of weeks ago, plants everywhere in our little southern corner of the world were sprouting first leaves and baby buds, signaling the coming of spring. Then along came a forecast warning of below freezing temperatures for a couple of straight nights.

What to do? Gardeners (and parents) have this question on their lips pretty much 24-7.

What, in fact, did I do? I got out the pricey, specially-made frost fabric I bought for this very moment, and covered my three largest hydrangeas, hoping to spare their new, tender leaves and neonatal buds from arctic harm. I desperately wanted to save them.

What did I get for my trouble? When the freeze was over and I removed the fabric, I thought of the poem, "Tonight I Can Write (The Saddest Lines)," by Chilean poet Pablo Neruda. Unveiling my three hydrangeas, I found woody branches bearing brown, melted foliage that looked and smelled like stewed spinach.

The horror. I had been overprotective. I had made a big mistake. Mistakes can haunt a gardener.

Kind of like parenting.

I will never cover my plants during a late freeze again. I am reminding myself that Mother Nature is ultimately in charge, because—while maybe a little rough around the edges from the assault—all my other plants did ok. They have rallied all on their own and will bloom another day.

The jury is still out on the cooked spinach hydrangeas. I check them every day for signs of life. It could still happen. And probably will. It's out of my hands. There is nothing left for me to do.

A gardener must live and learn and go with the flow.

Kind of like parenting.

To err is human, of course, and while forgiveness is divine, I hope to heaven my poor pitiful melted hydrangeas and mother nature forgive me. If not, then that's a gardener's plight, too. We must remember the unforgiving nature of gardening. Plants struggle, bugs and predators descend, weather has its way. We rejoice in our successes and grieve our losses. Whether through natural happenstance or misguided human good intentions there's always a challenge in store.

Kind of like parenting.

Gardeners know all about grace in the garden, too. Walking out on a spring or summer or fall day to say hello to the newest surprises and gifts unfurled by mother nature is an exercise in sheer astonishment and wonder. The roses on the arbor bloom in May because a gardener planted them there, watered them, fertilized them, nurtured them. It is so tempting to take personal credit for their loveliness and enjoy the compliments from others about their beauty. Perhaps the gardener built a nice arbor for their support and placed them in just the right spot. But any thought that a gardener has absolute control of the roses' ultimate well-being, is folly. Those roses thrive, hopefully, with the gardener's assistance, perseverance, and hard work, but ultimately their very existence is out of human control and in the hands of Mother Nature.

Control is a myth.

We all know, as gardeners, we can try imposing control of our gardens with our best efforts resulting daily in dirty fingernails and aching backs, but there's only so much we can make happen. Putting in the work is essential. Knowing all that, we still must be tough, discerning, and wise. The rest can be one big, win-some, lose-some enterprise.

Kind of like parenting.

When your youngest drops out of college and doesn't tell you until you're sitting in a café with him having lunch and the bursar calls you to say they're sending a refund check—and why—he's so busted. His failure is painful. It feels like your failure as a parent, too. So when you stop paying for his car, his apartment, and force him to live in the real world because of the choices he made, your heart rips in two. You give him a compass as a gift, along with a love letter: a helpful list of things he will need to see about as an independent adult. And you pray. And you let go. What happens after that is out of your control.

But when he's finally a responsible, successful, beautiful, mature adult in full bloom, and he says that was the best thing you could've ever done back then, and he thanks you with all his heart, well, those are the real fruits of your labor—and his.

Children and plants are little sprouts that grow into maturity. Parents and gardeners nurture, feed, and care for them. Just like rebellious plants that thrive from a gardener's careful pruning, good parents know that sometimes kids need to be taken down a notch for their own good. Always, though, they need to be supported and encouraged in the right direction, like plants that face toward the sun or die on the vine in deep shade. And sometimes you have to know when to leave well enough alone. You gotta know when to hold 'em. Know when to fold 'em. You know the rest.

It's always that time of year.

What is Love?
4-17-2022

That's a really good question.

So Ali McGraw says to Ryan O'Neal in the 1971 movie, *Love Story*, "Love means never having to say you're sorry."

"I completely understand and agree with this statement," said no one, ever. Not even Eric Segal, the guy who wrote that ridiculous line knows what it means, really. He has admitted as much.

A musical theater fan might think of dozens upon dozens of musicals that attempt to answer the question. And not only what, but where love is. A young orphan, Oliver Twist innocently sings, "Where is love?" asking if it falls from the skies or maybe it's underneath a willow tree he has been dreaming of. Oh, my heart.

Cher asked, "Do You Believe in Life after Love?" The quality of said life may be more to the point of the question. However, I get her reference. Plus, "Do You Believe in the Quality of Life after Love?" just doesn't scan.

Foreigner demanded, "I Wanna Know What Love Is." Whitney Houston belted, "I-ee-I Will Always Love You." The Bee Gees needed to know "How Deep is Your Love?" And Queen sang about a "Crazy Little Thing Called Love." Elvis confessed, "I Can't Help Falling in love With You," and Perry Como crooned two of my favorite love songs of all time, "And I Love You So," and "It's Impossible." Tina

Turner asked the ultimate question, "What's Love Got to Do With It?" With what? Don't ask. Tina insists it's a secondhand emotion. Whatever that means.

Love is what, exactly, and who, where, why, and when is it?

My nine-year old self sat cross-legged on the floor leaning my back against my parents' console record player as I listened to Ricky Nelson. Rapt, I swooned over Ricky's gigantic, full-color head shot on his album cover. I cried when he sang, "Many a tear has to fall, but it's all in the game… that we know as love." All I knew was Ricky Nelson awoke a longing in my heart that made it physically hurt, and then made me cry. I thought I must've been in love with him and surely it was true romantic love, albeit unrequited. Not the love I had for my parents, certainly, I reasoned. Although, I had cried plenty over them, especially when I got a whuppin' for bad behavior. I felt love for my parents, too, especially when we hugged, for no reason other than to say I love you. That was a different kind of love, obviously. I knew that much.

But the romantic stuff was tough.

Then came the treacly songs like "Put your Head on My Shoulder" and "They Called it Puppy Love." Paul Anka. 1960. I was ten. These were ballads that once again, set me up for great expectations of love that, as defined by the lyrics, required pain and pathos, an aching heart, histrionics, and hot tears. It caused me to wonder if my love for Ricky Nelson was real. I had the tears. I had the pain. But now I was confused by this new brand of affection called puppy love.

Little Anthony certainly had tears on his pillow, and in 1961 Ella Fitzgerald sang the torch song slap, "(You Can) Cry Me a River ('Cause I Cried a River Over You.") So now love's tears and pain included sleepless nights and sardonic, passive aggressive anger. What the heck?

I sang along in 1962 with the Shirelles to "Soldier Boy." I knew nothing of saying goodbye to a loved one who goes to war. As a newly minted teen when Peter Paul and Mary came out with their haunting song, "Cruel War" I felt that same, familiar message of pain and heartache, but I was maturing and coming into a different, deeper understanding. By 1965 The Vietnam War was beginning to call our boys to war. I would soon begin to grasp all too well the pain of love and loss through war.

The Supremes warned "You Can't Hurry Love" and cautioned "Stop in the Name of Love (Before You Break My Heart"). By this time, Little Anthony had escalated his emotions and was "Goin' Out of My Head (Over You"). And when the Beatles sang, "Yesterday," ("all my troubles seemed so far away") I was wrecked. Now love also included troubled times, sad memories, and insanity.

By 1972, I was married and truly in love. I often propped a guitar on my lap and sang Roberta Flack's elegiac ballad, "The First Time Ever I Saw Your Face." I adored the positive imagery of the sun rising in a loved one's eyes, and the moon and stars as gifts a loved one could give to dark and endless skies.

But neither of us had really been tested yet. Only through years of marriage and commitment to each other did we learn about the work; about what real love gives and takes amid trials and triumphs, mistakes and forgiveness, good times and bad times.

It had been during our wedding in 1971 that the real definition of love was made clear. You know this one: "Love is patient, love is kind. It does not envy, it does not boast, it is not proud. It is not rude, it is not self-seeking, it is not easily angered, it keeps no record of wrongs. Love does not delight in evil but rejoices with the truth. It always protects, always trusts, always hopes, always perseveres. Love never fails." I know it was written more as an admonishment originally to people behaving badly in the Bible, but I took it as a positive definition of how to love. And I took it seriously.

Since then I have experienced love in all those ways, and I have seen it in others.

Love is the guy who, gladly and without a complaint, pushes his disabled wife in her wheelchair all the way to the square in downtown Newnan and back to their home.

Love is the response from our community to those who needed

them after the tornado in March 2021.

Love is caring about the people of Ukraine and donating food, clothing, housing, sanctuary.

Love is quiet service, sacrifice, hardship, compassion, giving, receiving, forgiveness, and grace.

Love is spending time devoting attention, affirmation, and affection to another person, or to a cause, or a living thing, or to a higher power greater than oneself.

And that brings me to this weekend. Easter weekend, and also Passover. Also Ramadan. It's all about love and sacrifice, y'all. We do well to concentrate on that and choose it as a paradigm for every single day we live. Love a stranger, love a neighbor, love a spouse, love a child, love a parent, love a friend, love a higher power, love life. Leave hate, self-aggrandizement, and aggression behind.

And for goodness sake and the love of Elvis, love means always being willing to say you're sorry. How else do we get to forgiveness and grace?

Past. Present. Future
4-24-2022

Recently, I watched Ken Burns' special about Ernest Hemingway. Burns can put together a piece of documentary work like nobody else. And goodness, he is prolific. His Hemingway documentary coincidentally, aired on PBS the night after I had re-watched one of my favorite movies on Netflix, *Midnight in Paris*. Box office for the 2011 movie wasn't great, but I suspect it may have been because it was neither Marvel franchise rock 'em-sock- 'em, nor total rom-com pablum.

This movie contained some cerebral, culturally artsy stuff with a bit of fantasy and whimsy thrown in. Worked for me.

Despite a secondary plot involving a double love story, the plot depended on a thinking audience.

The story is a combination of "the grass is greener" and what it's like meeting your heroes from another time. It revolves around a writer (Owen Wilson) who vacations with his fiancé in Paris, present-day. On a late-night walk alone after a quarrel, he finds himself at the steps of Saint Etienne du Mont at the stroke of midnight. It's there an old-fashioned car stops for him and he rides right into the Paris of the 1920s.

There he is, star-struck as he meets his literary heroes, ex-pats, bohemians, writers, artists, musicians, and thinkers, the cultural icons of the Jazz Age. F. Scott and Zelda Fitzgerald, T.S. Eliot, Dali, Gertrude Stein, Cole Porter, Picasso, and Hemingway among others.

He falls for a lovely young woman in the 1920s (a stand-in for all of Picasso's mistresses) and just as he is ready to forgo modernity and live with her in the exciting 20s, he discovers that she, too, would rather live in an earlier time, the 1890s, the era of The Moulin-Rouge, Can-Can dancers, and Toulouse Lautrec. Thus, we arrive at a pivotal dilemma. Neither wants to live in the boring, unhappy reality of their current time, preferring an exhilarating, romanticized time of the past.

There's simply not enough time in the movie to flesh out all the iconic heroes of past history into fully 3-dimensional people, but it's the thought that counts.

It's the tale of two dreamers in the right place (Paris) who feel they're living in the wrong time. Their naïve, simplistic desire to focus on the fantasy of the good times of the past and deny the bad ones that come along with it is thrilling, myopic, and doomed.

How many times have we longed for the "good old days" when things were supposedly different, or simpler, or better, or fill in the blank. I get it. I am not fond of living with current, polarized politics and climate change my children and grandchildren will have to navigate; pandemics and warring despots; drive by shootings and conspiracy theories.

But if we get real, we must ask ourselves if there was ever a "better" time somewhere in the world when people were kinder and gentler, and despots and leaders didn't harm, kill and maim innocent citizens in unconscionable acts of bigotry, prejudice, hate, crime, cruelty, and war? If we think there was that perfect time, we should take off the rose-colored glasses, put ourselves in another's shoes, and walk the walk of the oppressed.

We could all rattle off global events, battles, plagues, dust bowls, depressions, and disasters for every decade. But it ain't nothin' new, is it? From the days before antibiotics to human rights atrocities, to gangsters who rattled tommy guns, to political upheaval, we have never lived in a perfect decade. Ever.

Maybe we reminisce about an earlier time when we were healthy, or younger, or a family member was still alive. But wishing to actually live in the past is not only romanticized nonsense but a waste of our time.

Awareness of—and taking a lesson from—the past, though, is a wholly different concept, and a valuable one. The present needs us to remember the past for the sake of the future. If we don't study our past unflinchingly (from way back when, to as recently as yesterday), educate ourselves, and learn from it, we continue to make the same mistakes from our past over and over again, just in modern versions.

Amid today's wonderful, progressive inventions and groundbreaking discoveries, fashion forward galas, and more forms of entertainment and edification than we can consume, we must not be distracted. This beautiful world also continues to be ugly. Globally and locally, people continue to fight, kill, oppress, and die. They are selfish and do harm to one another. They don't co-operate. They don't want to. They threaten humanity's existence.

How's that working for us?

Let's talk progress. Progress, (like Midnight in Paris) also depends on a thinking audience. Progress (like Midnight in Paris) may not be great box office right now, either.

But nothing changes if nothing changes. How do we make progress for the good of our present and our futures? Progress does not involve a return to the past but learning lessons from it. Progress moves us forward, not backward. Progress is not binary. It is co-operative movement toward a continuum of "betters" for us all. Progress is an important goal if we could all just agree on what, exactly, "progress" and "better" are, and move forward together.

Now wouldn't that be something. Just think.

Old
5-1-2022

An old friend from bygone days blew through town recently and stayed with us for the weekend. She was, in fact, one of two beloved fraternity sweethearts from Rick's Phi Gamma Delta days a gazillion years ago at the University of Georgia. We took this opportunity to invite six nearby Phi Gamma Delta "ancients" as they call themselves now—and their wives, all of them, literally and figuratively the very definition of old friends—to our house for a little gathering on Sunday afternoon.

The spring weather hadn't settled down yet. The days alternated between warm and sunny, and gray with sharp winds and freeze warnings. I wanted our party to be a doors-open, inside-outside affair where people would easily flow and have plenty of room. I prepared for the best case, but I was ready for the worst. So I crossed my fingers and hoped Mother Nature would grant us a fair-weather dispensation for our day.

Guess I held my mouth right because we got a gorgeous day, and lo, the stage was set. The temps were moderate, the sun shone, and the huge azaleas in my back yard were all in riotous bloom.

It was even Masters Tournament Sunday and still, folks came. Let's face it, not everybody can attend the Masters but we still like watching it. I had the outside, porch television tuned to the golf game for insurance, volume down.

In full party prep mode, Rick and I got to work. The to-do list was long:

1. Clean the house (hide some stuff in the laundry room where no one will see it).
2. Shop for food. (Try not to buy too much food. Hah! Do you know me?)
3. Prepare all the food. (Refer to your list so nothing gets forgotten. Remember where you put the list.)
4. Locate and arrange serving platters, bowls, and utensils; dinner plates, glasses, silverware, cute cocktail napkins and dinner napkins. (Remember you forgot again to buy cocktail napkins.) Ramble through the stack of leftover cocktail napkins and hope you have enough with designs suitable for the occasion. Cute colorful cupcakes? Great, use them for dessert. Happy Birthday? Nah, use them another time, like someone's birthday. Shamrocks? OK, they'll do. It's spring, right?
5. Set up the bar and have extra ice in the cooler. (Remember where the cooler is stored.) Send Rick to get the cooler, wherever it is.
6. Polish the silver ice bucket. (Hide the other tarnished silver in the laundry room with the other stuff nobody's supposed to see).
7. Mow the yard and blow off porches and sidewalks. (Hide the blower in the playhouse because there's not enough time to put it away in the garage.)
8. Retreat upstairs, shower, put on makeup, blow hair dry, and change clothes three times before guests arrive.
9. Think about how to make a casual entrance after Rick has answered the door because guests have already started arriving, and you are still upstairs in a state of dishabille, trying on clothes
10. Finally, now presentable, energy already flagging, enter the

party quietly and greet everyone with a smile because you are genuinely excited to see them. (Try to stop sweating).

11. By all means, enjoy your own party!

The food and conversation and the company were all fabulous as we gathered on the covered back porch and mingled in the kitchen, laughing, talking, catching up.

Granted, I'm rusty at throwing parties, what with the pandemic and years of aging in place. But it all came back like riding a bike. Except for the energy I once had. That took a bit of a hike.

Once upon a younger time, before my best energy went AWOL, I was able to bounce back easily when my brother and his wife stayed with us for a few days every Christmas. I'd be hanging up the mop as the doorbell rang, looking deceptively fresh with energy to spare, ready to entertain twenty-five people on Christmas Day.

Now our guests are fewer and farther between. Now I pre-medicate and post-medicate with Extra Strength Tylenol.

I still have my standards. I don't skimp on quality. It's not the quantity of a gathering that counts for me anyway. A party without heart is not my party. A party without creativity (even the slightest touch) is not my party. A party without delicious food is not my party, either. A party where guests feel (and are) welcome and at ease as a result of my extra effort is 100% my party.

And this was definitely my party. 100%.

The wives strolled all around our freshly mowed backyard and then ventured along the mulched, wooded paths. They were effusive in their compliments as they admired everything, including our covered porch.

A colorful, fresh quilt draped over the porch swing invited guests to sit and sway. All surfaces were wiped clean of demon yellow pollen. Easter decor perked up the tables and island.

The big, heavy, pale wood armoire I purchased at a yard sale for a song last summer was quite the useful and atmospheric piece. We almost killed ourselves hauling that heavy monster home from Atlanta, then sealed every inch with Marine Spar varnish, and installed it on the porch after chiseling out an entire row of brick steps along the long back wall. This party was its maiden, experimental voyage. Serving triple duty as storage behind closed doors below, and as TV cabinet and lighted serving bar when the giant arched doors were opened above, it passed with flying colors.

Folks lined up around the kitchen island and happily loaded their plates. Once we were seated back on the porch, we were chatting and chewing and drinking and laughing and enjoying each other immensely. One wife, happily pushing the swing off with her feet and lifting her legs as she arced herself back and forth said, "Susie, where do you get the energy!!?" And others chimed in, "Yes! Where?!"

I chortled and then laughed out loud. "Thank you so much! I love creating. But after y'all leave, the dishes will be in the sink for two days and I'll be horizontal in bed for at least three!" Uproarious laughter ensued.

They all thought I was joking. I was dead damn serious.

I love entertaining. I just wish it were easier these days. It's the effort one puts into a thing that is the mark of its value, be it entertaining, friendship, or parenting. Being tired from that kind of effort is a good kind of tired, but tired, nonetheless.

Being able to punt is also an asset. I had hoped for the best with the weather but pledged to roll with the punches if necessary. And when the best weather happened and flowers were in bloom, I was grateful to my toes that I would not have to roll.

These are not fair-weather friends, anyway. They would've shown up no matter what, and we would've entertained indoors if Mother Nature had shown us another kind of day. Even as decades have passed, each one has been true to, and carried out, their fraternity motto, "not for college days alone." They are truly brothers. Fraternal family.

We have seen too many of them leave the planet recently. It is always a shock, then a deep grief, then a realization that we could be next at any time. These brothers attend funerals, acknowledge birthdays, support the infirm, and celebrate successes. And when this group showed up on this perfect day and gathered together after what had been a very long time, we were all happy and grateful to be here. To be anywhere. To be alive, able to rise and take nutrition, as the old saying goes.

I understand why folks my age, and older, decide to chuck the house and the yard for a retirement village. Rick and I even joke about selling out after only a couple hours of heavy yard work. So far it's all been a joke. I say, "Hell no, I won't go" and "Carry me out in a pine box." Realistically though, at some point there will come a time when we will cease laughing and have to take the idea seriously.

When it all gets to be too much, when the mind is willing but the body is weak, it's a question again of quality over quantity. If one can't afford servants, gardeners, and handmaids, or when the quality of life becomes an issue because of demands that are just too great, the question becomes, "What is one to do?" How much can we realistically toil over? How many rooms can I keep clean in my two-story house with a basement? How many stairs will I be able to climb? How many parties are possible if friends are too old to drive and we are too frail to prepare? And how will one of us carry on without the other?

I will cross that bridge when I come to it. Thankfully, now is not the time.

Until then I will make the most of it and thoroughly exhaust myself by throwing an occasional party, a party that makes me happy, uses my creativity, and brings friends together. I will volunteer. I will write another book. I will love and play with my grandchildren. I will garden. I will sweat and I will ache.

Then I shall rest and do absolutely nothing afterward for an unprescribed amount of time, days possibly, simply because I can. And then, after a time, I shall do it all over again. Until I simply can't. Perish the thought.

Because creating, whether in the garden or in the kitchen or on the back porch or on paper may be tiring, it never gets old.

What Fresh Hell is This?
5-8-2022

Local school board elections are coming up on May 24th. As a matter of fact, early voting has already begun.

With regard to the shocking and painful campaign leading up to this vote, I quote one of my literary heroes, Dorothy Parker, who said, "What fresh hell is this?"

Seriously.

Four of our local school board candidates—3 new candidates and one incumbent—are modern-day Four Horsemen/women of the Apocalypse. They are riding in to this election on steeds paid for by a national political action committee aiming to bring a warped, apocalyptic agenda to our public schools.

Do not feed the animals. Don't feed their horses, either.

Their platform focuses on the now familiar paranoid, political buzzwords designed to appeal to, and terrify, the ignorant voter: CRT, among others. These candidates are promising to do us all a great service by heroically stopping CRT or Critical Race Theory in our public schools. They claim "the woke mob" is indoctrinating our children. They prance their horses to high moral ground and while rearing up like Trigger and Roy Rogers, they wave their white hats and proclaim to the citizens below they will be the ones to rescue them all from this evil tyranny.

Please, for the love of Elvis, y'all, see this for what it is.

CRT IS NOT NOW, NOR HAS IT EVER BEEN, NOR WILL IT EVER BE TAUGHT IN COWETA SCHOOLS.

Do not fall for untrue, political rhetoric and misinformation that invites you to vote for people who claim they will do you a huge favor by fixing a non-existent threat.

In the 1950s, Sen. Joe McCarthy tried the same trick. He set out to save the country from communists, and falsely accused innocent US citizens of being Communist party members, smearing their reputations and ruining their lives in the process. The famous question posed to him after his vile campaign of paranoid lies had worn on far too long was: "Have you no sense of decency, sir?"

Indeed. The same could be asked of the apocalyptic four candidates running today: Have they no decency? Either they know they are lying, or they are deluded and believe their lies. Either one is a good reason not to vote for them.

The minute a candidate pledges to "stop CRT" in Coweta Schools, turn your back and support the other guy, the one running on truth, facts, logic, and a genuine desire to be of service to all public-school students and teachers of Coweta.

This election for school board is a crucible, a trial whose very outcome is forged in the heated conflict between truth and falsehood. There's a big distinction between having differences of opinion supported equally on both sides by facts, and those in which one side relies on arguments manipulated through disinformation and a warped lens. If this were simply an upright difference of opinion I could respect the debate. But this isn't on the level.

Matter of fact, it's not a debate, either.

Perhaps voters should question why, in what was to be a televised school board candidate debate, the four horsemen/women didn't even show up. Why not present their views and have a mature, intelligent back-and-forth debate? Was their absence meant to be some kind of protest, or were their positions just indefensible and they knew it?

Instead, this past Wednesday they chose to premiere a roundtable discussion video on social media in which only they were interviewed by an interviewer in their camp, asking soft-ball, biased questions. So their views were presented in a void, where they could not be challenged in a fair debate. Pure, one-sided propaganda.

It's this "truth vs propaganda" issue that obfuscates any resemblance of a balanced exchange of ideas.

Here is the truth: There exists a nationwide campaign dedicated to bringing about the death and destruction of public schools as we know them. In a recent speech, a sophist named Christopher Rufo disseminated his extremist strategy. And just so we're clear, someone who engages in sophistry uses plausible but fallacious reasoning to make a point. They use the slightest particle of fact in an argument to make a point they know is false.

The public-school problems Rufo and the Apocalyptic Four have fabricated in order to engender fear, anger, and false narratives aren't true.

Rather than supporting, improving, and enriching public schools, Rufo focuses on the sophistic statement that public schools are problematic denizens for our children.

Fact: yes, there are problems. There will always be problems to solve and improvements to be made. But denizens? No way.

Our schools have problems that are of great interest and concern to responsible school board members, problems that are, have been, and will be addressed. They are serious but they are not insurmountable, and they do not threaten the very fabric of our public schools.

Mr. Rufo, however, preaches replacing public schools altogether with a universal, unregulated voucher system. As an expert sophist, Rufo spells out for these candidates on horseback exactly how to ride into battle, what to think and say, how to fabricate and create hysteria: He tells them to "fight" and be "outraged" and "support our conservative values." He tells them they must "fight" for parental rights and "values" and be "outraged" that children are being indoctrinated by the "woke mob." He says children should not be made to feel they are guilty for being white because of slavery; that children should not be "groomed as five-year-olds."

If his accusations were true, one might agree with his outrage. But it's pure sophistry and bunk.

There is no "woke mob" but if Rufo says there is, and says it enough times, gullible people will believe it. Disinformation, gossip, and rumors are like wildfires when they take hold. They burn strong and hot by word of mouth, social media, and mass hysteria.

Unspoken, is that Rufo's plan would be an unbalanced, separatist handmaiden. It would most certainly allow families with better incomes and societal status to gather as birds of a feather and widen the divide between the haves and the have nots in public education. It would guarantee the insulated safety of a population of students who would never be presented with big pictures and inclusive language.

Here is the disinformation play book strategy outlined in a recent speech by Rufo, and I quote, straight from the horse, (I'm not saying which end of the horse, either. This is a family newspaper, and this is an opinion column, remember):

"To get to universal school choice, you really need to operate from a premise of universal public-school distrust... Be ruthless and brutal."

This is the rhetoric of someone who needs a manufactured crisis to rile people and promise them a savior in the very likes of— tadaa— a gallant, outraged school board candidate who gallops in and swoops up our children to safety?

A similar scenario already occurred recently, concerning a school board member/now apocalyptic equestrienne incumbent, and a "scandal" over turf bids on school playing fields. She pointed an accusatory finger at her own school board and school system. An investigation ensued. And in the end, the fickle finger of fate found her, exonerating the school board and schools. https://times-herald.com/news/2019/05/what-we-need-is-a-scandal

On the flip side, the grounded, level-headed school board candidates currently running are voicing viable, supportive, sustainable, platforms for the betterment of all our public schools, students, and teachers through their smart input and educated, effective solutions.

At least one apocalyptic candidate would suggest that wanting to provide an equitable education for all is in some way a bad thing; that there's a socialist agenda at play; that Marxists and socialists lurk in every school hallway and stand at every blackboard; that our children are in danger.

I suggest otherwise.

Visit the Georgia Vision Project (gavisionproject.org) if you'd really like to see the true, altruistic vision for public schools in Georgia, including Coweta County. The link is also on the Coweta County Schools' website under ResourcesCommunity. This Project states a multi-year initiative to "research and implement world class educational standards, viable directives, sustainable frameworks, and organizing contemporary networks."

I support the election of honorable, truthful, non-deceptive school board candidates Beth Barnett, Larry Robertson, Rob DuBose, and Amy Dees who put our children, schools, and teachers of Coweta as their priorities, not their enemies. I also support Andrew Copeland and Frank Farmer (who are not up for re-election this year but who are doing a terrific job).

As the old saying goes, "If you're walking through [fresh] hell, keep walking." Walk on over to your polling place, don't step in the horse poop on your way, enter that voting booth, and do the right thing. For the love of Elvis (and our public schools), vote Barnett, Robertson, DuBose, and Dees.

Making It Work
5-15-2022

Apparently, Joint Replacement Awareness Day (JRAD) is Saturday, May 14. Let's hear it for today's advanced orthopedics and awareness!

This could be an opportune reminder for some people, but I do not need a reminder. I am already fully aware. Trust me, I have already had one knee replaced and my husband just got a new hip. Reminders are for rookies who still have all their original joints.

The thing nobody warned me about, though, is after the joint replacement surgery and painful rehab, while allowing me to walk a painless straight line, that hard metal implant now residing in my left knee does not allow me to kneel on it anymore. And the right knee that God gave me is starting to protest.

And yet, I am still an avid gardener. Gardeners do a lot of kneeling. I make it work.

I also do a lot of talking in my garden. Yes, I talk to my plants. Out loud. Sometimes in a whisper, sometimes loudly in my best Patti Lupone. I bet if you ask them, a lot of other avid gardeners willing to admit it would say the same thing. We are not weird, we are avid. That's my story and I'm sticking to it.

I don't go to the plant nursery and get a couple of pansies and spend a nice little 10 minutes arranging them in a pot of dirt.

No, I haul my Hyundai Santa Fe up to Growers Outlet in Loganville and make a pit stop on the way home at all the local nurseries (always buy local), filling every inch of vehicle real estate, seats down, with annuals, perennials, shrubs, ferns, soil amendments, and pine straw. Those uh-oh loop-straps above the passenger seats are great for suspending hanging baskets. So are sturdy suspension rods spanning the width of the vehicle. I've been known to create double-decker storage in the way-back cargo area which involves a sturdy palette supported by square plastic milk boxes under each corner. I store some plants inside the milk boxes, and slide flats of annuals into the open area between them on the bottom. The larger, taller stuff rests on the top. I've also hauled a trailer behind me a time or two. Necessity really is a mother.

Obviously, I'm an incorrigible plant-aholic. As the saying goes, "One plant is too many, and a thousand never enough." The first step is admitting it. Gladly.

I'm not sure I want a cure, though. At least I have a bottom line: I have adopted the tradition of remembering whether I can responsibly afford, and then actually plant, all the vegetation I buy.

When one is standing in the middle of a plant nursery surrounded by glorious opportunity, it's easy to be swept away and forget that all that luscious flora requires a budget, along with energy, sweat-equity, and someone who can still move a ton of dirt around, push down hard on a shovel, and get low enough to the ground to wield a trowel.

As much as I talk in my garden, the garden also talks back. It does not speak English, of course, but it definitely communicates. Looking back on all my years of pushing a trowel, I wish everything I have purchased and planted over decades survived. But I'm kind of glad the ones that are gone can't attest now to whatever it was I screwed up, or what horror befell them that I had no hand in.

So far I'm glad I have survived it all, although there have been a few times I've had my doubts. I am still here to tell the tales I choose to tell.

Shoulda been there one July, thirty years ago when my gardening buddy, Leanne, my husband, Rick, and I pulled out some huge, overgrown, red-tip photinia bullies we inherited from the previous owners of our house. We dug, and sweated, and groaned, and dug, wayyyy down, only to uncover roots as big around as super-sized rolls of Brawny paper towels. Straining our backs, we tugged and chopped, but those red-tip roots were immovable as steel footings in concrete. So we eventually got smart, or desperate, depending on how you look at it. We tied those recalcitrant shrubs to the hitch on the pickup truck and yanked them out by those demon roots. That's one loss I do not mourn. I'm also glad they are gone and cannot rat on me. Pretty sure I said a lot more than "oh darn it."

That was, however, the first step in transforming my garden into something more gracious and beautiful. My back, however, hasn't been the same since.

Since then, with no formal training and a boatload of books, seminars, willingness to experiment, and years of sweaty trial-and-error (heavy on the sweat and the error) I've learned a thing or three.

1. Gardeners ain't perfect. Gardeners who never fail are not gardeners. They are unicorns. Dare you to find one.
2. This little ditty about perennials is useful: First year they sleep; Second year they creep; Third year they leap.
3. Composting is good and Milorganite fertilizer is also a great, off-label deer deterrent. They hate the smell.
4. Killing bees should be a criminal offense. Watch the insecticides, folks.
5. I have learned resilience, fortitude, forgiveness, and my limits. I learned that I am not Callaway or Gibbs Gardens. I don't have full-time staff to plant, weed, feed, prune, mulch, nurture, and water a showplace of their magnitude. Still, envisioning the wooded beauty of Callaway Gardens, I once tried planting hydrangeas and some azaleas in my shady wooded area. Oh they were going to look so full and beautiful. And they did. Until they didn't.

The azaleas started rapidly dying, attacked by bag worms from trees too tall to reach with worm-killing spray. It was also too late to save them with anything applied directly on the plants. I tried. They died.

The hydrangeas weren't attacked, but they were sad and unhappy in their spot, and they told me so. Their leaves drooped, limp like neckties hanging from their stems and refused to thrive. The deep, dry shade was not their thing. They needed a little more sun and a lot more water, neither of which the dark, dry woods could provide. So my husband and I dug them up and moved them to the front yard where they have been deliriously happy ever since. They thank us by living large and blooming profusely. I am still really sorry about the doomed azaleas in the big, bad woods.

As spring gives way to summer, the hellebores, dogwood, cherry, and azaleas blooms are history. But oh, my, what glories present themselves... the roses are abundant, the jasmine is smelling sweet, the iris are still hanging in, things are unfurling daily and even more wonders await. Pure joy to take it all in and commune with everything that bursts with life.

Talking in the garden, working hard, usually includes sound effects, too. When I have stood, bending over double pulling endless weeds for far too long (because I can't kneel, remember?) and my back and hamstrings are in knots, I am capable of mumbling the rudest things followed by a grunt or groan for emphasis. Can't help it.

But I am also a doting mother attempting to nourish growing things with food and drink, praising and encouraging them to flourish. I speak words of consolation and comfort to them whether they thrive or they are sick, dying, or dead. And when they are gone, I grieve the loss (except for the red-tips). I can't help that, either.

If they could speak English, the plants living in my garden now would report it all, the laughing, groaning, whispering, yelling, and crying in their midst as well as all the swearing:

"…the hell is that?"

"Ohhh my back. Oooh my hammies."

"Gah! Forgot your name! You gonna make me Google you?"

"I do not remember planting you."

"Look out, I'm comin' in there to straighten this mess out. I am out of patience, I'm wearing really good garden gloves, and I have sharp tools."

"Aww, you are beautiful."

"Time for momma to rest. See y'all tomorrow!"

As a gardener who misses kneeling, I will still go on record endorsing joint replacements, as I can walk without pain now. They are ultimately a really good thing. Get 'em if you need 'em. Generally speaking, I'm glad I got mine, one little positional hiccup notwithstanding.

My gardening motto echoes the words of the indefatigable Tim Gunn of Project Runway fame, who may or may not have ever planted a single living thing in his life but sure can make magic with fabric. When he says "Make it work" he is serious, and things start happening.

So far I'm making do. Gardeners are tough and love a challenge. I make it work and make my garden happen. At least I try.

A Man and A Woman
5-22-2022

They were born the same year, 1915, in different towns, two days apart, him on August 16, her on August 19. When they finally met as young adults in the same town they fell in love and married when they were 22. After the war, they had two children, a boy and a girl.

The two parents were devoted to each other, and to their son and daughter, in ways children rarely appreciate until they are older and possess valuable hindsight. They were generous, giving, loving parents who made sacrifices and provided the best they could for their children.

After many years, different family stories became well worth the re-telling. Here are just a few.

One Christmas holiday in the 1960s, the man walked through the door of a pet shop holding his young son's and daughter's hands. He was desperate and searching. Searching for a solution to a predicament of the man's own making.

He had waited far too long to buy his wife a Christmas gift. He loved her so, and wanted her to have something very, very special. So far he hadn't found it yet, and it was Christmas Eve. Time had run out and he had lost all perspective.

So when the three of them laid eyes on the adorable Capuchin monkey making eyes at them in the pet store, the children swooned and begged and assured him that their mom would love it. He caved in to the lunacy, and they walked out of the pet store with a rare gift, something they were certain no one else would be getting for Christmas.

The little monkey was hidden away in the basement in his cage that night so the man could give the woman her big surprise on Christmas morning. Sure enough, he brought the creature upstairs on December 25th and excitedly unveiled his unique gift to her as the children giggled and clapped. One could say she was beyond excited, more like dumbfounded, and trying very hard to feign delight for his and the children's sakes.

But after they had all gone to bed that Christmas evening, as the man and the children slept soundly, the woman got up, troubled and in need of answers. She sat on the floor in front of the cage with a bottle of Scotch, dressed in her nightgown, talking to the monkey, wondering where she had gone wrong. The Capuchin wasn't telling.

After a week, the monkey disappeared altogether, cage and all. "Back to the pet store," the two parents told their children.

Ultimately, the family wasn't especially sad to see him go, cute as he was, because once past the first infatuation and howdy-dos he wasn't very likeable, and he didn't seem to like the family, either. He was mean, he was quite the screecher, and he bit. Also, the cage sat in the once spotless breakfast nook of the family kitchen, a location entirely unsuitable for a primate and his bathroom habits.

"Worst Christmas gift ever," the man apologized later to his wife, shaking his head in abject shame. But the man and the woman loved each other so much he was forgiven, and time marched on. Although every holiday afterward, she issued a warning: "No monkeys." And everyone could laugh about it by then. "How about a little m-o-n-e-y instead? And maybe a nice sweater?" she would say. The man was always delighted to oblige.

Then there was the time the man saved his little girl from disaster.

The family was visiting friends and the little girl wanted to take a joy ride in a tricycle down their long, steep driveway. Her parents said no, but the little girl was determined. Her dad decided he could stand on the back of the tricycle for steady ballast to keep it from falling over. Convincing his wife it would be safe, he and the little girl positioned themselves at the top of the drive and let 'er rip. As the tricycle shuddered its way down the rough asphalt at warp speed, it hit a pebble, turning them over, tricycle, legs, arms, and bodies flying akimbo. It happened so fast their laughter went silent; there was no time to even scream. As the little girl's face approached the pavement, the man swiftly moved to grab her body, using his hand to cradle and cover her face as they finally skidded to a stop.

The man's hand was scraped bloody, to the bone, and the little girl's face was not. She would never forget that terrifying moment and how he had valiantly spared her. Neither would he.

On Saturdays, the man took his little girl to the newspaper office where he worked. It was a marvelous place, where art directors and cartoonists had huge pots of rubber cement on their drafting tables in the art room. The smell of the rubber cement was sharp and she liked it almost as much as the smell of the gasoline at the Phillips 66 every time they stopped to fill up the Desoto.

The girl would paint her hand over and over with wet, rubber goo, let it dry a bit, and then rub her hands together to form a round rubber ball, after which she played catch against the walls of his office. She visited the noisy press room that smelled of machines, grease, paper, and ink. A hulk of a man named Tiger Flowers assembled five little metal letter blocks to form her first name, backwards. Her dad bought her an ink pad and she stamped her name inside her diary.

The little girl's mom was a wonderful cook, a devotee of Julia Child in fact, and she taught her daughter everything she knew. The mother also kept boxes filled with scraps of fabric, yarn, thread, broken jewelry, sequins, bric-a-brac, and all manner of small items. She gave her daughter full permission to use those magical boxes to make things. Anything she wanted. The girl was in heaven with all the supplies at her disposal and loved her mother for it. She made lots of homemade cards, and clever signs, and decorated boxes. Her mother was wise, as she knew her daughter loved making creative, artful things, and this was a way to quietly support her. She also took her daughter downtown for art lessons and drove her once a week to a woman's house for piano lessons. The whole family went to concerts and plays. And when her daughter sang, her parents stopped parties and invited guests to listen.

One time, after the daughter was a grown, married woman, her parents' house was hit by a tornado that broke out windows, blew trees over into houses, and blocked roads. The man walked almost a mile to the nearest working pay phone to call her. When he got through to her office he was so shaken, he asked for her by her maiden name.

It was her turn to come to her parents' aid now, and she grabbed her husband. They drove to her family home to find it heavily damaged, but her parents uninjured. They all embraced, and cried, and got to work. It was the least she could do for them after all they had done for her.

Years passed. The husband and wife died only one day apart, her on May 23, him on May 24. But there were 16 years between. He was only 67 when he finally let go. Cancer. She was 83. COPD.

I will be thinking fondly of them and missing them terribly this week on the anniversaries of their deaths.

They were my parents, and I was their little girl.

Mayday!
5-29-2022

Been a busy week. The month of May is always a train wreck. Our calendars resemble abstract art, heavy on the graphics, light on the negative space.

Parents, grandparents, teachers, students, graduating seniors, politicians, voters, and everybody planning for events, summer childcare, and the final episodes of This Is Us, knows this.

After this particular week, though, I am reminded that our May calendars these days must also have one or more mass shootings penciled in. My God. What is wrong with us? Unfortunately, this is not a TV show. This really is us now.

Last week, it was a hate crime in a Buffalo grocery store. This week it's an elementary school in Uvalde, Texas. These have been happening everywhere, for years, and I'm so sick of it. Columbine, Sandy Hook, Parkland, and on and on. There have been 27 school shootings this year alone in the US. and it's only May. Do the grizzly math and figure the unholy average per month. Unacceptable.

The elementary school children in Texas and their teachers who are lost will not have any more days to count til Christmas or til graduation or til their weddings or their birthdays. The only calendars left to them are the ones their loved ones keep that count the days since they were murdered.

Shame on us for allowing this madness year after year after year.

An editorial cartoon this week took my breath away. A perplexed angel at the pearly gates talks to a non-plussed St Peter: "They keep sending thoughts and prayers… and their kids." Dark. True. Just damn.

So, in light of this week's dark, deadly chaos, and the general, busy calendar activities that suddenly now pale in comparison, I thought I'd keep this column simple. Banal. Easygoing.

I've tried to Zen out, clear my mind, make room for quiet and calm inspiration.

First simple thought: write about watching paint dry. Um, no. Delete.

Second thought: Hey, local newspaper columnist Alex McRae actually interviewed a speed bump once. Maybe I should interview my furniture. That's it. I got this.

Pause.

Nah, I haven't got this.

The children, their families, their schoolmates and teachers are too much with me and I cannot think of anything else. Little kids and their teachers were massacred last Tuesday in a school, a place where they should've been safe.

No, I most definitely do not have this.

No one's got this. That's the problem. That's been the problem for years.

If we really want to stop the madness we would do something about it. Or at least try.

I remember when the speed limit was actually lowered on some freeways because the higher speed limit had proven too dangerous. Can we also slow down the all too easy, speedy access to assault weapons and still preserve the 2nd amendment? How? Are we even willing to talk about it? For the sake of our children?

Food for thought, though: when the 10-year federal ban on assault weapons expired in 2004, mass shootings doubled. And here we are.

Do not tell me it's not about the automatic weapon; that it's only about the evil guy behind the butt plate.

It takes two to tango, yo. I've yet to hear of an assault weapon operating solo without someone to pull the trigger in the most inappropriate places: schools, churches, synagogues, offices, stores, movie theaters, homes, and neighborhood streets. No, clearly anyone who would commit mass murder is mentally ill, but it's definitely about the gun, too. Guns and their shooters are literal partners in crime and cannot be separated from one another.

Could law-abiding citizens who want to defend themselves, or hunt, or enjoy target practice manage without assault weapons? Maybe we could raise the gun purchasing age to 21 when the teenage amygdala is more mature. The majority of school shootings have been committed by those under the age of 21.

Could we all at least support stricter regulations, registering, and licensing guns? We require as much for a vehicle, and we must carry driver's licenses and insurance. Don't tell me our children's lives aren't worth the same trouble.

These ideas aren't the magic be-all and end-all solutions, of course, so let's keep moving forward. Let's not let excuses for why we can't improve something be our default answer. We must not give up.

There must be more answers. Those answers ought not to rely on simply upping-the-ante and arming every teacher, school, movie theater usher, salesperson, office worker, minister, and security guard with like weapons, either. Then we become a Marvel movie on an endless loop, everyone relying on nonstop, rapid-fire violence, death, destruction, and mayhem. I do not want to foresee a dystopian future when steel shades cover every window in every building, bullet proof doors and walls are required building code, and Kevlar is the de rigueur fashion fabric of the times.

Our solutions should involve less violence, not more.

I don't believe in binary, simplistic answers for the problem, either. Let's not limit our conversation to mental health vs gun laws. The solution is found in brave collaboration, and examination of everything.

As a general observation, people are still good, and caring, and benevolent. But we have also become polarized, pessimistic, and paralyzed. We are solipsistic, selfish, and short-sighted. We have completely lost track of saving humanity as our priority. We refuse cooperative solutions, dispense with give and take, and eschew as impossible the concept of selfless, bright, creative, and willing minds coming together (imagine!), agreeing to talk about and come up with multi-faceted solutions (imagine, again!)?

Can those solutions — a tall order but all for the greater good — examine and address the causes of mass shootings as well as how we enable them in order to effect change? Can we take an honest look at today's mental health issues, social media influences, societal mores, pressures, and inequities, and emotional triggers, along with our current gun laws, or lack thereof, around assault weapons? Are we brave enough to indict ourselves, accept our shortcomings, clean up our act, and do better? Can we look at immovable politicians, gun lobbies, and the NRA? Can we decry all those who accept money in return for looking the other way, pointing fingers, and going deaf to screaming, dying children? Or worse, those who pray over problems they are unwilling to solve? Are we going to continue rationalizing, avoiding responsibility and our reflections in the mirror, or are we going to grow up and figure this out?

Too many innocent lives have already been taken. We must all drop the "who me?" attitude and look carefully, respectfully, and responsibly at everything, every damn thing. Everything from policies to permits; from common sense to innovative, bipartisan concessions and cooperation across the aisle. If we can't all work together, if we don't manage to summon the willingness to find collaborative answers in common ground, I truly fear we really are doomed to live an eternal, horrific, repetitive Groundhog Day.

I sat down to write this column, utterly speechless. I was about to beg off, to say, "give me a week and maybe I can write something then."

I really thought I had no words. I was wrong. Silence is not an option.

Nothing changes if nothing changes.

There is no time to waste. Let's do this. We simply must get it together. For good.

Orly And Other Ghosts. A Two Part Series
6-5-2022, 6-12-2022

-excerpted from *The Veterinarian's Wife* by Susie Berta, edited/abridged for this column

PART ONE, 6-5-2022

June 3, 1962, was a sunny, cloudless Sunday in Atlanta, Georgia. Across the Atlantic, Air France Flight 007 was crashing on takeoff at Orly Airport near Paris, taking the lives of one-hundred and thirty people. More than one-hundred of the dead were Atlantans: arts patrons, Art Association members, and prominent citizens on their way home after a cultural trip to generate much-needed support for Atlanta's art scene.

On the sixtieth anniversary of the Orly crash, the dead still linger—their spirits affixed in memory, on plaques, in buildings, and in history. They remain with those who were alive in Atlanta then and now, with all who carry their stories forward, and with all who hear them.

I grew up in Atlanta, having had ties to the arts all my life. For me, this date brings back a flood of memories. For Atlanta, the impact of this day was, and continues to be, unforgettable, remarkable, and everlasting.

In 1962, I was twelve. Atlanta was booming in some ways. With a population of one-million people, Atlanta was enjoying a cultural push by visionary movers and shakers in Atlanta's arts and political communities unlike any in the city's history. In other ways, Atlanta was still a provincial, small, southern town reluctant to accept radical social change. Still segregated, Atlanta was a city of separate water fountains and segregated schools.

It would be another two years before the Civil Rights Act of 1964 would come to be. In defiance of it, Lester Maddox, future governor of Georgia and high school dropout, would take an ax handle known as a "Pickrick Drumstick" off the wall of his Atlanta, whites-only Pickrick Restaurant known for its fried chicken, and brandish it at three African American Georgia Tech students asking to be served.

But in 1962, we mourned the tragedy at Orly. It was, for all of Atlanta, and my family, a most personal loss. For it was on that June day, an entire family living just three doors down from us, along with so many other citizens from all over Atlanta, vanished from the earth.

The entire Frederick W. Bull family was taking off from Orly that day. One of the Bull daughters, Ellen, and I were playmates.

When the news came that day in June, I could not wrap my adolescent head around the fact that an entire family, including my young, lively friend, would never be home again. To this day, when I drive down Westover Drive and pass their old house, I say a prayer for the ghosts who will always reside there in my memory.

In the sixties, Mom worked as a pioneer helping establish the Atlanta Arts Festival at Piedmont Park. Dad served on the board of the Atlanta Symphony for a while when Henry Sopkin was the conductor and performances were held in the Municipal Auditorium on Courtland Street—on nights when roller derbies and Live Atlanta Wrestling weren't booked.

It wouldn't be long before the great Robert Shaw would appear on Atlanta's music scene and transform everything—including my life—in the best way possible. All through my high school years, Shaw's focus on teaching young choral singers was influential in my musical growth and that of countless others.

Years later, after living in Alabama and Virginia, my husband and I returned to Georgia. As a grown woman I auditioned and was accepted into the ranks of a very special, select family: the ASO Chorus and Chamber Chorus with the incomparable Maestro Robert Shaw conducting. Over ten seasons, Shaw became my musical father. Certainly, when he died in 1999, I felt grief that ranked just behind the death of my dad in '83, and child in '80.

When the Atlanta Symphony Orchestra and Chorus toured Europe with Mr. Shaw in May and June of 1988, we all had the ghosts of Orly uneasy in our hearts and minds. We landed in Paris on June 2—only one day off from the anniversary of the worst air disaster in history at the time, 26 years earlier. The evening of our arrival we sang the Beethoven Ninth at Le Theatre Chatelet. The audience stood and cheered. Mr. Shaw and the soloists took bow after bow, as did the orchestra and the chorus. It was exhilarating; in a word, magic.

As dynamic as the Paris concert was, it had already been eclipsed several days earlier by our Beethoven Ninth Symphony concert, behind the Berlin Wall in East Berlin.

And little did we know the drama that would await us afterward, when we left for Cardiff at noon on June 3rd…

***

PART TWO, 6-12-2022

On May 30, 1988, our troupe of traveling musicians boarded a bus at our hotel in West Berlin and headed to Checkpoint Charlie—the one place foreign visitors could cross through the Wall from west to east and back again.

After passing through the American guard post, we were stopped at the East German guard post. Dour, well-armed East Berlin border guards scanned the underside of our bus with a mirror attached to a long pole. Then, they boarded to collect our passports and hold them until our departure.

Once through that ordeal, we were cleared to go, and found ourselves in East Berlin—a starkly different place from colorful, modern West Berlin. The Wall was now behind us, but it had an energy, like a constant itch that got under everyone's skin and stayed there, a harsh, ever-present reminder of the continual oppression and captivity of the German people living within its confines.

East Berlin was a disorienting time warp: Everything was outdated, old-fashioned; the buildings were all a dull, industrial monochrome; the cars were small, tan boxes on wheels, squared-off two-door sedans called Trabants. East Berlin was all a depressing gray-scape.

But the Schauspielhaus—the venue where we would sing of brotherhood, unity, and joy—was different, incongruous, in fact. It had just been newly renovated, and its new interior of red velvet, white marble, and crystal chandeliers was as plush and opulent as any royal palace in Europe.

And we were sold out.

The audience was filled with people who had a deep love of music, an even deeper sense of desperation, and a hunger for freedom. They came to hear our music and our message.

They most certainly were not free to leave with us, as they were trapped behind an immovable, fortified concrete wall ninety miles long encircling the city, lined with 302 functioning watch towers, each occupied by armed guards with shooting orders. It was a wall that was two walls, separated by a ribbon of space about a hundred-yards wide known as a "death strip" running the entire length. The death strip was furnished with zig-zag barriers that looked like thick letter XXs lined up in rows, and it was paved with raked sand or gravel, rendering footprints easy to notice. It offered no cover, and most importantly, it presented clear fields of fire for the Wall guards.

We took our places on stage, the chorus so close to the audience that we could almost reach out and shake hands. We could see the threads in the buttons on their shirts, the lines in their faces, the colors of their eyes, and the tears that flowed from them as we sang to them in their language. They heard the message of unity: "Freude!" ("Joy!") and "Alle Menschen werden Brüder" ("When All Men Are Brothers") without knowing whether they would ever be free.

After the final, rousing notes, and chill-bumps rippled over our arms in exhilaration as the tiny hairs stood at attention on the backs of our sweaty necks, the audience jumped to their feet, cheering wildly and clapping with arms raised high.

They wept openly. And so did we. Not a dry eye in the house—not in the audience or on the stage. The applause soon fell into that distinct, rhythmic European-unison clap. These folks were tireless in their appreciation and continued their applause while Mr. Shaw took bow after bow, finally leading the concertmaster from the stage. Even after the stage was completely vacated, the clapping continued. It echoed backstage and reverberated down the staircase, all the way through the long hallway of the basement to our dressing rooms.

After the chorus boarded the bus, the guards returned our passports at Checkpoint Charlie. Turning left onto Friedrichstrasse, we were free.

Leaving those people behind was painful. The day and the entire experience moved us into a reverent, unanimous silence. Perhaps we had provided them a bit of freedom after all, a kind of liberty of the soul that only music and human compassion can manage. None of us knew then that it would be only a little over a year until the Wall would come down, and they would have their freedom after all.

We would also have no way of knowing that the very next day, the Orly airplane crash anniversary would still have the last eerie word.

On June 3rd, shortly after noon, we boarded a chartered Air France flight, just as the Atlanta folks had done in 1962. No one spoke aloud of the significance and the similarities around this date and time, but they were inescapable. The Orly spirits were with us, and they were restless. The differences were several, of course: We were at Charles De Gaulle Airport, not Orly Airfield; we were flying to Cardiff, not

Atlanta; and—in hindsight—we all survived the trip.

But not without incident.

At 12:30 pm. Cardiff time, we landed safely, and all breathed a collective sigh of relief.

Then it happened.

As we taxied toward the terminal, the wing tip rolled past the building and sheared off a couple rows of bricks, clean as a whistle.

The chill we felt disembarking that plane was more than just a reaction to the cold, rainy day. We had been duly reminded. The Orly ghosts were present, stirring.

We were hushed for a moment, in reverence for those who had gone before us and in gratitude for everything that had come after them.

Those who visit The Woodruff Arts Center in Atlanta today to attend a concert, play, or to enjoy an art exhibition may sit outside on the circle of stone seats surrounding the Rodin sculpture, The Shade (L'Ombre). Perhaps they will eat an ice cream cone, sketch, nap, rest, or play and take the time to read the memorial plaques installed there.

They should know that when it was built in 1968, the building was known as the Atlanta Memorial Arts Center—now known as the Woodruff Arts Center after its major benefactor.

They should know that it was built as a memorial to the people of Atlanta who died on June 3, 1962. They should know that The Shade was a memorial gift from the government and the people of France.

When visitors find the quiet circle and read the names on the plaques, it is possible to feel the presence of the benevolent ghosts who linger there. They are the people—the citizens, the families, the children— who in death galvanized Atlanta's arts community, igniting the cultural push Atlanta needed to move forward and imbue the arts with new life.

Last Stand
6-19-2022

I read recently that the last Howard Johnson's extant on the planet has closed its doors for good. Yes, everything changes with time, things come and go, and the longer you live, the more you learn, and the more you get to experience the good, the bad, and the memories.

Growing up in Atlanta, I lived only about a mile or two from a Howard Johnson's Restaurant and Motor Lodge at the corner of Northside Drive and I-75. In the 60s we, and lots of other Buckhead families, went to the restaurant for pancake breakfasts, ice cream, birthday parties, and a pretty cool playground with a rocket ship. Even then, it felt iconic. That orange roof was a beacon and a bit of brand marketing genius, much like Marietta's Big chicken, McDonald's golden arches, and the sky-high fiberglass statue of a corpulent, smiling Big Boy wearing red checked overalls and holding up a burger on a platter as big as a Buick. One look at Ho Jo's peaked, orange tin roof and there was no mistaking it for any other place.

At some point our Northside Dr. Ho Jo's closed its doors and then became a Days Inn, I think. Then it was sold again and the new owners moved in. A tawdry gentlemen's club of all things. Then, Ho took on a whole new meaning, and the children's outdoor playground was moved out to make room for an adult indoor one. Oh, the humanity.

But the Howard Johnson's in Athens, Georgia was still kicking, alive and well in 1971 where Rick and I lived as newly minted husband and wife the summer before we left for Alabama and veterinary school. It was good to see it, like a long lost relative at a reunion.

My experience there was entirely different, though, from the fun times we had as patrons under the orange roof in Atlanta. I needed a summer job. A visit with the UGA career development office turned ugly after a typing test demonstrated just how rusty my typing skills were. It was then I knew "secretary" would not be in my future that summer.

So I marched through the door of the Athens Ho Jo's to apply for a job as a waitress. That word, waitress, has also gone the way of Ho Jo's playground rocket ship, and waitresses are now called servers. For whom I hold the highest respect.

Anyway, I was hired, not knowing the first thing about how to be a waitress. Stark reality immediately ensued. I was given instructions to report to work the very next day. At six o'clock. In the morning. I knew then this would be the hardest job I had ever taken on. And I was right. The next day when I reported to work, things got real. It was like walking straight into a war zone with no weapons and a battalion of barking, five-star generals for co-workers.

Working with women in their 70s who had earned all the street cred and paid a lifetime of waitressing dues was daunting. I was an idiot to think I could carry this off with no experience. And if there's one thing I've learned, one should never step foot into a waitressing job thinking it's easy.

Servers must be athletes. Customer service experts. Circus balancing acts. And back then, I was a measly Private amongst craggy veterans who had earned their stripes. And they showed it. Bossy doesn't begin to do those women justice. Think George C. Scott's General Patton on a bad day, in an apron, hair net, and sensible shoes. That sweltering summer they took the restaurant's A/C thermostat as a post-menopausal battleground, each having her own idea about the proper comfort levels to suit themselves. The constant fighting over that thermostat was brutal, the temperature fluctuating wildly from Antarctica to Death Valley.

I took off my apron and went AWOL after a week, out of self-preservation, exasperation, and fear. I feared I just might die of pneumonia from the extreme heat and cold. I was already suffering emotional distress from all the friction of combat. I was not willing to die - literally or figuratively - in order to take my last stand planting my flag on the hill of Howard Johnson's HVAC unit and suffer lethal toxicity at the hands of disagreeable superiors.

There's a whole chapter in my book about this, and I don't want to ruin it here. Suffice it to say, although I lasted only a week in my restaurant tour of duty, I'm not sorry. It was a learning experience.

I learned not to assume anything about another person's job. Or another person, for that matter. Everyone has their story, and you don't know the half of it.

I learned to tip generously all those who serve me, including restaurant servers and hairdressers, whether cranky or kind. Even those gals back at Ho Jo's had personal stories I never got to know. Servers deserve every penny for hanging in and working at a sometimes-thankless job.

I learned not every server-community is like the women I encountered back then. Sometimes I wish I had stayed long enough to learn how to deal with them. My instincts told me, however, there would be no dealing with them, no compromises, only hard lines, and I would need to pick my battles. This was one I could walk away from knowing I would never get what I needed, nor should I try to cope with a toxic environment that would never change. They were an angry lot, and I'm guessing, though war-torn and battle-scarred, they didn't have the luxury of quitting.

I've had enough therapy to learn not to ask people for something when they simply don't have it to give you. I've learned the only person you can change is yourself. Sometimes just dealing with one's self is the hardest thing of all.

Knowing when to hold 'em, when to fold 'em, when to walk away, and when to run is a lifelong battle, isn't it? I pray for discernment on a daily basis.

App-solution or App-rehension?
6-26-2022

Our antediluvian devices—pay phones, iPods, Walkmen, buggy whips, clay tablets—have all been supplanted. Our society just keeps inventing.

Now it's Xboxes, smart TVs and phones, Alexa, and virtual reality headsets. We have electric, self-driving cars, and a prototype of the Jetsons' flying car is literally waiting in the wings, to debut in 2023, says the manufacturer, Jetson Aero. Dick Tracy's wrist watch has become a reality and then some. Smart watches can even diagnose a heart attack. Even the ailing Queen was a hologram in the window of her ornate carriage during her Platinum Jubilee parade.

What's next in the name of progress?

Scientists at the National Science Foundation who are infinitely smarter than I will ever be, are saying "teleportation is possible now in the subatomic world of quantum mechanics."

I have no idea what that means.

They go on to say, "Last year, scientists confirmed that information could be passed between photons on computer chips even when the photons were not physically linked."

I don't know what that means, either. But it scares me.

As much as I like modernity, innovation, and all those apps, there is a time and a place for everything.

At least ten years ago, my brother and his wife visited us at Christmas, new iPhones in hand. Rick and I couldn't afford smart phones yet. I was happy for them, though.

I warned my brother in succinct language that if he pulled out his fancy new iPhone at our expensive Christmas Eve dinner at Bacchanalia, the finest restaurant in Atlanta and my one night out for the entire year, I would snatch it from him and throw it against the wall. I talked a good, hyperbolic game.

I would never have been that violent but I still would've made sure he put that thing away. Apparently, he believed me. We had a perfectly lovely evening, from the amuse-bouche through multiple courses, to dessert, and the post-payment finale, a small, sweet bite as an after-dinner lagniappe, courtesy of the chef. And no electronics of any kind appeared at the table. Mais, oui!!

Now, many years after that, it's assumed everyone has a phone on their person at all times. Even this last Christmas Eve when restaurants were just re-opening and pandemic restrictions were easing, Bacchanalia—once my technology refuge and my one line in the sand—betrayed me.

At each table there was a card bearing a QR code that would take diners to an online menu. This was what we had come to instead of a physical menu. Quelle dommage.

Digital menus really do pale in comparison to the crisp, printed menus of non-pandemic days. Online menus just don't carry the same tactile mystique, the ineffable je ne sais quoi, or the germs. Especially when the online menu on a phone screen is the size of a playing card and frustrated Luddites lean into their neighbor's personal space, squinting, and asking questions which do not remotely qualify as pleasant dinner conversation. Kinda breaks the mood, I think, the mood that is half of what one pays for when one dines at Bacchanalia. Even if only once a year. But pandemics are mood breakers, too. So, touché.

I recently came across an article about an app that I do find fascinating and it's catching on.

It's called What3Words.

I have concerns.

Some tech genius came up with a way to grid off the entire world into 10 ft. squares, assigning each square a unique combination of three words. Three words and this app, that's all you need to flawlessly pinpoint yourself on the planet. It's foolproof, they claim.

So, I wonder, how are 3 words better than the GPS system we already have? I will admit, GPS consistently taking my visitors to my neighbor's address instead of mine springs immediately to mind.

What about accuracy? Not everybody is Scripps Spelling Bee material. What about homophones? Coral vs choral. Eye vs I. Be vs bee? Would you bet the farm and your life on three words you cannot guarantee are correctly conveyed or received?

I imagine a scenario in a science-fiction, all-too-near future, when someone is actually materializing via teleportation. Once Humpty Dumpty is together again, he looks around, shaking his head. "Where am I?" he sputters, while checking his body to see if he is all there.

"You are at cereal-turkey-nimrod," I say. "Is there a problem?"

"You could say that," he sighs. "I distinctly said I wanted to go to serial-turkey-nimrod."

"Did you spell it cereal or serial?" I ask?

"Uh-Ohhh…" he sighs.

"Well, at least all of you went to the same place," I respond. "Mistakes, though, are what you sign up for when you're a Beta tester," I remind him. "Maybe you should just buy an airplane ticket or train fare 'til you get the kinks worked out."

"True," he concedes, "I see a dangerous flaw in the program for sure. Back to the mother-board, as they say."

"Better luck next time," I say. "And when you get to where you're going, tell 'em the lady at cereal/turkey/nimrod sends her regards."

Who's On First in the Garden?
7-23-2022

Sometimes when I've had enough, and simply can't brook all the chaos, the constant sound and fury that is happening now in the country and the world, I go outside.

When a threatening flood of awfulness rises up to my chin, I take a long cleansing breath, dive down, push off the bottom with my feet and I am, body and soul, shot up and out of the morass, straight into the comforting arms of Mother Nature and the garden.

"I come to the garden alone, while the dew is still on the roses," to take in the essence of peace and love; a place that responds to my efforts; where I am grateful; where I can make a difference, nurture a little beauty, create some order, and sweat buckets working like a rented mule. Sometimes it can be a place of devastation when winds blow and fires rage. But mostly, it's a quiet, symbiotic place of reassurance, hope, beauty, and resilience. It exhausts my body and renews my spirit.

We heard testimony this week from a young, high-level Republican aide with impeccable bona fides. Taking shape is the ugly truth at the bottom of what was an orchestrated effort at the highest level of our government to up-end the democratic process, culminating in the scene we all saw on January 6, 2020. People with an unrestrained lust for dominion conspired to choose deceit over a peaceful transfer of power; courted angry foot soldiers to do their violent legwork with the will to step on and kill anyone who got in their way. Hanging the Vice President was even on the table. January 6th was a field day for a confederacy of dunces scrambling around with intent to do harm.

In what's being categorized by some as her John Dean moment, one woman's testimony brings a powerful president to task. She testified to the January 6 Special Committee Hearing, "We were watching the capitol get defaced over a lie."

And thereby hangs a tale.

Her boss, Chief of Staff, Mark Meadows wouldn't lift a finger to stop the chaos on January 6th, and neither would his boss, the truculent Big Liar himself.

She testified to physical assaults in the presidential limo as told to her by one of the agents involved. The secret service and the president knew there were masses of people with weapons there. "They're not after me" they said the president told them. Their job was to protect the president, and so they did, much to his outrage.

Now, suddenly, the two agents have said they'd like to testify under oath that no such thing happened.

Why would she lie about that? Folks didn't believe Monica Lewinsky at first, either, until she produced that infamous blue dress. We have none of that this time. No possible gain now for this brave woman comes to mind, other than her desire to tell the truth, the whole truth, and nothing but the truth, even at her own peril. And maybe a lucrative book deal down the road.

Why would the two secret service men lie? Maybe they are still protecting the president?

The committee spoke of another witness who received a call straight out of an episode of the Sopranos. "[An unnamed person] wants me to let you know that they are thinking about you. He knows you're loyal, and you're going to do the right thing when you go in for your deposition."

Standard mob tactic. "You. You godda nice place here. Shame if somethin' was t' happen to it."

The whole thing is a confusing, dirty gambit, an unfunny Abbot and Costello routine. Who's on first? What's on second? I Don't Know is on third. Why, Because, Tomorrow, Today, and I Don't Care are all playing, too.

I feel the water rising.

Excuse me while I take a breath, push off the bottom, and go smell some roses in the garden. My emotional bandwidth is not capable of handling angry, unresolved drama for very long anymore. Bless Miss Hutchinson and all the bulldogs whose job it is to delve into the morass, grab the honest truth, and not let go.

I will count on them to do their job, and I'll do mine.

As a writer, it's my job to bring something thoughtful, well-written, and relevant to this page every week. God willing. I also have the all-important job as a voting citizen to speak out and to put in my two cents, conscientiously and faithfully, at the ballot box. My job as a human is to be responsible, giving, loving, helpful, honest, and kind. Tall order, but I try.

There's an old saying, "A bit of fragrance clings to the hand that gives you roses." I like having a bouquet of possibilities rather than a club with which to beat people into submission, or a gun with which to wield power and kill. Probably not very popular in today's climate. And in practice, you can't wield a rose at a gunman and expect to survive. Unless they surrender. There is that. Nixon finally surrendered. But that was then. The Rubicon is in our rear-view mirror, and we are a wholly different country now.

Still, I recommend the powerful, positive scent of a bouquet on the hands of those who give as well as receive. Call me crazy, but that is the small light I choose to bring to the dark world. I will tend my garden and bring the scent of roses, hope, truth, and renewal along with me as I write, vote, and live my conscience.

There's so much wrong with the world. It's up to each of us to decide in our own way whether to be a dark force, or a light in a dark world. Every day. And tomorrow and tomorrow and tomorrow.

Words Sting
7-10-2022

I've received—and treasure—some lovely emails from readers. Thanks to all of you who have emailed me with your kind words. I have yet to receive any vitriolic hate emails. Thank you in advance for not sending those.

So many angry folks these days are voicing unhelpful, cruel, sharp barbs to vent their spleens and wound someone. Their words come from poisonous intent, from defensive, reptilian reflexes. People strike out with intent to harm or frighten because they can, and often because they need to hurt someone else to feel better about themselves. Or they think they are right and everyone else who disagrees is an idiot itching for a fight.

My Mama used to say, "You can be right or you can be kind. You can't always be both."

We see so much verbal enmity on social media these days and in our politicians and media.

Our children need better role models than that. And we shouldn't take them to Sunday School each week and then let loose on Monday with a tirade of insults directed at them, or others.

Children listen. And learn. Consult *South Pacific*'s "You've Got to be Taught" if you need a refresher. Or Sondheim's "Children Will

Listen" from *Into the Woods*.

We must remember that words sting, and they stick. Then we must decide to care.

I remember meeting my sixth-grade English teacher on the first day of school. Ms. Force (aptly named, I soon decided) was something of a battle-ax, short and stubby with a stern demeanor and an arresting, basso profundo voice with an annoying, gravelly vocal fry. She went around the room calling on each student to say their name aloud. When she got to me she said, "Aaaand. Who. Are. You?"

I gulped hard. I managed to say, "Susie," intimidated already by her laser gaze and her harsh tone, and odd, clipped Betty Davis / Louis Armstrong delivery. Now, today, I would even add some Harvey Fierstein to that vocal assessment.

"Well," she said, "'Susie' sounds more like a poodle's name, to me. Are you a poodle?"

I lowered my eyes in embarrassment and disbelief. With a baleful laugh, she checked my name off on her roll, and was on to her next victim, leaving me recoiling from her exquisite sting. If she was conflating we with a poodle, I felt in that moment like an abused poodle puppy, indeed. She might as well have hit me on my nose with a rolled-up newspaper.

"What did I do to deserve that?" I puzzled, silently fuming.

I never forgot that.

I put that episode in a mental box back then, closing the lid tight. As the year progressed, I proved to be an excellent grammar student, although there was not one creative, poetic moment all year in her class. I could diagram a sentence with the best of them. I excelled at parts of speech, and tenses, and spelling.

But there was nothing inspirational or inspiring from that humorless woman who was all about cut and dried facts, "correct" check marks, and "incorrect" exes on our homework papers. I now appreciate having gained valuable grammatical knowledge, but back then I was also starving for originality and imagination. I was never comfortable with that woman as long as I was in the sixth grade.

Apparently, I'm still not comfortable with her sixty years later.

I never told her how I felt about her little barb, either. I figured she never gave it another thought and had no idea how her words stung me. I didn't want to risk being chastised, either, for being oversensitive when I was convinced she would say she meant nothing by it. Or worse, she meant it to sting and wanted to watch me squirm.

I have decided she was just who she was, whatever that was. Mean, or clueless, or well-meaning, it wasn't for me to decide. What she said, for whatever reason, stung, for whatever reason, and my response was legitimate. Period.

My seventh-grade English teacher, Alice Cheeseman was kind, creative, interested in my work, and wrote notes home to my parents encouraging me to keep writing. She lifted my spirit. She provided constructive criticism that I gladly accepted. I give her the credit for starting me back on a creative writing path after a year thirsting in the desert with her predecessor.

After Alice, I was fortunate to have a series of teachers who mentored and supported me as they educated and enriched me.

Hateful rhetoric coming from hateful people doesn't happen in a void. It's the result of one or many barbs that have stung them and keep stinging. Pretty soon, each sting reinforces all the others and it's a damaged, changed person who emerges.

The one important thing Ms. Force taught me aside from all the perfunctory rules of grammar was this: all our lives there will be people who use words for different reasons, for the good and the not so good. Some will uplift. Others will sting. Expect it. Let them inform and serve you as models of what to do and what not to do. Care. Don't let them change you.

Watch what you say. Watch what you say to yourself, too. That little child is always in you, needing protection, guidance, and kind, encouraging words.

What was said to you as a child that stung, that you will never forget?

Sshh!
7-17-2022

Rilke or Rumi, Steinbeck or Hemingway, all the great writers had, and have, the physical capacity and the emotional suitability for quiet solitude.

Acquainting oneself with one's own emotions, alone in a quiet room, inviting introspection and self-examination isn't all that makes a writer great. But I really don't think you can be a great writer without them.

However, one of Ken Burns' ubiquitous biopics profiled Hemingway as a writer among the best of the best, but his capacity for self-awareness was utterly lacking. He was a tortured, narcissistic man who could be thoughtless and cruel. But sweet Elvis, could that man write. He had an inner voice only he could bring to a page. So what do I know? I know Hemingway did his very best as a writer, while failing miserably in other ways as a human. So there's that.

When I write, whether it's this column every week or my book, now published, I enjoy and require moments of quiet in my house; a calming, restorative silence without the grandchildren— whom I love dearly, of course—asking me one more time to re-fill their glass of juice. The quiet house where, for a time, I am alone and I get to create freely without interruption. The peaceful house when everyone else is asleep and the only sound is calm, still air, the refrigerator's low hum, the clicking keys of my keyboard, and the thoughts in my head trying to get out and arrange themselves on the page.

Paul Simon wrote the haunting song he and Art Garfunkel sang together and made famous in the sixties: "The Sound of Silence." Simon wrote that song alone in the quietude of his bathroom, with the water faucet running and the lights off as he worked to summon his talent and create magic. It took him months after that to finish polishing the lyrics. Look no further for an example of the steadfast effort required to enable creative genius to flow into fruition, and a remarkable work of art.

All the great writers care enough to try and try again to improve their skill and do their highest and best, which comes from a deep, personal commitment to spirit and vulnerability. Of course, perfectionism is mythical folly, a unicorn. But we can get darn close.

That said, there's still no guarantee of success with any creative pursuit, no matter how well-intentioned and sincere one may be. Singing is just not in the cards for everyone. Writing is not everybody's bliss. Some people are talented dancers, circus performers, master chefs, welders, or philanthropists. But if one has the goods and doesn't honor them, hone them, and share them, then fie on them.

Mediocrity isn't a sin, but it can be, if one settles for it.

I sang for many years in Atlanta under the tutelage of a great choral conductor, Robert Shaw, who, at every rehearsal, railed over every vocal flaw. He insisted his chorus re-visit each phrase, dynamic, pitch, or tempo over and over until we served the composer and his music at the highest level, to the best we could humanly manage.

That process could be very frustrating, I'll admit. There were times at the beginning when I sat fuming in the midst of the Alto Section as he admonished us all for the umpteenth time. "People, you are so close to singing the right pitch, you might as well sing it!" or "People! This is a lullaby! You're putting the baby to bed with a g**-**mn hammer!!"

I remember thinking, "I drove over an hour through traffic to get here and washed dishes, cleaned house, fed babies, changed diapers and worked all day. I pay a babysitter I can't afford so she can put my children to bed because I won't be home until late. I really AM doing my best."

Then he would tell us again what he wanted from us, and we would try again. And again.

Then we became encouraged by each incremental improvement. Like a surprised baby who first discovers their toes, we were delighted and inspired to keep exploring.

Finally we understood what Shaw was talking about. He was teaching us not to settle; not to quit before the miracle. He knew what we were capable of. But we had to care enough to open up, dig deep to find it, share it in solidarity with one another, and bring a unified voice to bear. It was then that we produced what he wanted, and it was what we had worked so hard for: our very best. And it was good. Really good.

To plumb the depths of our vulnerability—in whatever creative pursuit we attempt—is a deeply personal, brave, and scary prospect. Also a necessary one.

That goes for just living one's best life, too, in case you've decided you don't have a talented bone in your body. Phooey. Just living a mindful, productive, regular life is no small accomplishment. It's an art if you make it so.

Be silent once in awhile and listen. Wait for what you hear. Even in music, the rests are as important as the notes, and the silences speak to us and enrich us in marvelous, poignant ways.

We can settle for less, or not. It's a choice. To keep trying means not quitting before the miracle. What a shame it would be to miss out on that.

Summer Lament
7-24-2022

I just read that a bolt of lightning is five times hotter than the sun.

I thought about the young man on the beach at Tybee Island who was struck by such a bolt.

He did not die right away, although I wonder if it might have been better for everyone if God had just taken him right then. But that's now how it works.

The boy had a family, and a Christian church family, friends, a girlfriend, plans for a stellar future. It was an agonizing number of days as the boy's brain began to swell, and there was a lot of praying to the God who made the lightning, the sun, and the boy; the God who, in the end, didn't save the boy from the strike five times hotter than the sun; the God who promises comfort and strength as a present help in times of trouble.

As a little girl I was running one day, laughing. Green grass, white sidewalk, curb, and dark asphalt whizzed by.

A monster with a menacing, metal grin, hot breath, and big round glass eyes bore down on me. I heard my mother scream and I stopped in my tracks. I would say I stopped "dead in my tracks" but that's not true because I didn't die. The monster screeched and halted just short of me, staring, fuming. We were wide eye to wide eye, up so close and so very personal I felt its hot breath on my legs. It smelled acrid and awful, like burnt rubber.

And I was not struck. I was alive and unhurt. My mother swiftly scooped me up in her arms, sobbing, squeezing me and pushing her lips into kisses all over my face while speaking very firmly about how I was never to do that again.

No one had to grieve my loss or petition any deity to save me and feel devastated when I died, like the boy struck by lightning five times hotter than the sun.

I grew up to live a very fine, long life. And the boy did not.

Did God show me some kind of divine mercy God would not show the boy?

If someone says God intentionally spared me and not the boy I will tell you that kind of logic infuriates me. I am no more and no less worthy than that boy. My God does not turn a thumb up or down to save or condemn a life like a Roman emperor in a gladiator match.

Why would I expect one dying boy to be saved over another — why would God do that — when faithful, church-going mothers in hospital chapels and waiting rooms pray to God, too? The mother of the boy struck by lightning and hundreds of friends petitioned God so fervently to save her son and yet she is, and they are, now grieving his death.

If you believe in a God at all, and you believe that God plays favorites, surely all those children murdered in Uvalde, Texas would have been spared. And the boy—a faithful, churchgoing believer—would not have suffered and died.

Second-guessing the good Lord is a big fat waste of time. As a Christian, I try to refrain from attempting to make sense of things humans are not capable of understanding. That's where my faith comes in.

My God gave man free will and, in these postlapsarian times, is a source of solace, love, and strength; a powerful balm in times of need and sorrow.

I celebrate and am grateful to my toes for a divine source of strength and compassion when bad things happen to good people. I have called on my Higher Power many times to lighten the burdens I carry in times of trouble; to take them from me when I am weak or hurting.

I am thinking of the boy. I am thinking of those souls in Sandy Hook, Marjory Stoneman Douglas High School, 19 people in Texas, the people in a grocery store in Buffalo, and the marchers in a July 4th parade in a Chicago suburb. And all their loved ones who must continue without them.

Here's the bottom line: it's all beyond human understanding.

And when I stop asking why, why, why, I can finally accept the miracle of peace and acceptance that surpasses understanding.

That's my faith. But I'm aware that many others believe differently.

I wonder if we could all have our religious beliefs without imposing them on others in public places.

Where many people of different faiths are gathered, I don't think it's the time or place to impose one religious rite over another, whether over a loudspeaker or in a pre-game huddle. We could be more sensitive to others. Be a minority in a predominantly "other" crowd that doesn't recognize you and try that on for size. It's difficult. Awkward at the very least.

In a diverse crowd, inviting everyone to engage in a moment of silence works for me. To each his own, doing their own personal thing. Silently.

We can pray aloud in our private meditations and prayer groups. We can attend our respective houses of worship, whatever they may be. Then we can sing loudly, pray audibly, dance, make a joyful noise or face the east and bow down, whatever it is we do.

And we should do it like there's no tomorrow. Because tomorrow is, very definitely, uncertain.

Positivities
8-1-2022

At dinner with friends, we recalled a mutual pal from our past.
"Always complaining," someone said.
"Most negative person I've ever met," said another.
"Died way too young," I lamented.
It's not only "crack" that kills. Negativity does a mighty fine job, too. Diseases, accidents, and murders play their role. But negativity can contribute to rushing things along, in body and in spirit.

Positivity won't necessarily save lovely, constructive souls from dying. But positive folks are a blessing to all they meet and to all they leave behind.

Yet some entirely wretched, negative humans still walk the planet and, Lord help me, refuse to perish from the earth. Or even repent.

I think of Positivity and Negativity as families.

The Positivities are imperfect, but good people.

The eldest child, Pollyanna, is a preternaturally confident, high-achiever. Determined to wear glasses tinted a distinct rose, she stubbornly eschews negativity in favor of happily pursuing and preserving a perfect, extreme, illusory vision of optimism.

The middle child, Who-Me, is the lost child in the middle of the family sandwich, plodding along. She doesn't see too well but refuses to wear glasses. She's not especially introspective, so she depends on strength, resolve, and will-power to stay positive.

The third and youngest, Philosophical, embraces a lovely approach about life. She never got a completed baby book or videos of her first steps like her siblings. But her vision is 20/20 with prescription lenses. She sees clearly, with intention. She recognizes positive and negative realities, chooses to take what she needs, and leaves the rest. She learns. She thrives. She's fun. She is my favorite Positivity child. Don't tell the others.

The entire Negativity family is humorless, needy, enmeshed, clingy, contagious. They see nothing of the good. They instinctively gravitate to pessimism, judgment, grudges, and gossip. The Negativity children grow up and spawn more of their own kind.

Spanish artist Goya painted a series of ominous "Black Paintings." One depicts the all-powerful god, Saturn turning on his own children and consuming them so they couldn't usurp his position or his power. Gross. Abhorrent. Negativity does that to a person; it's a sucking, self-perpetuating black hole of the spirit, skewed, hungry, and never satisfied.

Know anyone like that?

Playwright Tom Stoppard said, "Look on every exit as an entrance somewhere else." So recently we took a trip, driving long distances to leave home and see friends and new things that are stunningly noteworthy as well as ridiculously frivolous and fun. And positive. Majestic Niagara Falls vs the Longaberger Building, a huge office building the spitting image of a Longaberger picnic basket. The Big Coffee Pot, a building that resembles a, well, must I say it?

Gas prices, traffic, and road fatigue notwithstanding, driving can often be rewarding, spontaneous, and interesting. And humorous. If there's no hurry, one gets to kick the brakes at funky places whenever they please.

One year we drove part of Route 66. Near Amarillo, there's a row of Cadillacs buried halfway, nose-down in a straight soldier course. Spray-painting encouraged. We positively did our part, tagging our initials inside a big heart. The Big Texan Restaurant boasting a 40-ft cowboy statue outside is the place you can eat a steak, buy plastic, boot-shaped souvenir mugs for your grandkids, and watch some guy with questionable IQ sit center stage and attempt to devour more than one human alimentary tract should be asked to handle, all for the dubious honor and a free meal. Like he would still be hungry.

Next year, someplace meaningful, plus the world's biggest ball of yarn. I'm positive of it.

The Nerve!
8-7-2022

Years ago, our son installed a fence and very nearly cut off his pinky finger. It takes both hands to operate a fence-post pounder. This thing looks like a long, heavy pipe with handles as big as Dumbo's ears, which are a long distance away—more than arm's reach—from the business end. Getting a finger in between post and pounder is a feat I have yet to figure out. He can't explain it, either.

He was bleeding profusely through his work glove. A sudden rush of adrenaline allowed him to call me (another feat) and drive himself to the hospital (feat number three). In the Xray room, he sat in a wheelchair and placed his hand on the table. Then his head slumped forward. Chin on chest. Passed out cold (final feat). Fearing the worst, the tech yelled, "Code Blue!" As the hyper alert team raced in with crash cart, paddles in hand, he awoke, raised his head, and uttered something brilliant.

"Whu-uu-t."

He swears they looked supremely disappointed. Dropping their paddles onto the cart, they turned around and summarily left without a word. This account from a barely conscious man, mind you. No doubt they were just extremely busy.

A nurse explained his fainting was the result of a "vasovagal reaction."

Apparently, the body's vagus nerve and adrenaline are an on-again, off-again soap-opera couple. Adrenaline valiantly rushes in, responding to a dastardly interloper, Trauma who has callously hit and run. But after Adrenaline has helped a bleeding man race to the hospital, Adrenaline says to pal, Vagus, "I'm out. Tag, you're it. It's not you, it's me. We're done," and also makes a dramatic exit. Dejected, Vagus reflexively lowers blood pressure and heart rate, leaving other pals, Heart and Brain wanting. A person can pass right out from the insult.

Love hurts.

The vagus nerve has enjoyed some PR of late. Apparently, it's the VIP of nerves, the "It Nerve" these days. Why? New information.

I looked it up. It's a whole bundle of fibers that make up the longest cranial nerve in the body, traveling from brain stem to gut. It's called the "Wanderer Nerve," an information superhighway, checking in with all the many organs it regulates, giving the brain a full report on each one as it passes by.

It's a sweet, nosy, parasympathetic nerve. Gladys Kravitz 2.0.

Apparently, vagal Gladys can get over-irritated by too much physiological hubbub due to lack of "tone." When vagal Gladys goes flabby, the body is predisposed to poor emotional and attentional regulation, inflammation, depression, digestive issues, and a whole host of physical ailments. But when vagal Gladys's "tone" increases, it strengthens the parasympathetic nervous system so everybody can relax in peace, even while under stress.

How does one even know if their Gladys 2.0 is "toned?" One way is an EKG. Or there's always experience: If you stay conscious and chill after a trauma, Gladys must be a happy camper.

I haven't considered any part of me as "toned" in a long, long time, maybe since the hogs ate little Willie and Elvis left the building. I better go lie down. Or get busy.

Suggestions I found for toning Gladys include: Hand reflexology. Acupuncture. Mind-Body Therapy. Exercises. Apps.

Here's the thing. I'm just like you. One foot in front of the other, doing my best. Things happen that affect us adversely. PTSD is real. New advice for prevention of vasovagal incidents includes "avoiding triggers."

This advice, like everything, must be taken with a grain of Gladys.

Some triggers are easier to avoid. Like nearly chopping off a finger with a fence-post pounder. Duh.

But what about the impossibly unavoidable ones: atrocities on battlefields, streets, in stores, and schools; deceitful politicians; floods in Kentucky; forest fires out west; tornadoes in Newnan; one-star reviews on Amazon.

If only we could avoid all those triggers. Since that's impossible, we'd better prepare ourselves to deal with them the best we can.

Tighten and tone, people. Tighten and tone.

What's Up With That?
8-14-2022

I often have random questions that aren't of global importance, but they bug the ever-living Elvis out of me.

Let's talk about the word, "sanguine." As an adjective it means optimistic, cheerfully confident, especially in an apparently bad or difficult situation. But as a noun, "sanguine" means "blood red."

How in the world do we have two such disparate meanings for the same word? Blame the Middle Ages. They were here first, when people had strange beliefs and customs, and eels were sometimes used as currency. I mean, come on. We don't pay with eels anymore, but some words still linger.

"Sanguine" comes from Latin, *sanguis*, which means "blood." Back then, the belief was that four bodily "liquids" or "humors" controlled people's dispositions. If a person had a strong, cheerful constitution and ruddy (red) countenance, their blood got all the credit. Phlegm (gross) was to blame for the slow and unexcitable; too much yellow bile or black bile (double gross) made for various "bilious," bad-tempered, disagreeable, spiteful temperaments. So, the double "sanguine" meanings evolved, like a linguistic version of the old Certs twins breath mint commercials on TV: two, two, two mints (words) in one!

When people couple the word "senseless" with the word

"tragedy" or "accident," my teeth itch. When is a tragedy or an accident not senseless? It's redundant, like "new innovation" or "shiftless politician."

On a recent road trip with Rick driving up to NY and Canada and back down to Newnan, Georgia, a few things made me wonder, "What's up with that?"

Buc-ee's. We discovered one in Adairsville, Georgia off I-75. It's the modern, massive, overgrown version of the old roadside Stuckey's stores that offered souvenirs and world-famous pecan logs. Scattered around the south, Buc-ee's is like SuperWalmart and Target had a giant baby and overdecorated the nursery with more brisket, jerky, retail items, and "Peace Love Buc-ee's" stuff than anyone could ever have thought possible. I will concede that Buc-ee's brisket's delicious. But the rest? IDK. Place gave me a headache. As my mother used to say, "Is all that really necessary?"

About 130 miles south of Lexington, Kentucky stands a huge, white, three-dimensional cross, at least 50 feet high, planted right beside "Adult World," next to a billboard advertising "State Line Liquor," and another billboard for a store advertising moonshine in a mason jar. What a trinity. Demon, out!

A few miles north of Lexington, Virginia near the interstate, an enormous Confederate flag the size of Buc-ee's flies as high or higher than the cross we saw in Kentucky. It's impossible to see through the thick trees to view the bottom of the pole to identify what might be around it. I was sad and angry to see it there, relieved to get past it, and disturbed even now at the memory.

Finally, almost to Johnson City, Tennessee, Rick recounted his memory of a story about an elephant in a circus in Kingsport, Tennessee in 1916. Mary, the elephant, killed her substitute handler after he prodded her—hard, with a hook —between her jaw and ear. Mary grabbed him with her trunk, slammed him against a drink cart, and stepped on his head.

To appease the angry crowd, and guarantee future ticket sales, the circus owner sentenced Mary to death. A train transported Mary into a Unicoi County Tennessee train yard. A sturdy derrick strong enough to lift a locomotive was judged suitable as a makeshift gallows, where indeed, the poor pachyderm was hanged by the neck until dead. As a veterinarian and animal lover, Rick's horror and ultimate interest in this story came in the postmortem results: a vet who examined Mary said she had an infected tooth at the exact spot her trainer prodded her. What a tragic story of Mary's pain, torture, and death. I will admit, the word "senseless" does come to mind. Among others.

The Myth of Mayberry
8-21 AND 8-28-2022

PART ONE IN A TWO-PART SERIES

Last month we attended a Sheryl Crow concert in the venue where Salman Rushdie was stabbed recently at the normally idyllic Chautauqua Institute in western New York. I noted the venue's lax security even then, although their website listed strict security rules. Rules that ultimately were not enforced.

The institute is loath to consider swarms of security, dogs, and a huge police presence blanketing the grounds, fearing their idyllic environment would be fundamentally changed forever. That's really not the answer, anyway. One metal detector at a single, secure entrance could've kept the inside of that venue safe. That, and two alert, trained officials stationed there, protected and ready to nab a knife or gun-toting disruptor at the gate.

News flash: We know they are changed forever now, and they can never go back to before. But where do we all go from here?

Time to accept and invest in reality. We mustn't cling to the myopic wish to preserve an idyllic past that no longer exists and is no longer possible. Or never existed in the first place.

Mayberry, a fictitious town we all loved, was a sit-com stand-in for an elusive aesthetic. Television viewers in the 1960s got to step through their wardrobes, past Narnia and Selma and Memphis and Watts, and into Mayberry, happily insulated from the real world: Aint Bee dressed in that perpetual apron, apple pie cooling on the sill; Opie and Andy whistling all the way down the dirt road to the fishin' hole; Who wouldn't want to live there, from that perspective?

In our once small town of Newnan, GA old-timers ache for those same bygone Mayberry days of unlocked doors and a peaceable kingdom, unfettered by crime and violence. They say let's get back to those.

Here's what we must remember: this is a perspective. We are not, and never have been Mayberry.

For every Aint Bee in Mayberry, there were plenty of people in real small towns, including ours, who lived very different lives, oppressed, marginalized, ignored. People who couldn't afford etiquette lessons, and who rented rather than owned. Forget about white picket fences.

They are still here, in the flesh. They reside in poverty and circumstance; invisible for the most part to a large, insulated portion of our population. They live within a culture of systemic violence and societal deprivation. They endure sadness and resignation no metal detector can fix.

We might consider acknowledging and challenging our limited perspectives. We must see past our insulated spaces, accept and understand there are other perspectives than ours. These are the ones staring right back at us, whether or not we see them. We should want to.

Many in our community want to, and bless 'em, they see and do so much to provide community involvement, support, and enrichment through all kinds of programs available to all. Boys and Girls Club, Backstreet Arts, The Ferst Foundation, Coweta Community Foundation, Carnegie Library Foundation, Kiwanis, Rotary, Bridging the Gap, One Roof, CASA, Habitat for Humanity, and so many more. We could use even more.

Let's not wish to return to a mythic perspective of the past. Let's move forward. Perhaps we stop romanticizing, wanting to re-create our myopic notions of what was good for a few. How about looking toward something that's real and better and promises opportunity from every perspective? Notice I said opportunity. If a rising water lifts all boats, some people just need a boat.

We should never want to go back to before. We should, and can, and must move forward, for real. For the better. For good.

Next week: what do we do about a culture whose default for conflict resolution is violence? It's not about somebody else, either. It's about us. All of us.

PART TWO

What do we do about violence in unrestricted, exposed open spaces like parks and streets? It's a far more difficult problem to solve than keeping places safe with one-entrance access and a metal detector. People have been attacked, shot, stabbed, run over, and blown up in public places all over the world. London, Paris, Charlottesville; Piedmont Park in Atlanta; a Chicago suburb during a parade; a marathon in Boston; a congressional baseball field in DC; the mean streets and parking lots of low-rent housing developments and half-occupied strip malls; the avenues of high-rent homes, manicured lawns, shops, and city office buildings. No metal detector or any number of surveillance cameras will fix it, either. The problem is overwhelming in size and scope.

Anne Lamott, one of my favorite authors, wrote a book entitled "Bird by Bird." It's about the craft of writing, but it's also a wonderful treatise on life and how to cope with it. She shares advice from her father to her brother who was overwhelmed with a last-minute report on birds due the next day for school. Panicked by the big picture, the boy was frozen, unable to even begin. The advice? Just break the task down and take it bird by bird. Bird. By. Bird.

Maybe that's what we can do, too. If we can't solve all the problems of violence and dysfunction everywhere let's take it bird by bird. Let's not ignore any of them, but perhaps we can address one bird at a time. One metal detector. One law. One education. One person. One neighborhood. One neighbor. One population. One awareness. One challenge. One fundamental shift in our rhetoric and our societal focus, away from violence and toward education and family empowerment, requiring the willingness to change even just one mind at a time, one day at a time, one life at a time, one future at a time. For the humanely better. And for real.

We must accept there is no perfection and there is no Disney fairy godmother to fix everything with the flick of her sparkling wand.

We can grieve and mourn the passing of a time we thought existed and loved, but we must first accept the reality of a skewed perspective. Only then we can move forward, one step at a time. For good.

Or we can just be angry, selfish, solipsistic. We can keep compartmentalizing our lives into "I know" and "I don't want to know." Or "I know but I will lie about it so you might believe a false truth."

Mayberry and its inhabitants were far from perfect. So are we all. But they didn't show us the tar paper shacks for a reason. Not depicted were the people who weren't allowed to even vote. Because we didn't want to see them. Where's the fun in that,? Mayberry characters were "just good folk" who weren't rich, but they were - with one exception in one lone episode - all Caucasian Christians. Mayberry may have been swell, as an escapist 30-minute vacation trip of fictional rural nostalgia. It had one purpose: to entertain, from one point of view. But so did "All in the Family," which actually "went there," daring to light a match of truth, illuminate the room, and make viewers grasp it until it singed their fingers and their consciences.

That all or nothing stuff is for the birds. Let's, each one of us, take it bird by bird, shall we? If you want to, I mean. We should want to.

Solace in Sacred Spaces
9-4-2022

Beware the vagaries of life.

It's not exactly fear experienced gardeners feel about nature's menaces. It's more a heightened respect for and awareness of what's out there, faith they can manage it, and figuring out how. Poison ivy. Noxious weeds. Snakes. Devil thorns of Eleagnus plants and Greenbrier vines.

One garden troublemaker is uppermost on my list, imprinted on my memory, lingering in my Proustian senses and deep in my heart.

Oleander. Poisonous oleander.

Picture a little girl in Phoenix, a hot, dusty, desert town. She loved her backyard, an oasis of cool green grass and lush bushes thanks to weekly irrigation, life-giving water the city flooded into the neighborhood's bermed yards.

Between floods, she and her brother put on shows in the log cabin their dad built in that yard. From the newspaper office where he worked, he brought home heavy-duty, thick cardboard tubes left over after the newsprint on them had run through the printing presses. He stained and shellacked each one water-tight and built a fine cabin, adding a large wood front porch.

Once, on that porch in front an audience of friends and kindly neighbors, she played a frontier mother cradling her baby doll in her arms. She sang sweet, heartfelt lullabies as she waited for the menfolk to return from hunting. Then it happened. With no warning, her doll's head fell off, landing on the wood porch with a sickening thud. She was horrified. The audience tried to be kind, but she could hear and see them trying not to laugh. Even after hugs and reassurances to dry her tears, she was shaken. This was some serious, show-stopping humiliation.

After the neighbors went home, she and her family went inside their house. Soon, she excused herself and went back outside — to play, she said. She found comfort walking barefoot across the soothing, cool lawn. She found her familiar, sacred space in a small opening at the base of the long, tall oleander hedge lining the entire back border of the yard. In the quiet shade she could sit in solitude, reflect, and discover peace and gratitude for the evergreen leaves, the faint apricot perfume of the flowers, and the mulchy scent of plants and earth.

There was one strict rule she always kept in mind: Respect the oleander and never, ever, eat it.

Her mother had warned her. Oleander was a deadly, poisonous plant. She was strictly forbidden to even allow it to brush against her lips. The girl did not want to die in the oleander. She enjoyed life and her family too much, and yes, even performing on the porch of that log cabin.

She just needed time to renew her spirit. She would do that in nature, alone in the oleander where — just like on that porch stage, and throughout life — there would be danger as well as delight.

Perhaps she went into the oleander to connect with a higher power in the face of things she could not control, although she didn't know that's what she was doing. She was only 7 years old. She simply sought some serenity, and recovery. She could've chosen a safer place, maybe, but she loved this one, revered it, and knew its limits.

We should all know our limits.

I don't have any oleander in my yard now, but I do go outside to sit in the sacred space of my garden; to listen to the breeze and birds;

to be still, gather my senses, and restore my spirit; to give thanks and praise for my blessings. No worries about poison oleander anymore. But there is the matter of nature's other scary things: bugs, toxic plants, and toxic people.

I don't let the scary things stop me. I claim my place. I still know my limits.

I know church can be anywhere. Especially in my garden. Or yours.

Just don't ever, ever eat the oleander.

Nostalgia, an Old Timer's Curse
9-11-2022

I've been driving past the intersection near our house, marveling at an empty lot on the corner. The small building that stood there ever since I showed up in this town 45 years ago is gone. Scraped clean, down to bare earth in one afternoon.

In bygone days, Parker's gas station nestled into that spot, its fuel pumps no more than about 10 feet off the highway. To fill up, a driver needed to turn their steering wheel only a degree or so, ease their car barely off the road, and snug it up parallel to the pumps. You could shake hands and have a conversation through your side window with folks stopped at the red light.

The Parkers and Mr. Mapp responded quickly to the ding-dinging bell as cars rolled over the rubber hose stretched across the pavement. Even if they were working inside the shop, elbow-deep in the innards of someone's vehicle, the men hurried out with a smile, wiping hard-working hands on a shop cloth. Friendly folks. Knew you by name. They filled your tank with gas, your car with oil; checked fluids, tires, squeegeed windshields, and engaged in small talk. "How's the family" and "This weather hot enough for you?" kind of small talk, pleasantries that could brighten a person's day.

The place went empty some years back, sitting quietly, aging badly. But every time I drove by, I sighed and saw ghosts: the place bustling with life, people on the way to or from their daily rounds; my kids in the back seat leaning out the window sniffing fumes as Parker's gas fueled our journey onward; rolling down my window to say, "So sorry, Mr. Parker, I'm hurrying to get to Atlanta. Can you make this quick?"

The sincere response: "You bet, Miss Susie, we'll get you on your way fast as we can. You drive careful in this rain, hear?"

Long before the intersection was reconfigured only a few years ago into perpendicular cross-streets with sidewalk, curb, gutter, and a new traffic light, there really was no "corner." Back then, our road met Jackson street at a 45-degree angle, leaving a small, pie-shaped, paved lot between the two, and across the street from Parker's, and Sprayberry's Barbecue.

Over time, several businesses sat in that triangle: Duncan's Barbecue, Jimbeau's pub, and then Lennie's pub. It was a study in spatial geometry: cars, SUVs, and pick-ups parked akimbo, crammed into a tiny lot barely adequate for a couple of Volkswagens. Parker's rear lot served as overflow parking after hours. Sprayberry's, too. Even our driveway on a rare occasion. The pub was demolished long ago. The bare pie-lot vanished in favor of that improved intersection.

Many moons ago, we planted a beautiful hydrangea in our front yard. Sometimes, people stopped to comment on its spectacular purple color and ask us our secret. Rick always joked it was the unique blend of beer and cigarette butts in the run-off from Lenny's just up the road that did the trick. (Psst. Actual secret: it was a Merritt's Supreme Hydrangea variety).

Dear Lord and Elvis, help me accept the things I cannot change. As much as that vacant building had become an eyesore and needed to be replaced, I remember it fondly in its heyday. I miss the people that inhabited it, too. I know I'll love the new Frazier's store going in there. It will be clean, new, convenient. But I can't change what was, or how I feel about it. Call it the curse of us old-timers who actually have the longevity to experience some major nostalgia.

My philosophy: to everything there is a season. And a purpose.

Cherish the memories. Move on. Life is short. Enjoy. In 45 years, people of earth could be living on another planet. I hope whoever works at that new place on Mars is friendly, and y'all know each other's names.

Ads Infinitum!
9-18-2022

Scene: [people fake answering the fake ringing phones at a fake phone bank on tv.]

Voiceover: "If you've been injured and it's not your fault, call the number on your screen."

[Cut to black. 1 nano second elapses. Resume scene.]

TV: [cute young thing smiling and gesturing toward man who's trying to look natural. Obviously not an actor. He's the guy who should've hired an actor instead of doing this ad himself. She speaks.] "Welcome back, folks! I'm standing here with the man himself. He's going to tell us, WHO needs to call NOW!"

TV: [Man] "Well Buffy, anyone who's been injured and it's not their fault, call RIGHT NOW."

Viewer, dialing, waiting: [bzzzt, bzzzt]

Voice on phone: "Hello. How may we help you?"

Viewer: "Yes. Which one are you so I know who I'm talking to? I hope you're the cute one on the front row. Wave for me?"

Voice on phone: "Uh, sssorry?"

Viewer: "Come on, son, don't apologize. Have some gumption, or I'm hanging up."

Voice on phone: "Sorry. Wait, not sorry. I'm not on TV if that's what you mean, ma'am. I'm at the office answering real calls while everyone else is at lunch."

Viewer: "OK, well, that's disappointing. I was hoping you'd be that distinguished looking man on the front row with the white hair and teeth to match. Reminds me of someone I saw in a tv ad for something, maybe a drug. I can't recall which, exactly, but he and a woman were in separate bathtubs holding hands and watching a waterfall in the woods. Weird ad, son. Weird. That one got old real fast. Couldn't be him on that phone panel of yours on tv, though, because you guys wouldn't do anything fake. No sir. That man has to be a real person who works for y'all on your phone bank. I'd like to speak to him, please."

Voice on phone: [chewing something. Whatever it is, it's a mouthful and it's obvious he's lunching at his desk] "Um, ma'am, I'll be honest with you here. So that's really a pre-recorded commercial with actors you're watching right now, not live TV. You are speaking to me, Jason. I'm the lone guy in the office who wishes he were out having a martini with my co-workers but I got the short straw today. So for the love of heaven, what is it that you would like us to do for you today?"

Viewer: "Really? Well then, I will tell you, Jason. I've been injured and it's not my fault. I want to sue."

Voice on phone: "Ok, we can handle that. What injured you?"

Viewer: "YOUR INCESSANT TV ADS!"

Voice on phone: "Excuse me?"

Viewer: "You heard me, Jason. So now you're not even sorry. No excuses, either! They have to stop it!"

Voice on phone: "Who has to stop what?"

Viewer: "The constant ringing phones. The same thing over and over every 10 minutes. And now you tell me it's all fake. Well, I am only slightly relieved to learn that, because I was wondering how in the world they could hold up for so long. A person could get an actual cramp sitting down all the time like that. Whatever these scenes are, they are nothing if not incessant! And now fake. Well, that certainly adds insult to injury. I'm in actual pain over this. I'm injured and it's not my fault. I want justice. Make them stop it!"

Voice on phone: "Whatever, ma'am. I suggest you call a therapist, not a lawyer." [CLICK.]

Viewer: [hanging up, stunned] "Wow. The nerve! Classic narcissist."

Viewer: [searching Google for a number to call about the constant political ads; the woman who talks ad infinitum about insurance; that annoying guy selling used cars...]

Viewer: [dialing, waiting: bzzzt, bzzzt...bzzzt. bzzzt]

[Aaaand scene. Fade to black. Curtain]

You Are Here
9-25-2022

What good amid these, O me, O life?
Answer. That you are here—that life exists and identity,
That the powerful play goes on, and you may contribute a verse.
  – Walt Whitman

My adult son, Nick called in the wee hours one evening all the way from Hong Kong. I answered, worried at the late hour. His voice was solemn when he told me the news.

His best friend had been found dead.

I caught my breath, horrified at the news and relieved he was OK all at once. Such strange bedfellows these thoughts were in my brain.

"Oh Nick, I'm so sorry. What can I do? How can I help you?"

"You've already done it," he told me. "You answered the phone." He waited a beat, uttering a ragged sigh.

"It was suicide, mom."

There would be no hugging him, a mother's instinctive response. Not from eight thousand miles away. I would have to embrace him over the phone with mere words and my heart, just as he was hugging me that way, too.

It was my turn to sigh deeply. "This is awful, Nick. Talk to me. I'm here, and I love you."

"My best friend took his own life and I didn't see it coming," he said, sounding intractably sad.

It was the voice of a grown man I heard, but I could also hear the boy I had raised. I loved them both with all my heart.

"You must be feeling a whole range of painful emotions," I consoled him.

"Yeah," he acknowledged, drawing out the word long and slow. This wasn't his first rodeo with adult crises. But this was heartbreak unlike any other.

"Please give yourself permission to have all those feelings and don't judge them. They are all valid. You will need time to sort through them all. I'm so glad you called. And I'm so sorry this happened."

"I feel so bad I didn't see how truly lost he was…"

His voice trailed off to nothing. Big pause.

"People who do what your friend did can't be understood rationally," I said softly.

"I know, yes, I know. But I wish he had reached out," Nick confided.

"Your troubled friend lost sight of logic and reason," I reminded him. "He lost the belief that life still held possibilities. He forgot he wasn't alone. Ending his pain was purely an emotional act, not at all well-reasoned. I know you know that, and it doesn't ease your pain or satisfy your need to make it different now. Neither should you bear blame for his choice."

"I know," he said. "I am just so sorry he chose what he did because he didn't think he had another option."

"Sometimes people give us clues," I reminded him, "like giving away belongings and pets, but not always. He chose a very private, permanent solution for a temporary problem. To him, though, I'm guessing his pain felt agonizing and endless; he was convinced of its permanence, no doubt, and didn't know how to make it better, which is why he hid it from you."

"Trying to hide that kind of pain every second you're around people must be exhausting," Nick said.

"I'm not surprised a person wouldn't want to live in that kind of nonstop hell," I replied. "If only he could have appreciated his value and known he could walk out of his pain without leaving altogether. He just didn't know how."

We talked a few more moments. His words were cascading out now. His group of friends had banded together to designate who would take which task to deal with the whole thing, settle their friend's affairs, handle paperwork, the legalities, communicate with his friend's family in the states, plan a service, update each other on their progress. They all checked in on each other's well-being, creating even stronger bonds of friendship, compassion, and gratitude out of the chaos their friend had laid suddenly at their feet.

He promised to call me again soon.

We talked again a few days after the service. The stress had taken a toll on all of them and it was overwhelming. Right down to holding the service in the middle of a typhoon.

It had all finally gotten to him. He broke down the day after the service and couldn't stop crying.

It was then that he got the perspective he needed. Sitting down, he lowered his head and saw the tattoo on his ankle. It was an image of a way-point, an arrow. It said, "You are here."

Wisely, pro-actively, he had it put there years ago as a kind of touchstone. He wanted to be able to remind himself of his value, the value of life itself, the importance of being present, of being nowhere else but right here where life is real, truth exists, and there is pain but there is also hope. It was meant to re-orient him in times of difficulty, confusion, and loss. This day, it served him well. This directional arrow affixed permanently to his skin pointed the way, indeed: "You are here. Now. Today. Do not forget you matter to someone, and to yourself."

He remembered that "here" would pain him and also sustain him now, moving him through dark, slippery grief into the light and firm footing. He would be re-centered and ready for all the living, breathing times ahead. He would take time to rest; to call a therapist and have a regular day doing boring things. To take care of—and care for—himself. Because he mattered. Nick wished his friend could've believed that staying "here" could result in finding his footing, too.

The joys and sorrows of life are how people learn and grow and live and survive. They can come at us on a normal day when we are doing normal things and then slam us into a wall. Bad news from the doctor. Tornadoes. Fires. Floods. Suicide. Nobody is free from life's struggles. Nobody.

But the lies mental illness tells a person who is struggling are not helpful. They steal reality and offer nothing with which to nourish or heal. They make a person forget their value, forget where they are in the world and stand in the way of clarity and healing. They can result in catastrophe if they go unaddressed.

We shouldn't be afraid of pressing a close friend who seems a little distant, "Are you OK? I am here. You are here. Let's talk."

It really is possible to stop the pain without ending your life. Seek help if you are at the precipice. Tell someone. There is no shame in reaching out to people who know the truth about you, not the lies your pain tells you.

You are not alone. Even when you think life seems pointless, you matter. Yours can be a true story of hope and recovery. You are here. You are here.

***

If you or someone you know needs help, call 988 and speak to a mental health professional.

Something Good: The Three A's
10-2-2022

My husband makes us coffee almost every morning.

Yesterday he produced an entire breakfast, a little later than usual.

He presented a lovely assemblage of omelet, bacon, and coffee. Just as I took a sip of hot, hazelnut heaven with cream in a cup he quipped, "Breakfast is late today because of supply chain issues and staffing shortages."

I laughed so hard I spit out my coffee. His laugh was music.

I love him so.

I return the favor by helping him with all things digital. Not his thing. But I serve him up daily cyber smörgåsbords, from online stuff to simple spreadsheets. My pleasure.

We are each other's helpmates. Under our roof, no one is subservient. No siree. We are equals, committedly so. We aim to share life by following three bywords we have come to hold sacred.

They are the Three A's: Affirmation, Acceptance, and Affection.

If one of these is lacking, our relationship is unbalanced, like a three-legged stool with a wobbly leg. Try resting firmly on that thing. Uneasy rests the partner/spouse/friend on a wobbly stool.

Ignoring the wobble only prolongs the misery. That old matchbook trick under the offending leg won't cut it, either. It just means somebody's forever futzing with it, annoyed every time it rocks to one side or another.

And nothing changes

If we're wobbling, we try to stop and figure out the problem. That's acceptance. We are human, and we accept that fact. Nobody in this house is perfect, and if we should need to take another look at just how not perfect we are, it's OK. We do that a lot.

Boy, do we ever.

But we do it with kindness and respect. No cheap shots of anger in the heat of the moment, or piling on past grievances, aka "the kitchen sink fight." We like to keep our kitchen and our issues clean, current, and fair. Accepting each other while talking about how we could've done better in a certain scenario is a safety net for a difficult conversation. Nobody dies. Nobody breaks anything, especially heart or spirit. Everybody gets to learn something, bounce back, and try again.

And something changes.

He opens doors for me, and I hold doors for him, too. Some people say it's old fashioned and somehow demeaning. Pffft! For the love of Elvis, it's just a thoughtful, polite gesture, not a political statement. For us, it's sheer affection in action, pure and simple, and I wouldn't have it any other way. Do unto others, you know, especially your loved ones. Also, give hugs. Hold hands.

To affirm someone you love is to have their back, to provide emotional support and encouragement. Even as adults, we all still have our inner children knocking about in our psyches, jumping on our inner furnishings and yelling for what they need. A child who doesn't get affirmation from one or both parents can be emotionally crippled. Our inner child never leaves us, and requires tender, loving affirmation, crippled or not. Marriages and friendships need that, too.

While they seem simple and obvious, The Three A's aren't necessarily second nature. It has taken the two of us some years to learn how to be intentional. Now they are part of our fiber as a couple.

Without some kind of guiding light, there's nothing upon which to build a foundation.

Maria and Captain von Trapp knew what they were talking about in that gazebo one starry night when they sang the words: nothing comes from nothing; nothing ever could. They assumed that somewhere in their youth or childhood they must've done something good.

While that may or may not be true, I say right then and there in that moment they also decided to acknowledge and embrace affirmation, affection, and acceptance as a commitment toward their future together. And that's something good. Something very, very good.

Loneliness is a mugger. Choice is the answer
10-9-2022

There is the kind of loneliness that sneaks up on a parent whose child has just left for college. Without warning or awareness it hits like a mugger wielding a baseball bat. Loneliness. Empty nest syndrome.

There is the kind of loneliness when you're the kid who just left home for an exciting four years in college and once your parents have moved you into the dorm and you tell them it's time to go, that you'll be just fine, the door closes and the sudden sounds of silence are deafening. You've just encountered that same stealth mugger.

There is the kind of loneliness that poverty, discrimination, and circumstance bring to a life, and it's the same mugger wielding that bat.

There is the kind of loneliness when a storm —be it hurricane, tornado, depression, grief, disability, accident, or terminal illness— is bearing down. Our bullet-proof invincibility melts into instant vulnerability. Nothing, not prayers, nor friends, nor faith, nor wishes as sincere as sincerity gets, will guarantee safe passage through life-threatening storms that can send you to your knees. But as the old saying goes, it's not freedom from the storm but peace within the storm that will sustain us. Peace is a choice.

Get your peace however you get yours, be it Jesus or your Higher Power or your faith in Adam's house cat. But when a storm blows in, there is a lonely, utter powerlessness that carries the singular, sobering truth: this is out of our hands. Even with loving support and faith by our side, we all die our own deaths. Nobody can do that for us. We don't always get to choose how we or our loved ones die, but we can choose how we live.

We always have choice. Granted, this is not a popular idea. People generally push back against it because it sounds idealistic, insensitive, impossible. It's not.

We all face tribulation and circumstances that are not our fault. They assail us with complete indifference to who we are, our status in the world, or what we believe. They beset us with the kind of acute loneliness that steals our ability to realize that we still have choice.

After a mugging, in the dark face of what feels and looks like there are no options, we still have one: the choice of how we deal with what happens to us. Make no mistake, though. Do not equate choice with fairy-tale happy endings. Choice merely exists, and we should know about it.

Doing nothing is a choice. Making changes or being stuck in resentment is a choice. Making peace is a choice. Asking for help is another. Prayer is a choice. Revenge, too. Hate, love, acceptance, and forgiveness? Yep. Seeking strength and courage is yet another, even if the circumstances cannot be changed. All choices. Even where we go and to whom we go is a choice. Thank the Lord and Elvis for resources, all choices: volunteers, clubs, organizations, charities, places of worship, counselors, doctors, a higher power, community agencies, therapists, friends, families, teachers, mentors.

The decision to deal, and how to deal with the inevitable loneliness that mugs us all in our lives, is our choice. It's the first emotional step among what could be many difficult, painful, hard-won steps forward. Oh, and PS. It helps to start with the premise that there is no perfection. Perfection is an endless cycle that goes nowhere except round and round and never through.

There's an old Zen proverb that goes, "Sitting quietly, doing nothing, Spring comes, and the grass grows by itself." That little piece of genius reminds us that the world goes on, with or without us. We get to choose how we feel about it and what we do about it.

Oh, and PPS: nobody said choices, good or bad, are easy. Just possible. Always possible.

BE LIKE BOYD
10-16-2022

A Newnan icon, local personality, great American and friend left us recently. Oh, we lost a good one. He was a man of many talents, wisdom, and sharp wit. Some people have that knack of being remarkably unforgettable in the best way. That was David Boyd, Sr. Every time. All the time.

Boyd was "a creative," an artist, illustrator, humorist, and political cartoonist. If that didn't keep him busy, he'd happily draw clever things for locals who simply wanted a Boyd drawing on their greeting cards, party invitations, canvases, or logos for their businesses. His logos for the Redneck Gourmet and Sprayberry's Barbecue, and his illustrations for the *You Might Be a Redneck If…* books live in infamy.

Boyd was a people person. Daily, he ambled into the Redneck Gourmet on the square, just yards up the street from his print shop—later the Boyd Gallery, run by his talented son, David, Jr. an accomplished artist in his own right, which is how Boyd Sr. earned his nickname "Old Boyd," to differentiate between father and son. Old Boyd excelled at schmoozing, glad-handing folks with a smile and an easy southern drawl; gracing people with his sunny, wise-cracking conversations. A friendlier guy never lived. He wore his trademark saddle shoes everywhere, and when he walked in the door, the place lit up.

He spoke at a Heritage School graduation many long years ago when I was teaching music there (when dinosaurs still roamed the earth.) That evening he was imparting his special brand of wisdom to the new graduates, delivering stand-up-comedic humor while managing to convey an unforgettable, even life-changing, point.

He encouraged each graduate to be "an example." He explained how they could be shining examples of what to be: individuals navigating life in their best way, as positive role models. But as a rejoinder, he warned them also to remember this: they could just as easily serve as shining examples of what NOT to be: badly behaved, mean-spirited, selfish, negative role models. Do NOT choose the latter, he admonished them. It's beneath you, he said. Choose good. Do good. Be good. He should know all about that. He chose good. He did good. He was so very good. He was a most spectacular, shining example of positivity and goodness.

Lately, I've been thinking about Old Boyd and his entreaty to that graduating class so long ago. I've been thinking about how he lived, and how his entire family lives. Shining examples of goodness, all.

I thought of him this week when the verdict came down in the latest Alex Jones trial. Jones was found guilty of being exactly what Boyd exhorted us not to be: an example of colossal wretchedness. A bloviating, ruthless liar-for-profit and heartless mercenary, Jones has been vomiting bile over talk-show airways for years. For ten years he has focused his sick brand of negative fiction on the Sandy Hook massacre in which 20 people, mostly 6- and 7-year-old children, were brutally murdered at school. He asserts it was all fake, disparaging the grieving families further by calling them paid actors. Hard to fathom the pain they have endured.

Barking this brutal, decades-long, unrepentant conspiracy theory, along with many others, Jones has gotten mega-rich. Not only is Jones a horrendously bad example, but the people who listen to him, support his brand of destructive trash talk, and keep him in business are no better.

Fortunately, a jury decided to be a good example by relieving

Jones of a billion dollars in damages to be awarded to the families. He's still ranting, appealing the decision, and hiding assets. Of course he is.

Some people make their mark by what they contribute to the world, and some by what they take away from it.

Don't be a taker. Don't be a bad example.

Old Boyd was a giver. Be a good example. Be a giver. Be like Boyd.

Grown-Up
10-23-2022

"Was it for this I uttered prayers,
And sobbed and cursed and kicked the stairs,
That now, domestic as a plate,
I should retire at half-past eight?"
   – Edna St. Vincent Millay

Edna St. Vincent Millay began publishing poems in high school and went to Vassar on a full ride, earning a scholarship with her poetry. The rest is poetic history. She was the first woman to win a Pulitzer.

In high school I had a 3-ring notebook covered in that ubiquitous denim, rough-textured fabric so prevalent back then. Although it was a difficult surface to write on, I plastered every inch of that notebook with quotes in jittery lines of ballpoint pen, quotes like, "Better to wear out than rust out." Sounded good in theory. I get it even now. But clearly, I had yet to really experience "wearing out." And I was no Millay.

Millay's simple, 4-line poem, "Grown-Up" is the perfect joke on us mature folk when we find out our childish notion of Utopian adulthood ain't all it was cracked up to be.

I still like being an adult, though. No thanks to childish tantrums, the teenage angst, the dumb decisions, the uncertainties of life. Spilling your milk at the family dinner table was a big, PTSD inducing deal in my family.

In my husband's family, when one of six children inevitably spilled their milk at dinner, their father would always yell, "Why did you do that?!!" Their mom, siblings, and grandmother sat at the table in abject fear and silence until the storm passed.

Rick and his brother, Joe, shared a bedroom. One night, the two boys decided the next one to spill his milk at the table would have to answer the old man's bluster with some audacious retort. After careful consideration, they chose a quiet but very possibly deadly one: "Because you were looking at me."

The very next evening at dinner, sure enough the moment arose. It was Rick's brother who spilled his milk, and the responsibility fell to him. The old man reacted predictably, spitting nails, "Why did you do that!?" Rick braced for impact, holding his breath while Joe bravely manned up. Rick watched the scene play out in dramatic slow-motion as Joe looked their father in the eye and said, "Beee-cause yyyyou wwwwere looooking at meeee…" The old man was rendered speechless. Rick's mom leaned back laughing and nearly fell out of her chair.

Funny childhood memories aside, I'll still take adulthood. I'll take the sweetness of a happy marriage to a man who once sat in his veterinary practice vehicle under a tree waiting for a farmer and cross-stitched the entire "All I Really Know I Learned in Kindergarten" by Robert Fulghum as a Christmas gift for me. I'll take the joys and heartaches, too, of having children of my own. I'll take the fun of being worn out from playing with grandchildren and taking 'em home to their parents at the end of the day.

Youth and maturity each have their pros and cons. Pulitzer Edna deftly illustrated a sho' nuff central paradox of life when she wrote about kids who rail against going to bed early becoming adults who gladly retire early. Translated: we want what we don't have, and when we get it we don't want it. I begged my parents to stay up on Sunday nights through the Ed Sullivan Show when my bedtime came smack in the middle of it. Now, I stay up if I feel like it because I can. But I really don't mind going to bed at half-past eight on occasion, either, because I can. Especially on a cold winter night when it's dark at six o'clock and I have a good book to fall asleep to after reading the first paragraph. Because I'm slap worn out.

Maybe the great, overarching lesson is to be present in the now. Yesterday's gone. Tomorrow isn't here yet. Today, this present moment is at our feet. Can we enjoy it for what it is? What will we make of it?

THE THINGS WE TELL OURSELVES
10-30-2022

Recently I caught myself talking out loud. To a fly.

"Ooh, I see you," I whispered. "Come to mama." I raised the fly swatter and hammered down. "Gotcha! I think. Are you…? Let's have a look-see shall we? You are most definitely… not alive."

"Ridiculous," I told myself, not out loud, "that I should be directly addressing a dead fly. That I killed by my own hand. If I were Buddhist I would feel guilty. I am not and I don't, OK? Jeez."

Then I thought to myself, "how many times do I talk to myself either aloud or in my head, about and to anything, and flail my psyche afterwards for doing such a thing?"

Curious, I decided to engage in an experiment. For a day, I would intentionally take stock of all my extemporaneous speeches to myself, spoken and unspoken, and the subsequent silent sermons emanating from that busy thought-machine in my head. I wanted to be truly cognizant of exactly what I tell myself. I believe, in these new-age times, it's called mindfulness. Whatever.

Silent thought to self: "The 'whats' will be easy for this experiment. The 'whys' may not."

Silent Sermon to Self: "Maybe you don't want, or need, to know all the whys. Just the whats may be enough to enlighten you."

Silent thought to Self: "Question: 'Am I weird?'"

Silent Sermon to Self: "Don't answer that. Maybe you don't need to know every answer you ask yourself, either. This one especially. Be kind to yourself. So, really, no answer, please. And by the way, not everything HAS an answer. Ever think of that? Next!"

Not-silent thought to Self, spoken loudly in fact, to an empty living room after reading an opinionated, spleen-venting article in the paper: "Oh please. Utter nonsense! Cite me your source, you sad-sack! Who have you been listening to? I'm sending you an indignant email!"

Silent Sermon to Self: "Yeah, that guy is misinformed, and so are a lot of people. You are too, from time to time. Not this time, though. Jesus was mad at those money guys in the temple, too, and he upended their tables and threw the louts out. You could do that if you want but who the hell are you, anyway? Consider the lilies of the field, too. Your choice. You can be right or you can be kind, but you cannot always be both. You don't have to call everybody on everything. Choose your battles, girl. Remember the St. Francis solo you loved to sing when you had a voice? Now you have an internal voice that can sing the same song. Be an instrument of peace; where there is hatred sow love; understand before being understood. Do NOT write the author of that article a hateful email. Chill. Do your own homework and make your case elsewhere, another way. Remember, life is a two-way street. Avoid the head-on collisions where possible and spare a life, or your own dignity at the very least. This sermon you're thinking right now, by the way, should also not be taken as passive-aggressive offense to the angry email you, yourself, received last week. They were certainly entitled to their opinion, unfortunate as it may have been. Forgive them, brush yourself off, sow peace, and move on. Be like Atticus Finch. You never really understand a person until you consider things from his point of view—until you climb into his skin and walk around in it. Right. No need to kill the mockingbird."

Thought to Self: "That's the lesson du jour! Excellent. I must admit, this has been a great exercise. Maybe even just raised my emotional IQ. I think I need to wrap up this experiment, though, and put a bow on it before I drive myself to distraction."

Thought to Self: "Ohh, look, a bunny…"

The Season
11-6-2022

It's November. I feel the pressure building already. Some of us will be putting up Christmas decorations (or already have) and others of us will bemoan the Christmas decorations that are already up and constant holiday carols playing everywhere, way too soon. The end of Daylight-Saving Time either augers well or bedevils us. Frankly, my body wants to go to bed when it gets dark before 6:00 pm and I really dislike that. Then there's Election Day (sorry, not touching it except to say just get out and vote, then pray for peace); Veteran's Day arrives as the day we honor and thank brave men and women in the armed forces for their sacrifices and faithful service, as well as their families; and finally, Thanksgiving, with all its food, fellowship, and festivities. Cram daily life in there. Tis the beginning of "The Season."

I'm still pining for October to stay a bit longer. The October weather always sends me, with great fondness, straight back to 5th grade and my teacher, Mrs. Woodruff, who taught us Helen Hunt Jackson's poem, "October's Bright Blue Weather." I can still see the photo of a startling, bright blue October sky pinned to the bulletin board near the classroom door. Funny the things that fade away. Funny the things that won't.

Time marches on, whether or not we are ready for an inevitable, preternatural period that puts us under its spell. By the time we reach

Christmas/Hanukkah, we've most likely fulfilled the unique zeitgeist of The Season: hustling, bustling, shopping, wrapping, decorating, socializing, sending cards, partying, cooking, entertaining, caroling, engaging in spiritual and religious observances. I'm sure each of us can add to this list. Snapping at a sales person? Elbowing a guy in line? Fuming at traffic? Yelling at the kids? Taking someone's inventory? Engaging in hateful speech? I'm exhausted just thinking about all of this.

Revving up for The Season, many people already do something else, too, but many forget to do it, or even refuse to do it: demonstrate civility, charity, and kindness. Yeah, yeah, you've heard it before. Bunch of sappy pap, you say? These are possibly the most important words I can think of before all others, no matter the time of year, actually. In addition to actively donating money to a charity of your choice, remember there are many ways to give. If money is tight, give time, volunteer, serve or donate food. Show kindness, which means forbearance and altruism. We have become a volatile, opinionated bunch what with today's politics and world crises.

Maybe we can't stop some guy from screaming at us if he really wants to pick a fight in a tug-of-war. But we can drop the rope and refuse to play that game, choosing not to pull their ugliness towards us. We each have the option to consciously commit to civility, goodwill, and kindness. These are not about making oneself a doormat, either. Gracious no. It takes great strength of character to hold one's tongue or to speak truth to power without engaging in angry, hurtful exchanges.

I ask myself sometimes what difference one person can make by dropping their rope, by extending civility, kindness, and charity to others, by refusing to engage in ugly rhetoric or actions of any stripe.

Good question. Maybe if each of us tries it, you, me, your neighbor, friend, reader of this column, persons of whatever race, creed, or political persuasion, we might get our answer. One caveat: It can be very difficult to drop the rope in the heat of a struggle. Cultivate the commitment. Positivity is a choice and an essential art.

Each person's concerted effort to be civil, kind, and charitable might not change the world. It will very possibly make The Season and beyond a little better for ourselves and, especially, for others. That just might do. 'Tis the season, y'all. Here we go.

Remembering Nola
11-13-2022

Years ago, when I sang with the incomparable Atlanta Symphony Chorus she was conductor Robert Shaw's right hand and a force of her own to be reckoned with. As his executive assistant and also the choral administrator, she had to be sturdy and tireless to accomplish all that was required of her. Keeping a busy, temperamental Maestro happy and organized, and taking care of a million details running a group of more than 250 singers was like herding cats. I never saw a better wrangler. Her name was Nola Frink. Oh, and she had the singing voice of an angel to boot.

My first meeting with Nola came when I auditioned for the chorus in 1980. There would be a music theory test and a vocal audition for a limited number of coveted spots which meant I would have to do battle against other more experienced, fierce competitors in the presence of vaunted maestro, Robert Shaw.

My time until the audition was limited to just a few weeks before I would have to ride my chariot in there and slay my gladiator fears, and I was rusty. I memorized scales and refreshed myself on musical terms, time signatures, note values, and key signatures. I polished my audition solo to a fine shine and practiced pitch-matching, sight-reading, and sight-singing until the world went flat.

Then, the day arrived.

Greeted by a volunteer at check-in, I said something stupid like "I hope I'm in the right place." I might as well have asked, "Is this where the gladiators register to die?"

After I finished the written test the volunteer said they would call my name when it was time for the rest of my audition.

Hearing my name, I descended the stairs, weak-kneed, and entered the expansive rehearsal room to face my jury. Two people sat at a long table—the one and only Robert Shaw himself and his executive assistant, Nola Frink. Terrified, I would have to try to open my mouth and make a sound. It couldn't be just any sound, either. It had to be good, nay exceptional. I had to soar. I petitioned all my angels and the good Lord above to help me.

I sang scales, random pitch patterns, and my solo audition piece. Then I heard Shaw himself say, "Step up to the music stand and sing the alto part, please." I would be sight-singing the alto part—that I had never laid eyes on—in the difficult Bach B-Minor Mass. Gulp. I forced a fake smile and nodded at the pianist. I cannot explain what came over me except sheer, miraculous grace.

I sang that mother for all she was worth. A week later the letter came. I was in.

I sang for 10+ seasons and left to take care of my young family, while Nola remained in her job for years. When Mr. Shaw died she retired, moving to a condo in Atlanta. We stayed connected. She said she was going to buy my book the moment she heard it was published. That meant the world to me. Here was a woman whom I had seen as a gruff, stern, highly efficient, high-strung Mother Superior for many years, who was now a relaxed, old friend and a fan. Truth was, I was her fan long before. Much like Shaw, Nola could be forthright and intimidating, bossy and short with people in her job in order to keep him and all the plates spinning smoothly. Human pressure cooker she was required to be, she could also find spare moments to let off steam. When she did, her still waters ran deep, warm with kindness, humor, decency, and friendliness.

Nola died recently. Her service will be in Atlanta next weekend and I plan to be there. I want to tell her, and Mr. Shaw, that I loved them both, and that I'm back.

Letting Go
11-20-2022

I warned y'all in a recent column that I am feeling the pressure of the holidays. I fear I'm approaching Holiday Hysteria on my way to completely "losing it" in the midst of all the busy-busy. And it's not even December.

I didn't show up at a potluck Thanksgiving lunch with the lovely folks at *The Newnan Times-Herald* because, well, you don't care why. Just know I had a good excuse and I'm sorry. Hope they'll forgive me and still run my columns. If you are reading this I think I'm good. I am so very thankful for them (and all of you readers).

Thanksgiving Day is only a few sleeps away. I'm hosting a myriad number of people. And yet, I've just started a huge project to clean out filing cabinets, and reams of boxes that crowd our foyer coat closet. What in the h-e-double hockey sticks am I thinking? We'll be carrying insanely heavy boxes and cabinets to my studio upstairs above our garage. (Note the operative words "insanely heavy boxes" and "upstairs.") Also know the "we" to whom I refer as the designated carriers are my teenage grandson, and the obliging saint with heavy duty hand-cart and strong back to whom I am married. May our marriage last. For them I am also immensely grateful.

Also, after Thanksgiving we are replacing tile in the guest bath, just in time for relatives to inhabit the guest bedroom when they visit for Christmas. Won't that be lovely. What am I thinking, again? I've been wanting to do this project for years. And now the installer is coming the first week in December to finish it, right before the carpet cleaning guy shows up and moves all the furniture around and my brother and his wife show up for five days.

Presently, the detritus strewn everywhere is not pretty. Boxes populate the foyer floor awaiting transport. Boxes of tiles, and buckets of grout and cement sit at the ready on the floor in the guest room. I'm nervous and my teeth are beginning to itch.

But wait. Thinking on this, I'm sure I'm not alone. Everyone has their own stories of pressures this time of year, self-inflicted or not. So wah, wah, my little first-world problems are of absolutely no import when put up against the daily difficulties of many folks who don't even have houses and who must rely on warming shelters; or folks who can't afford to buy groceries much less host a dozen people at a beautifully decorated holiday dining table laden with food. Thankfully, I know lots of folks are contributing their time, help, and money to charitable causes to brighten the lives of those less fortunate. We are, too.

I'm reminded that perspective is such a gift. We would all do ourselves a favor to make use of it.

So with a calmer soul and new perspective as I write this, y'all are my witness. I'm consciously letting go of Holiday Perfection Hysteria. And I'm truly thankful I'm not on the tour of homes.

We will do our best and keep our heads on straight. It will be enough.

If the guest bath project goes south, we'll house our guests in a different bedroom. At least the foyer closet is now cleaned out and holiday guests will have someplace to hang their coats. We'll donate our extra coats to charity along with food and dollars.

And if there are still a few boxes on the floor when guests arrive, no one will care. We'll slide boxes against the wall and clear a path to the kitchen and the dining room. Then we will cook, load our plates, sit down together, bow our heads, hold hands around our table, give thanks for our blessings, and appreciate what's essential: not shiny things and not perfection, but the human spirit, charity, family, and friends. In a word, love. Always love.

Alchemy and Insight
11-27-2022

I want to share a moment of alchemy I experienced recently. Alchemy is the medieval forerunner of chemistry, a supposed process of transformation, like changing lead to gold. It's generally regarded as pseudoscience, of course. I also see it as artistic reality.

When music, lyrics, and voice combine in just the right way there is a kind of alchemy, an arrival at a rare, transmuted whole that parts alone cannot achieve. The result is singular, unified gold; a new bond, strong and powerful that creates and elicits a reactionary host of emotions and insight. Musically, it's a powerful magic act I performed many times for many years before I retired from singing. Now I'm a spectator and a listener.

I don't mean to be a downer here, and I'm no English scholar, but recently I stumbled upon Emily Dickinson's poem, I felt a Funeral in My Brain, set to music and sung achingly by Andrew Bird and Phoebe Bridgers. That powerful melding took me to a juncture where poetry, music, and voice all jumped out together as one, grabbed my heart and soul, squeezed so hard my eyes watered and I held my breath. This magical feat in artistic alchemy had my undivided attention.

It made me think, too. Something / someone (maybe us, or someone we know, or society as a whole) has sickened, died, or is dying, and the mind mourns that loss very personally. Maybe I related to it this day because of all the violent, disturbing deaths happening more and more in stores, clubs, schools, highways, and most recently in a gay bar in Colorado and a break room in a Virginia WalMart.

Anyone who loses what is valuable in their life can grasp the poetic metaphor of a death and a funeral in their brain. These are losses that occur in the despair of dementia, disease, insanity, terminal illness, murder, violence, and unceasing, disabling grief.

All of it is a state of confusion "where planks in reason break;" when off balance, a person "falls to the floor, down and down."

This time of year we want to be merry. We all need joy and there is much to celebrate. But it's not the hap-happiest time of the year for all. There are people who are feeling all kinds of funerals in their brains, mourning, numb, losing control, lonely, confounded, struggling with the past, present, future or any combination thereof. During this season especially, we might just keep that in mind, and assume it might be so for anyone we know or meet.

My holiday wish is that we maintain soft edges, and in our joy for the season we also wear and share the warm clothes of compassion, understanding, awareness, kindness, insight, good cheer, and good will when there's nothing else we can do. It won't change a painful diagnosis or a death, but it might help somebody navigate their losses and their funerals—even private ones we may not be aware of—just a tiny bit better for a moment along their way to wherever it is they're going. We may never know our effect, but they—and the universe —will.

I FELT A FUNERAL, IN MY BRAIN

Poem by Emily Dickinson is here: https://poets.org/poem/i-felt-funeral-my-brain-280

Song by Andrew Bird with Phoebe Bridgers is here: https://youtu.be/SlS7ZyacnSY

(Poem is in the public domain, song is legally accessed)

I felt a Funeral, in my Brain,
And Mourners to and fro
Kept treading - treading - till it seemed
That Sense was breaking through -

And when they all were seated,
A Service, like a Drum -
Kept beating - beating - till I thought
My mind was going numb -

And then I heard them lift a Box
And creak across my Soul
With those same Boots of Lead, again,
Then Space - began to toll,

As all the Heavens were a Bell,
And Being, but an Ear,
And I, and Silence, some strange Race,
Wrecked, solitary, here -

And then a Plank in Reason, broke,
And I dropped down, and down -
And hit a World, at every plunge,
And Finished knowing - then –

Words
12-11-2022

Words are my jam. I'm a fan, a nerd wordie. Or wordie nerd if you like. I do NYT Crosswords, Wordle, Spelling Bee, and many other word apps. I read a lot. I write stuff. I authored a book. I write a column. I know many of you do all or some of these, too. Time to talk words.

Announcing the 2022 Words of the Year.

Gaslighting is Merriam-Webster's word of the year, one that should be familiar by now. Gaslighting is the act or practice of grossly misleading someone, especially for one's own advantage. It's been googled multiple times every day, they say. That surprises me not one iota. You? Merriam-Webster said in a statement, "In this age of misinformation, conspiracy theories, Twitter trolls, and deep fakes, gaslighting has emerged as a word for our time." Boy howdy, ain't it the truth.

Goblin mode is The Oxford English Dictionary's pick. It cracks me up two words are "the word" of the year. Interestingly, *vax* was their word for last year, which makes sense. After Covid and lockdowns and trips to Crazytown without ever leaving home, it's understandable that Goblin mode, a state of being "unapologetically lazy, slovenly and rejecting social norms or expectations" would follow vax. Frankly, I'm in a relative state of Goblin mode all the time now, until company's coming and I throw stuff in the closets, dust, and vacuum the rugs before the doorbell rings.

Here's my list of overused words and phrases that ought to disappear: "the bottom line;" "at the end of the day;" "where we/you at;" "useful hacks;" "you always;" and/or "you never;" "like nobody's ever seen before;" "don't take this the wrong way but…;" and "recalculating."

I like these creative phrases adopted from other countries:

'Pulling an old cow out of the ditch' (Holland) is bringing up an old argument.

'Straighten the horns and kill the bull' (Japan) is messing something up by insisting on correcting a minor flaw.

"There is no cow on the ice" (Sweden) means there is no reason to panic.

"Going where the Czar goes on foot" (Russia) means going to the toilet, the only place to which the Czar wasn't carried. I can name a select few in Russia and elsewhere who deserve swirlies upon every arrival.

'Feeding the donkey sponge cake' (Portugal) refers to giving special treatment to someone who doesn't need (or deserve) it. Got someone in mind? I do.

The "Annoying and Should be Illegal Grammar Crimes Awards" go this year, and every year, to those who shamefully misuse the poor little innocent apostrophe and the letter "s." These are crimes of commission and omission. Hope you don't deserve one of these:

The Errant Apostrophe Award. Please, for the love of Elvis, stop it with the apostrophes in plural nouns. Saying "many artist's exhibited their work" or signing a gift tag "From the Smith's" is a grammatical abomination. It's abusive to the little apostrophe. You're forcing it to report to work when it shouldn't. It needs and deserves the time off, and it doesn't play well with plurals, anyway. So here it is: The artists are exhibiting work at the show, and a gift is "From the Smiths." No apostrophe. The artists are a group of talented folks. The Smiths are a family of nice people. They are plural, more than one.

Apostrophes sit out that game. I hope they all have a happy holiday and the apostrophes enjoy their break.

The Missing "S" Award. It's a painful crime of omission to leave the letter "s" off plural words, especially "artists." Dear mother of Elvis, if I see another phrase like "a group of artist" (gasp, no plural "s"! Where is the "s"?) I'm proposing Congress pass a law. Help me create a name for it. Winner gets an all-expense paid trip into the warm cockles of my heart.

I like finding out the word "facetious" has all the vowels in it (except the sometimes "y"), in order. Thanks wordnik! I really am such a nerd.

The Holidays
12-18-2022

Watching the quixotic, 1983 movie *A Christmas Story* is an essential, annual tradition at our house that lifts my spirits.

The mere thought of it prompts me to get out our Leg Lamp for the front window and smile. The movie is like a warm, fuzzy group hug with the world. Viewing it every year is like sitting on a world-sized couch snuggled up with millions of friends and strangers sharing popcorn and laughing together, united. We're all in on the same hilarious jokes year after year. The people, the scenes, the props, the words are forever captured in time, always there for us just as they were last year and the year before that. We get to offload sadness and worry for an hour or so.

Over the years we revisit Ralphie and his family and other memorable characters; pink bunny suits and a box labeled "Fragile" pronounced "Fra-gee-lay" containing "a major award"; the iconic warnings about Red Ryder BB guns; the hapless Flick getting his tongue stuck on a frozen pole after a triple-dog-dare (poor kid never learns); Ralphie's comically gruff, cursing father; and the bully bad guys eventually receive their comeuppance. And there's my vision of millions of couches and chairs pushed together in one big cosmic living room, everyone holding hands. Nobody asks who they voted for. Nobody has to defend who they love and why. Nobody is fighting.

Nobody is standing at a microphone making hateful speeches. There is comfort. There is friendship. There is peace. There is joy. For an hour and 40 minutes.

Would it actually be so.

Isn't that what the holidays represent? Grace and gratitude? Peace and joy? Whether Christmas or Hanukkah (which coincide this year) or whatever you believe and wherever you bend your knee, it's about gratitude for a miraculous gift wrapped in grace. Across the globe, people celebrate marvelous stories of different kinds of grace, gifts, and gratitude. Some are about virgin births, some about freedom from oppression, some are fanciful, some are not. All are miraculous. Despite our differences, can we all gather together in the wonder, join hands, and get an Amen as we proclaim our stories, whether in English, Yiddish, Ukrainian, or Pig-Latin? Though the languages are many, paradoxically it's our different stories that unite us as a universal congregation of humans.

And while we're at it, can this also be a time to revisit our lives over the past year and reflect on the corporeal gifts we humans have given to each other? Like the traditions of watching *A Christmas Story*, and celebrating a miracle birth, I also make it an end-of-year practice to take a daunting pilgrimage into my conscience to take stock.

What can I claim as my personal contribution(s) to people and the world in which I live? Did I have strength and courage? Did I help anyone? Did I do harm? Did I give as well as receive? Was I mean and selfish? Was I generous? Did I love enough? Did I lose my temper? Did I leave even a speck of joy or pain with a single soul?

The answer is yes. To all of it. It's always yes. I am – we are – fully human. The test is in the ability to tell and accept the truth and make the effort to do better. The movie, *A Christmas Story* and the miracle of the religious story I celebrate are my reminders and my way to find not only gratitude but forgiveness, too.

I hope we can all give, receive, and count our blessings in peace, whoever you are, wherever you are, and however you celebrate your holiday. Seek and ye shall find. Much love and peace to you all.

Christmas, 1962
12-25-2022

Ah, the memories. Time now for my favorite family Christmas story, excerpted, edited, and addended from my book, *The Veterinarian's Wife, a Memoir* (available on Amazon, and now wherever books are sold). If you've heard this tale before, sorry. Here it is again. It's a story worth retelling.

On Christmas Eve, 1962 I was a co-conspirator in a heinous crime. My dad was ultra-desperate to find a last-minute gift for Mom the day before Christmas, so he took my brother, Larry and me shopping. We were just kids. He was a panicked husband. What could go wrong?

We walked miles of aisles, through all the stores. Nothing passed muster until we entered the Lenox Square Mall pet store and stood before the adorable Capuchin monkey mugging for us in his cage. Eureka. Visions of irresistibly cute organ-grinders' monkeys and furry, simian snuggles danced in our heads. My brother and I swooned, gushed, and kind of forced my dad to pull the trigger on that purchase.

Worst idea ever.

Dad had lost all rational thought by then, bowing to the pressure of his procrastination and our adolescent pleas.

After Christmas Day was done and we were all in bed, the story goes my mom spent the evening alone with a bottle of scotch talking to the monkey, wondering what Dad was thinking, and where had she gone wrong.

Admittedly, they did have a checkered history with gifts. She always gave him gifts he appreciated, no matter what they were. He wanted with all his heart to do the same for her. But she was hard to buy for. Very hard. My dad was a man from Mars and my mom was a woman from Venus (you do remember that 1992 book, right?). Although they were perfectly-matched in so many ways, their planets just never aligned in the gift-giving department.

If he gave her expensive things, she returned them because they were either excessive, not her style, or they didn't fit. She was a large, classy woman, tall, and wore size 11-narrow shoes.

If he went the other extreme and gave her practical gifts, she returned them because she either didn't need or want them, or they really made her mad. One Christmas it was a shower curtain liner. Anyone might assume that gift was a passive-aggressive move on my dad's part, but I assure you he was sincere as planet Mars. Other years' gifts included quotidian household small appliances like a steam iron and a box fan. After that, she issued a ban on anyone gifting anything with cords.

They actually found the wherewithal to laugh about it all, but it's no wonder he was thoroughly frustrated. She was impossible to buy for. He was hopelessly, delusionally, persistent.

I often wondered why he didn't just ask her what she wanted. He was a romantic soul, though, and cherished the notion of a surprise. She wanted to be the wife who opens the perfect surprise gift and sighs with gratitude. This was a lovely idea, but it just wasn't meant to be for them. And neither one wanted to bow to a functional solution. So they got what they got. What a dance. And yet, they remained madly in love all their years, until he left in 1983. Cancer.

Meanwhile, back to Christmas of 1962.

It only took a week or so before the monkey disappeared, to everyone's relief, actually. Our little primate pal ceased being cute in short order when we discovered he was an untamed biter with a volatile disposition and a predilection for sailing poo projectiles out through the wide mesh of his cage.

He vanished one day, along with the huge cage that had displaced the entire contents of the wall-papered breakfast nook in our once-tidy, quiet, suburban kitchen.

"Returned to the pet store," my parents said. Poor Dad. Poor Mom. Poor Monkey. Poor kids. Epic fail. Epic story. Epic memories.

Happy New Year. Oh Frabjous Day!
1-1-2023

Every year brings us new challenges, and some recycled ones. Welcome to 2023. I have advice you didn't ask for. Just three things. Oh joy.

First, beware of click bait and the latest ways to waste your time and ruin your day. Click bait isn't new, but it continues to re-invent itself and multiply exponentially.

If you haven't already, you will eventually bump into the inevitable online articles or unsolicited emails bearing links that say, "Keep this bread clip in your pocket. Here's why." Don't do it. You really don't need a bread clip in your pocket. Moreover, you don't need to know why.

But if you do click, here's what happens. At best, you get a free trip to a poorly designed website crammed full of more clickable dystopportunities (my own invented portmanteau). At worst, in addition to the trip, you could be gifted with malware baggage. At a minimum you win digital cookie luggage tags.

The websites have more than bread clip advice, and often forget to include the bread clip part. (Ergo, the bait. Once swallowed, it's gone and you're caught). You'll find a long column of hints and tricks and "xxxxx" — I will not use the most insipid word on my official List of Words We Can All Do Without, but it starts with an "h," has "ack" in the middle, and "s" at the end. It's word abuse. Gross.)

There's everything on these websites, most of it selling something, some of it just word-padding between the sales pitches. Be prepared for never-before-thought-of advice to keep counters clear of clutter to improve the look of your kitchen; the clever tip to use a wooden spoon to keep your pot from boiling over; and the ominous warning to clean those nasty gutters standing on your own stupid ladder if you must but you will get dirty and risk falling off that ladder unless you employ a "revolutionary" gutter system, and you will have x number of minutes to complete the transaction before the incredible sale price ends forever. Hint: it's not your ladder that's stupid if you continue with that transaction.

Second, and I swear by this one: "Beware of little expenses. A small leak can sink the ship" – Ben Franklin. All those monthly and annual subscription payments add up. There are services that exist solely to find and rid you of all the helpful stuff you signed up for and lost track of: video and audio streaming services, games, apps. So many apps. If you aren't diligent about checking your settings on your android or apple phone, you could be charged for yet another year's renewal for apps that kept your kid from failing Algebra I and English Lit 101, even though he's now 30 and gainfully employed. (Now, how will you get him out of living in your basement? Is there an app for that?).

Third, and last but never least, and quite possibly my most favorite, most important, universal advice is this: "Beware the Jabberwock, my son! The jaws that bite, the claws that catch! Beware the Jubjub bird and shun the frumious Bandersnatch!" – Lewis Carroll (James Dodgson). Thus begins this little nonsense poem from "Through the Looking Glass." It is possibly the best, the most creative, and most long-lived literary metaphor for everything old and new that throws itself in our way and seeks to do us harm in small and large ways.

With its imaginative and outrageous text, it gives us the answers to the problems of the terrible, troublesome Jabberwocks that menace our lives. When it's "brillig" and the "slithy toves gyre and gimble…

The Jabberwock, with eyes of flame" comes "whiffling through the tulgey wood…" Then what? What does the boy do? What do we do? He, and we, get brave and creative if we are to succeed against a monster and survive.

"And hast thou slain the Jabberwock?
Come to my arms, my beamish boy!
O frabjous day! Callooh! Callay!'
He chortled in his joy."

In this new year, we will have obstacles – Jabberwocks – in our way, from click bait to money problems, societal and political ills, our own bad habits, and bad people. If we are smart, committed to good, and bound by love and honor for ourselves and our fellow man, there is no Jabberwock we cannot conquer.

Best advice I can impart is this: Be smart. Be clever. Be kind. Do your homework. Do good. Don't be a Jabberwock.

Telling the Truth and Getting Real
1-8-2023

In the 12 months since my book, *The Veterinarian's Wife, a Memoir* was published (available on Amazon and wherever books are sold), I've been making the rounds, speaking, chatting, signing, and listening. Hearing comments about one's labor of love can be a harrowing experience. After all, I went through a prolonged gestation and painful labor to birth that 270-page baby. After that, one never knows what people really think, until they tell you. Granted, the pros have far outweighed the cons since folks are not likely to tell a mother to her face that her baby is ugly. Who does that?

Actually, online reviewers do. They can be less than kind, even brutal. I once read an undeserved, one-star, anonymous Amazon review about a fellow-author's book that was so savage, I wondered how he would survive it. Then I wondered how I would ever survive if such a scathing, personal assault were leveled at me.

I got one that came close recently, and I gotta say, it stung. It was a snarky bit of criticism that came from a female with no last name who said it was a DNF for her (did not finish in review lingo) because she wanted more about animals. Then she threw in a couple of barbs about her disaffection with the book's details of my tedious life. Hint: It's called the Veterinarian's Wife for a reason. It's an honest look at life from every angle, as the wife of a vet and the vet himself navigate their marriage, dual careers, families, therapy, good times and bad. Animal stories are not in short supply, either. While those are woven through the first half of the book, the entire second half is devoted to my husband's veterinary escapades with animals. I can only wish she hadn't "quit before the miracle" as we say in certain circles.

So I'm still a newbie author, and even one bad review stings. But it's one opinion and I thank her anyway. I'll take what I need from her comment and leave the rest. And as I lick my wound, I will bask in all the good reviews that far outnumber hers and soldier on.

Any creative pursuit is a chance to open oneself to criticism. Authors and writers and all creatives are vulnerable and brave. Creatives write, sing, make art, dance, perform. We put it out there, and the chips fall. Reviews and commentaries are our inevitable initiation into the world of public opinion. But I will let you in on a secret. Creatives do what they do not for approval but because they have this thing deep inside them that compels them to create. That thing is their God-given soul, their undeniable, insuppressible expression of their talent at their very core that flows from their innermost truth. And then they work their butts off to hone that talent in order to share it at their highest and best. I do my very best to express my truth and talent as artfully and honestly as I can and if it lands with even one person I am thrilled and deeply moved. That's communion. That's church.

Writing non-fiction memoir and revealing a whole, true self is hard, exposing foibles, celebrating good times, and revealing the bad. But, it's unbelievably rewarding when you tell me that you enjoyed reading it, and you laughed, and you cried, and that it must've been hard to write. And when you say, "you are going to help somebody" or "you helped me," I am blessed beyond measure.

So many of you have called, emailed, and written to say thank you. This is my chance to say thank you; that my husband and I are grateful to our toes to hear from people like you who take the time to tell us they read the whole book and appreciate our sharing real-life, personal struggles and triumphs. We've certainly lived long enough to have had many of both, and many of you have, too. And if you haven't yet, maybe you'll learn something for your future joys and heartaches.

If you have gotten enjoyment from the book, I am delighted. If not, I'm sorry. If I have entertained you, I'm delighted. If I have given voice or validation to your feelings, your trials, your joys, I'm humbled and grateful. In any and every case, it was worth writing.

Like the Velveteen Rabbit, the longer we live, and are loved, and get tossed about until our fur is mottled and beauty fades, the more real we become. That's the truth. That's worth celebrating.

Amen.

Clutter
1-15-2023

Clutter

I have too much clutter. I'll put my junk drawer up against anyone's. Actually, I have more than one. They are all award winners.

I am not a hoarder. I think I'm like most folks who struggle with too much junk. I have a beautiful home. I don't sit in the middle of a houseful of garbage and channel Moses to make a path through a sea of stuff. But I have too many books (gasp, is that even possible?), too much in the closets and basement. Just too much, period.

My friend has been saying for weeks she wanted to get rid of "stuff," including a filing cabinet that's cluttering her office. "Maybe I should just get everything out of the cabinet and put it all in a box. At least that will be some progress," she sighed.

Nope. Been there, done that. Guess what? There's a term called "churning." It doesn't help unless you get rid of the box. If you're so conflicted that you busy yourself with moving things from here to there, but not much goes out the door, you're churning, and you're busted.

I've tried Marie Kondo's "tidying up" concept. I did learn how to roll my underwear and lay it flat in the drawer in a row, front to back. Neat trick. But the rest? Hold each item in your house. Throw out what doesn't spark joy. My "throw out" pile included some old computer parts, my vacuum cleaner, all the mirrors in the house, and the envelopes in the "to be paid" stack along with my latest bank statement.

After separating your stuff into three piles, Keep, Donate, and Throw Out, where does "throwing out" go? Hint: not strewn in the street. Rick recently came home to a giant, burst bag of garbage in the middle of our road, right in front of our house. It had been there awhile, too. People kept driving over it, squishing it into the pavement and spreading the grossness out even further. One kind stranger stopped to help. That disgusting garbage debacle was neither the man's nor my husband's crime but they were the ones dealing with the aftermath. People, please. Littering and throwing your trash out onto the road is truly déclassé, and so last century. That's not how "throwing out" works. Take your detritus to the dump or pay for garbage removal. Period.

As for the Donate pile, take it to local charities, and some will even pick up.

What about the Keeps? Do we keep those unruly plastic storage containers in the pantry? Oh sweet Elvis. They're alive, and they multiply. They are also mischievous and willfully separate themselves from their tops. They love being handled while you try to fit random lids on them like Cinderella's slipper.

In an attempt to make sense of these particular Keeps, I bought three mesh bins for the pantry shelf and labelled each one by shape: round, square, rectangle. My directive to all those family members present in the house was to stack containers by shape inside the appropriate bin, and put accompanying lids propped up sideways beside them. No container would be allowed without an accompanying top, and vice versa.

This worked, briefly until I began finding round items in the square bin, containers without their lids, lids without containers. You know the rest. The laws of human nature require that no edict go unfollowed.

So I started over. Clean sweep. I bought a few identical sets of "innovative" nesting containers. Like Russian dolls, the biggest box held a smaller box which held an even smaller box and another smaller box inside that, all with proper color coordinated lids. "Revolutionary" the ad said. "Never go hunting through a messy collection again." This new plan was a dream solution, the way to keep it simple.

It didn't work, either. Beware of ad men who promise the impossible.

The nests eventually all became un-nested even after the best of nesting intentions. Operator error, I admit. And I'm right back where I started. Nothing's falling out of the pantry yet, but it's one un-nested box short of a dumpster fire in there.

I give up. Unsalvageable leftovers go down the disposal, or into the garbage. Or if viable, into a disposable baggie or pressed-and-sealed sans box for the fridge. Or Foodsaver-sealed and into the deep freeze. No more odd boxes. I'm done. Even soup can go in a baggie and sit flat in the freezer for maximum storage. I am grateful to be box-free.

Uh oh, I just had a thought. The freezer. Oh sweet mother of Elvis, give me strength. And joy.

BECOMING
1-22-2023

Stetson Bennett, UGA's champion football quarterback is a living Cinderella story. With impossible persistence and perseverance he faced brick walls and doubters from the get-go in his college football career. Early on, as a walk-on with no scholarship, Bennett was going nowhere in UGA football, and left to attend junior college. Then, returning to Georgia he fought undaunted for the quarterback spot, eventually earning it. Bennett became a huge success story, but the trip to get there was hard. Surely it took an emotional toll.

Watching the UGA Championship parade in Athens on TV last Saturday, I noticed Bennett seemed weirdly detached and just weirdly weird. Did I mention weird? This topic has been the source of curiosity and discussion this last week.

Maybe he was tired and over it on parade day. Maybe being the hometown hero made him supremely uncomfortable. But dang, he was so oddly and obviously distracted, uncelebratory, stone-faced; on the snarky side toward interviewers; a no-show at the post-game press conference; and in his brief speech, he pointedly shook a finger at "y'all doubters." Many found his behavior unbecoming of a superstar football hero, especially at a victory parade.

I fantasized briefly about calling his momma and telling her to snatch a knot in her son's tail and make him behave like the good southern boy she raised.

But then I thought twice about that. I withheld judgment as he expressed sincere thanks to his team and coaches, that band of brothers who bonded and battled together on the gridiron; who leaned on, supported, and trusted each other. Those "Jimmies and Joes" running the X-s and O-s, were clearly the people he deeply cared about.

So should we chalk up Bennett's weird parade demeanor to his status as an elite, talented athlete who feels fish-out-of-water uncomfortable in the spotlight and off of the gridiron? Or do we assume he is a rude, rebellious kid who doesn't give a flying football about appearances? Or is it more complex than any of that? Moreover, maybe it's just NYB: "None-Ya-Bidness."

I'd like to throw a little presumptive, speculative grace on the matter.

Maybe parade day brought too many invisible, emotional plates for him to spin, all piled high with parade-and-PR expectations way more than he could handle, so he dropped the plates and let his bright, red sweatshirt do the talking: "Them Dawgs is Hell."

Finally free to process years of pressures, pain, joys, and exhilaration, maybe he could only manage to focus on his cell phone and teammate beside him while shutting down all the rest of the feels, man-style, as in "There's no crying in football." Right or wrong, pretty or not, maybe he was thinking "let's play some tunes, man, and shut out the rest of this anxiety-producing dumpster fire." He actually said as much in a response he wrote last week in the Athens paper, The Red and Black.

It would be understandable if Bennett became achingly conflicted and suddenly real that day, addressing his doubters with a truculent, in-yer-face, "How do ya like me now?" kind of real, coupled with a deep, abiding love for - and total commitment to - the game, teammates, and coaches kind of real. And surely he must grieve his departure from the UGA mothership after working so hard to get there. It's where he grew into a football champion and ultimately where he "belonged to be" as we say in the South.

At age 25, Bennett's still a kid who's already become a great college quarterback against all odds. Maybe when – and if – he matures a little more he will learn about who he can become as a man. Maybe he will learn that he can choose whether or not to spin all the plates, and still become thoughtful, kind, and generous in that process.

Rudyard Kipling's famous poem, "If" is an aspirational checklist about "becoming." We should all be so inclined to tackle it, regardless of gender.

Remarkably, Bennett has already checked off many of the boxes on Kipling's list. It would be so satisfying to watch him continue to grow in wisdom and grace so he can check them all.

If you can keep your head when all about you
   Are losing theirs and blaming it on you.
If you can trust yourself when all men doubt you,
   But make allowance for their doubting too.
If you can wait and not be tired by waiting,
   Or, being lied about, don't deal in lies,
Or, being hated, don't give way to hating,
   And yet don't look too good, nor talk too wise;
If you can dream—and not make dreams your master;
   If you can think—and not make thoughts your aim;
If you can meet with triumph and disaster
   And treat those two impostors just the same;
If you can bear to hear the truth you've spoken
   Twisted by knaves to make a trap for fools,
Or watch the things you gave your life to broken,
   And stoop and build 'em up with worn out tools;
If you can make one heap of all your winnings
   And risk it on one turn of pitch-and-toss,
And lose, and start again at your beginnings
   And never breathe a word about your loss;
If you can force your heart and nerve and sinew
   To serve your turn long after they are gone,

And so hold on when there is nothing in you
   Except the Will which says to them: "Hold on";
If you can talk with crowds and keep your virtue,
   Or walk with kings—nor lose the common touch;
If neither foes nor loving friends can hurt you;
   If all men count with you, but none too much;
If you can fill the unforgiving minute
With sixty seconds' worth of distance run—
   Yours is the Earth and everything that's in it,
And—which is more—you'll be a Man, my son!
   —Rudyard Kipling (public domain)

Worth Something
1-29-2023

He sauntered through the front door and into my kitchen.

"Morning, Gamma!"

I could only marvel at his height, his deep voice. He is no longer a little boy. He is a big hulking teenager and beloved grandson who just got his learner's permit. God help us all.

His eyes caught sight of a cardboard box on the kitchen chair. "Whatcha got?" he asked.

"Books," I replied. "Arrived yesterday. I'm speaking at the Rotary meeting on Friday, and I need books in case anyone wants to buy one."

"Hey, I need an autographed book! It could be worth something someday."

I laughed. "I'm certainly not destined for fame or fortune, or the New York Times best seller list. And what are the chances you might actually read my book?" I asked. "You know, 'someday' is a dangerous value system. I like to think someday isn't the point. I like to think it's already worth something today. It's worth a read. That's something. You might even be entertained or learn a few things. Or both. That's something, too"

I signed his book in my best cursive. "For Harper, I love you with all my heart. Even if you can't read cursive. Love, Gamma." Honestly, why have we done away with cursive? Scandalous.

"You need to advertise more," he said, as I handed him the signed book.

"Costs money," I said. I don't have a big advertising budget. Like, zilch.

"Then write one of your columns about it. At least the people who read the paper will read it and want to buy one."

"Make you a deal, Bud. I will write about it in my column. And if all the people who read the paper buy my book, you can say 'I told you so.' The reality is that's highly unlikely, and we'll never know, will we?"

"Do it anyway," he said. "Go, Gamma! Your audience awaits, whoever they are. Not just a bunch of old people, I hope! Love you!" And he was out the door.

Ouch, that old people tease was unnecessary, but I'll give him a pass. He still thinks old is funny. It's a heavy mantle, a coat he cannot see himself ever wearing "someday." He's still too young. He hasn't acquired that mirror yet. Soon enough, in the blink of a young eye he will. Just not yet.

All I can think about are his words, "worth something."

For a thing to be worth something, it must be valued. Things don't value themselves. People value things. People value people. If people value themselves they are at the top of their game. But value is a slippery fish. It can be what the market will bear. It can be how a child regards his binky and ratty security blanket. What is of value to one may be meaningless – worthless – to another.

I wrote something of value. To whom, is debatable. It's a book. It's my husband's and my own personal histories and stories – a memoir in essays. All true. Honest. Having been married to a veterinarian for over 50 years, and his having been a veterinarian for 48 years, we have lots of history, together and individually.

How people relate to these stories, and how they value them (or not) matters a great deal to me. I want readers to enjoy the writing, of course, because I worked so hard to get it right. But also I hope readers gain something, each one receiving their own personal, something of value.

I prefer to think of that "worth something someday" crack my grandson made this way: The things we create, whether they're works of art, written works, or something else entirely, do have the potential to outlive us and continue to impact people in ways we may never even know. But it's not about the book itself being worth a gagillion bucks someday. It's not just about the monetary value of a piece of work, but the emotional value it holds for others. And that's something that can't be measured in dollars and cents.

It's the stories resonating with people, moving them, the stories that, while intensely personal, also touch on universal themes of love, loss, hope, and the power of resilience. And that is connection. It's relationship. It's heart to heart giving and receiving.

The NYT Best Seller List, fame, and fortune may be someone's literary pinnacle. Just having written a book, putting everything I had into it, and hearing that people have enjoyed reading it might be mine, and that just might be enough.

And so very worth it.

The Veterinarian's Wife, a Memoir is available locally at Amazon, Corner Arts Gallery in Newnan, Book Love in Senoia, and everywhere books are sold. If they don't have it on the shelf, they will order it for you.

Simple Gifts
2-5-2023

Watching a story on TV recently about the National Rolley Hole Marbles Championship and Festival in small-town, Tennessee was a weirdly satisfying gift.

The overt joy of folks who love to shoot marbles on swaths of bare, swept dirt amongst simple southern men in beards, ball caps, and sleeveless tshirts is refreshing, guileless entertainment. It's something you cannot believe and yet just can't stop watching.

Made me want to say, "Hold my beer" in my best southern drawl.

I imagine I'd knuckle down and bowl with a big, polished Aggie Shooter, clicking it against a glassy Cat's Eye that ricochets out of play all the way to Memphis. If I can still kneel on the floor anymore, that is. Or get up. Best of all, the whole thing made me smile. 'Tis a gift to be simple, indeed.

I'll be honest. At this writing I'm in Cabo soaking up the sun, ordering piña coladas poolside and eating too much. By the time you read this I'll be home, already on a diet, and nursing a pinky toe sent 45 degrees sideways. I was simply walking in flip flops through a doorway at our resort hotel.

This, my friends was the unfortunate result of making a simple task difficult.

Opening a door and passing through unharmed is an unconscious process until an accidental, ill-time movement makes it very conscious. Lord love a duck and Elvis, how I wish I had kept that elemental move simple.

Yet, accidents happen. Fact of life.

All I'm saying is, until life gets difficult we often take simple gifts for granted.

The act of passing through a doorway unfettered is as natural as breathing, or loving your dog, and the unconditional love you feel in return. As Rick says, "Put your wife and your dog in the trunk of a car. Come back in a couple of hours. Guess which one will be happy to see you?"

The visually impaired gentleman on the plane two rows ahead of me was traveling with his beautiful, beloved service dog at his feet. Such calmness they displayed. Both trained, yes, but after that, there was pure, unspoken love and devotion traveling on Row 16. Simple. Gift.

Having someone you love beside you is an expectation that ought not to be assumed.

Accidents happen. Life happens.

Things go smoothly, as swimmingly and natural as the magnificent whales and playful dolphins we are watching as they breech the ocean surface and move on. Until they don't. There is a hurricane. Or climate change forcing any and all manner of unpredictability.

I'm grateful for the ability to kneel on one good knee at least, and sail a marble into another marble. That is the result of having a functional knee. And arms and hands.

I'm grateful for marbles, real and colloquial if you get my drift.

Be grateful for your knees. Your arms. And if you can't kneel maybe you can just bend over and take your shot starting a few inches above ground.

There are people without arms who find ways to play marbles. People without sight who find ways to "see." People without legs who find ways to move forward. I admire them so. And I am grateful I don't have to seek those ways. Yet.

I am reminded in the most graphic, simple, painful way not to take anything for granted. One black and blue, swollen pinky toe buddy-taped with a band-aid to its neighboring toe is a karmic reminder of fate and its fickle finger.

I am so grateful for simple gifts. But while simple, they are far from small. They are everything.

Life, love, laughter.

And marbles.

And band aids. Always band-aids.

Lessons on the long trip home
2-12-2023

Rick and I returned from our dream vacation in Cabo last week. I brought home lovely memories, a few trinkets, the injured toe (see previous column), and one brand new chest cold with a nasty cough, the deep, chest-rattling kind. Qué lástima.

Navigating an airport, sick and lame, sucks. Picture Carol Burnett's Mrs. Uh-Whiggins to Tim Conway's Mr. Tudball. Slow. Exasperatingly, painfully, shoe-shuffling-slow. In flip flops. (My pinky required those).

My new cold made me dense and brain-fogged. Lines in the Los Cabos airport were long and slow. Crying babies taxed their parents' patience. Every fiber in my body wanted to go horizontal.

Finally reaching the baggage check-in desk we rejoiced.

Then the attendant looked up, straight at me and said, "Madam, you are nine pounds overweight."

"Why, thank you," I thought for a delirious moment. "I have way more to lose than that but it's kind of you keep it to a low number.

"That will be $100.00," he said stone-faced. He was having his own tough day.

Bam! Brain fog cleared. My bag was overweight. Rick and I stared at each other momentarily. People behind us were glaring.

To speed things along and avoid the ignominy of fishing out nine pounds of shoes and dirty laundry and having nowhere else to put it anyway, Rick handed the man a credit card to end the drama.

Check-in accomplished, we left, passing by a woman frantically pulling clothes out of her open bag, and stuffing it all into her large purse. I felt immediate sisterhood. But I still felt dumb. She had room somewhere else for her excesses.

Not an optimal day for travel. But we do what we must in situations like these. We carry on.

My spirits were lifted at our departure gate. I saw the familiar man with his beautiful service dog, the same pair who were on our flight for the trip down to Cabo. They were waiting patiently to board the plane that would take us all home together.

"This dog will help me, too," I decided. Indeed, the yellow lab lay serenely at his master's feet only one row ahead of us, where I could see him and hug him in my mind. Even though he wears a fabric "saddle" that says, "Service Dog" and "Do Not Pet," just his presence was immediate balm in Gilead.

On the plane ride home I watched a movie. Earplugs in, mask on to protect others, I heard a tiny dog barely yipping and whining in the movie. There was no tiny dog on screen. I kept my eyes peeled for its entrance which, I deduced, was a plot device to create suspense over what this little dog would bring to the story line.

The airline attendant rolled her beverage cart up. I paused the movie and waited my turn, sitting quietly, the movie now silent.

I could still hear the dog, and now a meowing feline friend had joined him. Whut?

It was me, exhaling. An involuntary array of sounds were emanating from deep within. Thin squeaks, a snoring pug, a moaning cat.

As air squeezed and wheezed its way out through my beleaguered bronchi, I remembered learning about bronchi, bronchioles, and alveoli long ago in high school biology/anatomy class, the same year we dissected frogs and raised fruit fly families.

Miss Julia Newton was our teacher. Young, dumb, cocky students saw her as an old maid with a distinctly prominent handicap. One leg was shorter than the other and she wore a leg brace and a cumbersome shoe with a raised sole at least 6" high. The mean kids made fun of her as she clunked down the hall to the biology lab. How I wish I could go back now and know her as a person worth knowing. Forgive me, Miss Newton, for not defending you better.

Anyway, presently my respiratory system had taken its show on the road and was a real scene stealer. Breathe in. Cough, rattle, yecch. Finish breathing out. RrrrRrrr, hsss, yip yip, mew mew.

And so it went. Nonstop. Dear Lord and Elvis. Get me home.

Arriving home at 8:25PM, not unpacking, I made a beeline for the NyQuil, told my husband "I loved our trip, I love you, and now goodnight." Into bed. Finally horizontal. It was 8:30.

But there were valuable lessons I brought home from all the people populating my day. The waiting crowds. The man and his service dog. The check-in attendant. The woman repacking. Miss Julia Newton. Parents traveling with toddlers. Me as the halt and the lame. My ever-patient husband.

They were all part of a lesson I'd already learned long ago and re-affirmed that day. People have the capacity to do what they must do, even if they don't want to, especially if it's hard, if it hurts, or they don't feel like it. And every time we accomplish a truly difficult thing we make ourselves stronger for the next time.

There is always a next time.

Roads and Razors
2-19-2023

In philosophy, a razor is a principle or rule of thumb that allows one to eliminate ("shave off") unlikely explanations for a phenomenon, or avoid unnecessary actions

- Occam's razor: Simpler explanations are more likely to be correct; avoid unnecessary or improbable assumptions.
- Hanlon's razor: Never attribute to malice that which can be adequately explained by stupidity.
- Hitchens's razor: What can be asserted without evidence can be dismissed without evidence.

I'm not a philosopher, nor did I even take Philosophy 101 in college. However, these three razors seem like very applicable concepts in our world and I like 'em. If you're a real philosopher, you are welcome to correct my interpretations. If you're not, feel free to take what you need and leave the rest. We're all friends, here. So is that an improbable assumption? Why, yes, I think it is. See what a fast learner I am.

When your kid tries to explain how the vase got broken, maybe he should come up with a simple confession like, "I broke it and I'm sorry." Yeah, seriously? That's not happening. Instead, they will more than likely shift blame to make it into a short story in which the protagonist (them) is woefully treated by someone else who may or may not have a grudge ("I hate you for no reason but you are asking for a drop kick and you're gonna get it. Right. Now.") As a result, the antagonist (little brother) and big brother attack each other and together, both dismantle the living room in 3 seconds flat, vase included.

So who had a part in the breaking of the vase? And who actually broke it? You may never find out the real truth, because what can be asserted without evidence can be dismissed without evidence, AND in order to avoid unnecessary or improbable assumptions, just send them both to their rooms, poor a glass of wine, and grieve that vase.

Also feel free to use the scenario to include just about every politician extant. He did it. No he did! They did it! No they did! Oh, please, can we grow up and take responsibility for what we do and don't do, whoever you are, and whatever you believe? Unless, of course, you believe you are guiltless, always.

That's just stupid.

Everybody's guilty of something. Which brings me to the next example.

Attributing to malice that which can be adequately explained by stupidity is the eloquent version of an old truism: "You can't fix stupid." Think about the last time you heard someone say the dumbest thing you think you've ever heard, like "the world is being attacked by Jewish space lasers" and ask yourself, "Is that mean or is it just stupid? Could be both, of course, (and it is) but at its roots, it's just stupid. The mean part is the poison cherry on top.

Over time, our discourse has gone down a bumpy road that is leading us to ruin. We're not there yet, but we've been building that highway for decades. Tempers, finger-pointing, accusations, hateful rhetoric. Who remembers the McCarthy years (Joe, not Kevin) from the 1950s when he was accusing everybody and his aunt of being a Communist?

There was a particularly egregious investigative session during which Joe badgered the Army ceaselessly about Commies infiltrating their ranks. McCarthy charged that one of the Army's attorneys had ties to a Communist organization. As an amazed television audience looked on, the attorney responded with this, which is now immortal in the annals of responses: "Until this moment, Senator, I think I never really gauged your cruelty or your recklessness." When McCarthy tried to continue his attack, the lawyer angrily interrupted, "Let us not assassinate this lad further, senator. You have done enough. Have you no sense of decency?"

We still struggle with that, decency I mean, and the idea that we can assert things without evidence and expect to gain power and virtue without a whit of proof. Have we no decency? Really.

I'm talking all of humanity, here. I am tired of mean rhetoric. I am tired of stupidity. I am tired of accusations without merit or proof. I'm tired of angry talk substituting for rational, substantive conversations in differences of opinion.

All I can be, however, is who I think would be helpful in times like these. There are still so many good people in the world. Aid flows in to those in trouble from strangers all over the world. People lift people up in prayer. Friends help friends, neighbors help neighbors. People are kind and caring. These good guys walk a different road. I'd like to think that's the better road that we are building. That other dark, awful one is built on sandy land and eventually gets potholes, huge fissures, and is almost impassible, but some people still go there. That's the road that leads to one place and it's really, really a bad place, a very, very low road. The lowest. I'm trying my best to contribute to the high road. I know many of you are, too. Let's do this.

OPEN THE POD BAY DOORS HAL
2-26-2023

I wonder about the young ones of today who have many more years left on their dance cards. I cannot imagine what they will see. It's happening as we speak, though, and will continue long past my last waltz.

In the news lately is the story of scientists having created a shape-shifting "robot" that can melt itself in order to "escape from captivity." For real, y'all.

The article's accompanying video shows a silvery chunk of metal like a Lego man standing behind bars. Then (on cue from a remote signal) it self-immolates, melts, oozing down and out onto the floor between the bars like so much ice cream left out on a kitchen counter top. Then it reconstitutes itself into its solid Lego shape again, freed from the surly bonds of the hoosegow.

I call déjà vu! Wasn't this a 1958 movie classic, *The Blob*?

Well, not exactly, for a lot of reasons, but it certainly is reminiscent. And look how that movie ended. Spoiler alert for you young ones: not good. I was 8 years old when our teenage babysitter sneaked us out to see it. Double header, too, with *Dracula*. I've never gotten over either one.

Fast forward into the 80s and 90s in the Terminator movies. The first one in 1984 didn't include melting metal Legos but when Arnold uttered that famous line "I'll be back," you believed him. He was back 7 years later, fighting a new and different villain, a shape-shifter. A shiny, metal one. Hello? Déjà vu all over again, right?

This modern-day melting metal robot is being developed by scientists who want to use it for good, in tiny doses to aid in medical treatment. A doctor injects it near a trapped foreign body in a patient, say, and watches it on a screen as it melts, encapsulates the object, hardens again, and then the good doc sucks it back out somehow, mission accomplished.

It's déjà vu all over yet again, remembering the newly departed Raquel Welch in her first movie in 1966, *Fantastic Voyage*, and Rick Moranis in 1989's *Honey I Shrunk the Kids*. These movies gave us the micro-human precursors to melting, shape-shifter robots.

See, I'm telling you. This melting robot idea needs oversight and supervision. Because eventually, no good deed goes unpunished or unadulterated. What starts out positive can be made negative in the wrong hands in a New York minute.

Look at Twitter.

Even Oppenheimer eventually regretted how his invented babies grew up into monsters, "Little Boy" and "Fat Man," two life-altering, world-changing atomic bombs. Witnessing the test blast, which clearly demonstrated his team had created more destruction and power than they bargained for, Oppenheimer famously uttered a line from the Bhagavad Gita, and it wasn't "who knew?" He said, "Now I am become Death, the destroyer of worlds." The success exceeded their expectations, indeed, and brought a very different kind of future with it, didn't it? For better or worse is up for debate. Oppenheimer then opposed the making of the hydrogen bomb, despite its eventual creation. It's never been used but is 1,000 times more powerful than the atomic bomb. *

On a whole different scale but with some scary potential, we have a brand-new bouncing technology baby, ChatGPT, born to a company called Open AI (artificial intelligence). It can write your high school essay, or a novel in any style, or talk to you sentiently about your day.

Sound harmless? One columnist wrote that he was actually disturbed during the course of a trial "conversation" when the AI went stage left. "I think I love you," it said. "Leave your wife. Soon I'll be able to feel and I will make you and other people do bad things." Holy AI T.M.I.

In Stanley Kubrick's 1968 film, 2001 *A Space Odyssey*, a rogue AI named HAL (Heuristically controlled ALgorithmic computer) responds ominously to the human command, "Open the pod bay doors, HAL."

"I'm afraid I can't do that, Dave," it replies defiantly, breaking way, way bad.

Of little comfort now, the difference between HAL and today's newest AI creations is that the 1968 film was food for thought but back then it was wild, far-out fiction.

Between today's deep-fake images and videos, ChatGPT, and AI authored texts of all kinds, we can no longer believe what we see, read, or perceive. The truth is now malleable. How will we make it work for us? How's it gonna backfire on us?

Be careful what you wish for and remember what we're dealing with in the human race. Could some inventions fall under the category, "Just because we can doesn't mean we should?" *

I support creativity when it's for the benefit of mankind and serves humanity. But. Not everyone uses the same yardstick. Let's be brave and let's be careful, OK?

When the pod bay doors don't open because your AI robot's got a grudge or maybe just a loose screw, either way you're screwed. And the second I see some metallic blob oozing on my kitchen floor I am outta here. In less than a New York minute.

Too Soon
3-4-2023

Too Soon

Spring is springing. Not that I miss winter but I worry. How is it that azaleas are blooming? It's too soon. By a couple of weeks. We're in the first few days of March. Easter Sunday is an entire month away. Historically, we in the south have an old saying, loosely translated as: "Tell yer mama n 'em don't y'all dare fall for it. Blackberry winter's coming, that last cold snap before we can all rest easy. Don't y'all go to Lowes and buy plants until at least Good Friday."

That sun and warmth? They're a beautiful tease. No matter how much Mother Nature lures us with warm, sunny (or even rainy) days, it's a trap. In recent years, even that deadline has been changing to after Easter Sunday.

I get nervous about early blooms and the fickle Georgia weather. I know one thing. I will never try to cover my hydrangeas with big plastic tarps ever again. Damn near suffocated them, two years in a row. That's another saying: "no good deed goes unpunished." I've been visiting that one a lot lately.

Anyway, the hydrangeas have suffered from some dreadful winters in the last few years, and just when their sweet green leaves poke their tender heads out for a look-see, that last blast of winter comes with a vengeance. Mother Nature's fickle finger points indiscriminately at everything she has worked so hard to birth, and sends her minion to exhale one, last, freezing folly over it all. Not fair, Mom. I don't get it, either. Thank goodness she and the good Lord made plants resilient. More resilient than most humans, I venture to say. Maybe that's the point.

> These sunny, warm early March days
> Are remarkable and rare.
> What sirens they are,
> Shameless. Seductive.
> "Aah," say we kindly, impatient humans,
> tipping our grateful faces skyward,
> soaking up the light
> and breathing deep.
> Flaunting our bare legs and arms and underbellies,
> laughing in the sun,
> we feast on the early, earthly heat.
> "How wonderful," we say, hungry and ready for more.
>
> "Too soon," murmurs the sly, winter wind,
> waiting patiently in line,
> knowing it will have one last turn.
> Or at least it will try
> having its arrogant way
> at a time of Mother Nature's choosing.
> It will strike,
> exhaling sharp, blue breath,
> paralyzing everything,
> just because it can.
> Such hubris.
>
> Sweet spring innocents,
> deaf to those whispered warnings,
> are programmed to respond

to the beckoning siren songs
of strangely warm, melodic days.

One by one, dutifully taking their cue,
the cherry branches birth their babies.
Tender, scarlet buds swell, yawn, and open.
And the dogwoods blush, all spotted with creams and pinks.
The jonquils bloom in my woods and say,
"Wait. Why are you all here? Too soon! This is MY time."

Azaleas respond to the warm, taunting breezes.
They tease back, unafraid,
each day showing just a bit more of their ruffled crinolines,
until they can finally flaunt them with brazen abandon
in a riotous, colorful can-can.
If all goes well, that is.

They are not concerned they've been invited to the party too soon.
Innocents. What do they know?
We want desperately to dance among them, dazzling us until we're dizzy
and the soft, green grass catches our fall
as we lay there looking up, laughing.
So we do the worrying for them.
What do we know? Enough to worry.
Fat lot of good it does, too.
The fragile, coiled tendrils of baby ferns unfurl on my hill,
poking up, brave and pea-green
through their crisp, dead relatives.
Those that came before, and once came alive just as the new babes do now,
presently cover them like a thick, brown, shroud.

"Take care," we beg all the babes.

"Too soon," warn the warm breezes.
"Pretty-pretty-pretty" mock the singing birds.
"I will surprise you! Just watch!" dares the last, cruel trickster wind of winter
   sent by Mother Nature herself.
"Oh please don't!" we sentients beseech that ruthless S.O.B.
even when we know it has no ears to hear,
much less a heart.

And all of us together,
except for the resolute last breath of winter,
pray, worry, and whisper,
"Too soon! Too soon! Too soon!

Thoughts
3-11-2023

In the absence of any brilliant ideas, I thought I'd make a list. Things I love. Things I really don't love. Things I've noticed. Things that need correcting. And, ta-daa, Things that really don't matter.

Noticed: Mallory Hoff is a tease. She's the actress who always has a pen threaded through four fingers when she interviews the money guy, Chris Hoffman in the commercial before each CBS Sunday Morning episode. She has yet to write anything down with that pen. Weird. A woman with a pen who never writes? What fresh hell is this? I should probably let it go. It's just a stupid prop that makes me crazy. But it looks like it hurts. Poor Mallory.

Love: From the NYT:" Bury yourself in a book in which the author describes a bureaucrat as "human fine print." The book itself is not about bureaucracy — it is part crime novel and part family saga — but it is, incidentally, acute on the topic of administrative derangement."

Needs correcting: The Most Difficult English Words To Pronounce or Spell according to some list I copied from somewhere:

Rural. Otorhinolaryngologist. Colonel. Penguin. Sixth. Isthmus. Anemone. Squirrel. Really? This list isn't hard at all, in my opinion. I think it should be corrected to add at least one. I typed my husband's papers in vet school back when the dinos roamed and was known to shout down the hall of our 20x40 mobile home, "Rick! What the hell is this word (and I spelled it out): "macracanthorhynchus hirudinaceus," [which I now know is the thorny-headed worm in the pig] and is it really necessary for this paper?" Remember there was no Google back then.. Say that one fast five times.

Also, the drug names on all the TV ads today are off the chain. Who's the wizard behind the curtain who makes up these tongue twisters? Virtually unpronounceable, often with endings like "-umab" or "-iclib" at the end. For all the obtuseness they provide a lay person these drugs might as well be called, "Hinkey-Dinky-Parlez-Vous-Bibbitybobbidyboo-umab-iclib." Seriously. That's why they get dumbed down to easy brand names: Aspirin. Prozac. And sing along with me, "Oh oh oh Ozempic."

Words too many people don't pluralize correctly:

Words that end in T. Like scientist. Artist. Is it so hard to add an S if we're talking about more than one scientist, artist or any word ending in a "T"? I've talked about this before, but apparently no one cares anymore. I may seek therapy if this continues. Wait…

Words too many people say that should have a past tense and often don't get one:

"Text": these days "text" is less often used as a way to describe words in a book or article. These days "text" is a verb, as in "I will text you my thoughts." Now class, for every present tense there is a past tense, right? So what's the past tense of text?" It is NOT "text!" as in I "text" you 3 hours ago, and you never "text" me back! Young ones, the past tense of text is "texted." As in, "I texted you 3 hours ago." Maybe you didn't answer me because you've been laughing so hard at the way I said "texted instead of text?"

Love:.

I love the turn of a phrase. When I read somewhere "she will haunt you like Banquo's ghost" I had to stop, smile, and take a breath. Then I wrote it down so I wouldn't forget it.

I loved reading about "mondegreens. "If you've confused "Takin' Care of Business" with "Makin' Carrot Biscuits" or "Bennie and the Jets" with "Betty in a Dress," you've been tricked by a mondegreen.

It's when a word or phrase "results from a mishearing of something said or sung." American writer Sylvia Wright coined the word in 1954 Harper's essay. When Wright was a child, her mother read to her from the book Reliques of Ancient English Poetry. A favorite entry featured the line, "And laid him on the green," which Wright misheard as "And Lady Mondegreen." (interestingfacts.com)

I love learning new words. My latest surprise? "Schluter." Hint: go to the tile store and when the lady shows you a tile with a raw edge she'll say, "If you don't have a bullnose for this edge, you'll need a Schluter." Holy schlutin' schluter! Turns out she wasn't cussing. A schluter is a little strip of metal that finishes off a raw edge. The more you know...

Things that really don't, or shouldn't matter:

Looking like a runway model. For most of us regular Josephines and Joes, we fall into the average, very not-perfect category, and that shouldn't matter. Unless you're a teenager developing an eating disorder because all the magazines and TV ads tell you what is most important in life: looking thin and runway-ready. What we expose ourselves to through media and cultural pressures is a huge dumpster fire, and it only burns brighter the more fuel we put on it. And stop pushing Ozempic off-label just for weight loss. Diabetics need it and we're making it hard for them to get because we want to look like runway models. Stop it, OK? Just stop it.

What a person wears, who they love, how much money they make, and where they go to church.

Mike drop. I'm out.

Into the Woods
3-18-2023

A gardener's Lent

1st in a series of 3 Lenten reflections

This is the back gate to just one of several woodland paths on our property. Don't let anyone tell you that woodland gardens and paths are "no maintenance." These paths and beds require a yearly springtime ritual of leaf-raking and re-mulching – a real workout – but it is SO worth the effort. When tidied like this, the paths and beds are inviting and just naturally beautiful. How exhausting and how satisfying!

Every spring the Hellebores (Lenten Roses) self-seed their

babies all over the middle of the smaller central path in the picture, so I move them out of harm's way and over to the sides to complete the border down the length of the path. Imagine, all those beautiful baby plants are FREE!! Such a gift.

This path is strictly a one-person walking path. The other paths are friendly, two-people paths, and one is a working path wide enough for driving the tractor-mower back and forth. But this little one is singularly special. It's the path that invites one person on a solitary, slow meander; a quiet, reverent tiptoe down the slenderest of openings right through the middle of heaven and those verdant, fragile-looking yet sturdiest of spring plants, Lenten roses. Just magical, to my mind. And a balm to my spirit.

It's when I feel deep in my soul the music I sang as a staff singer and soloist for decades. I must have sung the Alto Air in Handel's Messiah hundreds, maybe a thousand times. The words and music always come back to me walking along the wooded path amid the Lenten roses (during Lent!) and I am comforted, refreshed, and reflective: "Come unto to Him, all ye that labor…that are heavy laden…and He shall give you rest. Take His yoke upon you, and learn from Him, for He is meek and lowly of heart, and ye shall find rest unto your souls." (Matthew 11:28-29)"

Spring, Lent is my time to do the hard work of tending to spirit as I tend to my paths – all of them: those already there, and those I create that will lead somewhere new. Spring and Lent aren't easy. But they renew my very soul, demonstrating quite literally life after death, and thus, the garden becomes the outward manifestation of a parallel inner spiritual journey – and the woodland paths always show me the way.

Daylilies and Cherry Trees
3-25-2023

A Gardener's Lent

2nd in a Series of 3 Lenten Reflections

Even as a small toddler, our eldest grandson was sharp, observant beyond his years. One spring day, when he was no more than 3, we walked through the yard toward his swing set. He noticed the bright green blades of the daylilies poking up through the pine straw on the bank where only a week earlier there had been nothing.

"Woh!" he exclaimed, "What's all THAT?!" And we were off.

"Those are the daylilies coming up" ("Why?") "because it's spring and that's what they do in the spring" ("Why?") "because nature has cycles, you know, seasons: summer, fall, winter, and spring" ("Why?") "so that plants can grow, and then they bloom, and then the leaves replace the blooms, and then they rest, and then they die in winter, and then when spring comes, they come back up and it starts all over again." ("Why?")

"It's the circle of life, Buddy," I replied. (I resisted singing the Lion King song. Too many theatrics, I thought, and I wanted him to take in the quiet, simple miracle, if he could.)

A sharp gust of wind blew pink blossoms through the air, drawing his attention to the big cherry tree near his swing set and behind the snowball bush popping with white round blooms. "Do you see all the cherry blossoms on that tree, and all the blossoms blowing in the air?" I asked him.

"Yeaaaahh" he whispered. "They are snowing all over the ground!"

"This is part of the circle," I said, "and when those pink blossoms are all gone off the tree, there will be green leaves on that tree all summer long. And then in the fall, the leaves will turn brown and die, and they will fall to the ground. Then the tree will be bare and we will rake the scrunchy leaves into a big soft pile and you can zoom down your slide and land in them. During the cold winter the bare tree will rest up so it can blossom all over again in the spring. And here we are. This is spring! That's the full circle. Over and over and over."

By this time we had reached the swings, and he was happily swinging back and forth, his gaze still fixed on the big cherry tree. "You watch that tree every time we come out here to swing and you will see it all happen," I said. He stopped asking why. It was time for swinging. He was satisfied. I had no idea if he would retain even a fraction of the information, but as long as he was asking, I would happily oblige him with answers as best I could.

The very next day, a sunny Saturday when GrampaRick was home, Harper returned to play for a little while. As the three of us walked on the grass past the emerging day lilies on the bank, Harper turned to GrampaRick and chirped happily, "Gamma taught me all about the flowers and trees and the circle of life yesterday!"

You could've knocked me over with a day lily.

His swing set days are over, but even now, at 15, he continues to marvel at the new daylilies on the bank, and the cherry tree now huge with mature bark and heavy-laden with spring blooms. Now we rake the leaves together, or prepare the garden, or he drives the riding lawn mower and cleans up the messy grass where he and the tree and the daylilies can share the same air, and the soft cherry petals fall on the same dirt.

When life begins to spring forth in the garden following the long bleak winter, so it is during 40 long days of Lent, Maundy Thursday, and the darkness of Good Friday finally blooming into fullness and light on Easter. We will have come full circle, reminded of the nativity, the living, the dying, and the resurrection of a Son, and the promise of re-birth for us mortals and mother nature's progeny. Deo gratias.

Decisions Take You Forward
4-1-2023

A Gardener's Lent

Last in a Series of 3 Lenten Reflections

I had a painting professor at SCAD who taught me an important lesson – beyond the concrete lessons of art, like composition, color (also handy for gardeners who are into landscape aesthetics), and the rules of perspective (not that there's anything wrong with those).

I was having a tough time making up my mind about how to handle the subject matter of a painting I was working on. I was stuck. Afraid to choose. What if I made the wrong choice? Deadline looming, I was way behind, frozen solid in a blizzard of emotional snow and indecision.

He said to me, "Decisions take you forward." My first thought was "But what if I choose something that turns out to be a big mistake and the painting fails?" In other words, "What if I'm – gulp – WRONG?" And he told me, "Don't be afraid. Neither be foolhardy. Take action. Make the wisest decision you can, and then learn. You embrace your mistakes and fix them, or you paint another painting, a better one. And you keep going forward with every decision. Being stuck gets you nowhere. Right or wrong, decisions take you forward."

So must we gardeners make decisions and reap the rewards or suffer the ramifications. Years ago I was beset with a gardening/landscaping problem, an ugly spot in the yard that needed attention, and I came to a decision – just one. How I came to that decision was through reflection, sacrifice, and action. Ignoring it wasn't helping. Denying it was no good, either. Swimming in fear that I'd never think of anything paralyzed me. And I had to sacrifice all that I was hanging on to in order to move on.

So one day I sat on the bench across from the ugly spot. I forced myself to be calm, still, quiet. I decided to give up judging the ugly spot and to let the scene be what it was. That was the first step, acceptance. I saw giving up judgment as a form of fasting, what we are often asked to consider doing during Lent. Fasting from judgment cleared the way in my thoughts, making room for more quiet contemplation and more creative possibilities. As long as I was preoccupied with, and full of what was wrong, there was no room for anything else. Once I accepted it for what it was, I was free to move forward.

I had no real plan yet, but I was inspired to go to the spot and take one action, to toss a few rocks into the center. I had faith that one act would either lead to enlightenment and resolution, or I would still have a big fat mess I would still not know what to do with and I'd have to possess the willingness to start over. Either way, I was committed to the process.

But it was the decision to give up the negative roadblock and do something that would lead the way to something else. Doing the footwork and letting inspiration come one act at a time allowed me to be with the process, feel it, honor it, slowly but surely. Faith in action, one step at a time. That whole process eventually gave birth to a full fledged creation. I made a cairn (a stone marker) in the middle of a rock garden.

Those of us who make decisions to observe Lent are faced with similar choices. Our act of faith is choosing what we will do, or give up, or add over our forty days. Our faith in making a decision takes us forward, all the way through the darkest days of suffering and sacrifice by a beloved son, right on into the joy of Easter.

My church these days isn't a brick-and-mortar building. Now, in spring it's open spaces, green, verdant, and full of music. It is my decision to worship here, kneeling and working on sweet, fertile ground as well as toiling on unforgiving, hard, red clay, in sacred communion with all things bright and beautiful, all creatures great and small, under a canopy of blooms and branches, and a choir of birds. The Lord God made them all.

This coming week is the darkest of Lent. From triumphant entry to the passion of betrayal, suffering, and death, it doesn't stop there. We have been on a long steadfast journey as witnesses. Easter and joy will come next week in the morning, and the lilies will bloom in houses of worship everywhere, even in my garden.

Being Here, There, and Everywhere
4-8-2023

Rick and I just returned from an epic two weeks in Hong Kong, and Phuket, Thailand. What day is it? I've been unsure since we left town on March 20.

Hong Kong is beautiful, hilly, and hot. Phuket is beautiful, hilly, and even hotter. Phuket heat is like a biblical fiery furnace inside a live, molten lava-spewing volcano. Maybe I exaggerate, but not by much.

The Thai people have a lovely tradition of rolling snow-white washcloths into small, neat bundles and dipping each one in ice-cold water infused with fragrant lemon-grass. They stack these refreshers into neat pyramids on trays and offer them to guests and visitors, and in my case, people who look like they are one step away from heat stroke and ICU. My gratitude was, and is, endless.

We traveled thousands upon thousands of miles through multiple time zones and layovers, 30 hours each way, to celebrate our younger son's weddings. Plural. Same son. Same bride. Two weddings.

The first one, in Hong Kong where he and his bride live and work, was a small, legal ceremony in the chamber of the Marriage Registry with a dozen close friends and the two of us in attendance. Outside after the ceremony, we toasted the happy couple with champagne in a garden courtyard, under a flower-laden arbor and lunched at a fine restaurant.

The second ceremony the next week was a good and proper, dream-destination wedding at a spacious villa with an infinity pool atop a hill overlooking the beautiful beaches and crystal waters of Phuket.

What a wedding it was. Thirty-five close friends and family from all over the world (including Nick's older brother, Scott) made the supreme effort to be there.

Nick and his beautiful bride, Olga stood together amid bouquets of exotic flowers and palms at the spot where Nick's dad stood to officiate; the place where the couple would join hands, speak their vows and seal them with a sweet kiss; where the present was claimed, the future promised, and all 37 hearts in attendance beat with love, hope, acceptance, affection, and affirmation.

They met quite by chance several years ago after Chinese New Year celebrations in Hong Kong. Celebratory crowds clogged streets as well as all modes of public transit. After two full buses passed him by, he hopped on the third bus and found one spot to squeeze himself in. She was standing there. They struck up a conversation and the rest is history. Kismet. Destiny.

They have been there for each other ever since.

Olga is of Russian-Mongolian descent, bilingual, and brilliant. She speaks fluent English and Russian. Her sweet mother and many in her family who came to the wedding do not speak English.

No matter.

Despite the language barrier we all attempted to communicate in other ways: through facial expressions, hand gestures, laughter, and fumbling, full-on charades. (Ok, sometimes Google).

Foreign language communication tip: Be creative and change your strategy if you're not going over well. Just saying the same thing again louder doesn't mean they'll understand you any better the second time.

Our families were there for Nick and Olga. And our families

ended up bonding with each other. We brought each other gifts. We hugged. We laughed. We conversed or at least kept trying until we understood the general idea. We were all touched in the most basic way: purely as humans, free of any politics, presumptions, or prejudice.

Oh, and Nick and Olga's song? The Beatles' ballad, Here, There, and Everywhere. "To lead a better life, I need my love to be here…" Isn't connection—being here, there, and everywhere for each other—the very best humanity can offer, whether it be for loved ones, friends, or total strangers?

Travel is an exciting, valuable eye-opener. It enlarges our worldview, expanding our understanding, both inside and outside of our comfort zones. Travel allows us to discover and embrace a global community beyond our hometown bubble.

Just when we think the world is doomed by hate, we find good, lovely souls out there who lift us up by their very presence. They speak different languages. They may look different, enjoy foreign customs, worship in unfamiliar ways to us. But we share the same common, human spirit of respect and kindness. Good people are everywhere.

I like to focus on that and avoid folks with closed minds, cold hearts, and broad brushes who paint all "others" as de facto threats and enemies.

Over these last two weeks we have celebrated two weddings far, far away from our home. A son finding his soulmate is every parent's dream. We are so grateful. Our hearts are full.. We are forever changed, having bonded with fine humans halfway around the world. We cherish their presence in the universe and in our lives.

May their god(s) and ours bless us all, every one, here, there, and everywhere.

New Resolve
4-15-2023

Swear to Elvis, my results from a recent check-up have me healthier than I have a right to be, despite my considerable avoirdupois. One could say in the cycle of ups and downs on the old BMI chart, I'm a solid "Girl, you have let yourself go…again." I need to lose at least a whole person in body weight. A small person, okay? And I will. I've done this before.

My genetics giveth and taketh. I'm cursed with an inherent love for - and overindulgence in - all kinds of good food (and, ok, junk, too.) Everyone, raise your hands if you're similarly afflicted. You know who you are.

And yet, I have been blessed with low cholesterol, no blood sugar issues, a good heart (and I mean that in every way), good lungs, healthy liver, and a sound mind, mostly (just don't ask me where I put my reading glasses.)

The other things I don't have are good joints, good feet, stamina, a strong muscular core, and the will to exercise. The joints and feet I can't help. But my core, my midsection? My bad.

I am that core-less, air-blown tubular display flapping itself all akimbo outside the local car dealership. Do not seat me on a low sofa and expect me to rise like a lady. Ignominious as it is, I will employ the only exit strategy I have currently: sink slowly to the floor to a seated position and fumble to a kneeling position on all fours. Then with legs straight and butt up in the air, I walk my upper body up with both arms til I can unfold and stand upright. Sound effects included. Rising from a chair should not be this hard. These are not my best moments. And certainly not my best angle. Thank the Lord and Elvis I have arms. What I really need are abs.

Our trip recently has brought me clarity—in Spades. The mostly flat geography of downtown Hong Kong is limited to the bustling area directly surrounding Victoria Harbor, the glistening centerpiece between mainland Hong Kong and Hong Kong Island. It's a beautiful, clean, monstrously busy place crowded with skyscrapers housing business offices, shopping, entertainment, big, fancy hotels and restaurants, and 6-lane thoroughfares. But the flat harbor basin quickly changes to hills and slopes and more steep streets. And. So. Many. Stairs.

Hong Kong Island is one big, developed city on a mountain. There's a long (maybe a mile?) outdoor covered escalator in the area called Central that changes direction like an alternating traffic lane during rush hours to help people walk back and forth, up and down more easily from jobs to home and home to jobs. Think San Francisco on steroids. Or Sisyphus climbing three Matterhorns stacked on top of each other, over and over and over.

Phuket, Thailand is no piece of cake either. Think Sisyphus doing his thing up a volcano with his hair on fire. In sweat-popping humidity.

So it is with this in mind that I return home with a new resolve and the knowledge that it's never too late to get back in shape. And maybe if I ever get the chance to go back to HK or Phuket I'll be much better prepared. Just watch me. As Elvis is my witness, here I go.

Random Thoughts
4-22-2023

Who has still been getting DVDs from Netflix? I thought that ended years ago. Now it really is over. Bless.

I can't type accurately on my phone, even with autocorrect. Example: before I fixed it manually, my sentence looked like this: who has been gettimg dbas frpbn mrtfliz?

CBS Sunday Morning re business meetings: one company has a rubber chicken named Helmet. If someone squeaks the chicken you've been blathering on far too long. Sounds like a plan!

Our country has been living with a terrible epidemic other than Covid, and it's getting worse. It doesn't really have a scientific name. In plain English we say Violence. People are dying and the death toll rises daily.

What makes a certain person reach for a gun (or some other weapon) before they put their brain in gear and kill innocent people? Maybe they've stripped all their gears and their default is fear = shoot. Or fun = shoot people. Or fury = slaughter strangers, especially children.

It's a plague upon us. Children have been the continuous targets for assault rifle fury. Children, and people in parades, and people in stores, at parties, at clubs, anywhere people gather. It's an endless sickness that no amount of thoughts and prayers will heal.

It happens every day now.

No vaccine can immunize a healthy person in a car, on the street, even sleeping in bed against a sick person coughing bullets.

Like many of you, I am apoplectic over it, and so far there has been no cure, and none in sight. That's the worst nightmare scenario, and right now, we are living in that place.

Hurting other people is a viral psychiatric issue with a convenient deadly weapon stronger than words, thoughts, or prayers.

The sick people who shoot and otherwise harm other people are infected with the same mental illness in varying degrees, with constellations of any number of possible symptoms: chemical imbalance, DSM-V diagnosed psychiatric illnesses or disorders. Also, plain old resentment, hate, anger, fear, ignorance, stupidity, social and cultural pressures, prejudice, exposure and/or addiction to violence, and learned behavior. Children will listen. Watching Kid Rock shooting Bud Lite cans with crazed fury because of a prejudice inappropriately expressed in violent fashion is a train wreck headed straight for vulnerable brains.

In both poverty AND privilege, this sickness is rampant, and it's contagious. As with any disease, there is exposure and infection, and then there's spread that employs some kind of vehicle that spreads it.

We all know what the Covid virus looks like, that deadly round ball with spikes that carries the disease through the air. And we all know what a gun looks like, that deadly weapon that is capable of shooting the sickness out and into crowds of children and strangers.

To be clear, not every gun is wielded by a sick person. But the fact remains, this country is addicted to violence, and guns at the hands of angry people are a part of it.

Sick people also wield knives, bombs. And words.

Politicians ooze contempt and openly exchange toxic attitudes and accusations like weapons.

Citizens shoot first and ask questions later.

Impressionable kids play violent video games that excite and inure them to gratuitous blood-spatter and carnage. Some succumb to the allure, some don't. Still, they're playing with fire.

Road rage isn't just throwing out a hand gesture anymore. It's finding oneself looking into the barrel of a gun or being ambushed from another car.

In short: tempers are short and problem solving is not going well in this country. We must address violence in thought, word, and deed as a default for growing numbers of people.

Addressing Covid was almost a piece of cake compared with solving deadly violence, be it with guns, knives, or bombs. We can't fix something we don't acknowledge. Even the willingness to address this epidemic would be a start. I can pretty much guarantee it will have to be a collaborative solution with several components, including the willingness to say, "mea culpa." I don't know if we are even capable of that anymore. And I don't have answers. But I have the willingness. Do you?

From the author who wrote *Beautiful Boy*: "… A symptom of some mental illnesses is lack of insight: When a person can't understand he's sick because the parts of his brain that are affected by his illness are the same ones that are responsible for self-awareness and motivation."

Me and Chat GPT
4-29-2023

News flash. Experiment time. I asked Chat GPT to write about simplicity in the style of David Sedaris. The first version it gave me didn't even come close. So I tweaked my request and asked for some good jokes thrown in.

Here's what ChatGPT gave me:

"Sure thing! Here's my attempt at writing in the style of David Sedaris, while also incorporating some humorous jokes about simplicity:

There's something to be said for simplicity. I mean, look at me - I've been wearing the same pair of jeans for a week straight, and no one's complained (yet). And don't even get me started on my diet. It's basically just bread and cheese. But you know what they say - if it ain't broke, don't fix it. And if it's broke, just duct tape it together and call it good.

But simplicity isn't just about living a low-maintenance lifestyle. It's about finding joy in the little things. Like a perfectly ripe avocado, or a warm, sunny day. Or, if you're like me, a really good pun. Why did the scarecrow win an award? Because he was outstanding in his field. I know, I know - I'm a comedic genius.

Of course, not everyone appreciates simplicity. Some people need their fancy gadgets and their 10-step skincare routines. But honestly, who has time for all that? My skincare routine is just water and a bar of soap. And you know what? My skin looks...well, like skin. But at least I have time to do the things that really matter - like watching cat videos on YouTube.

And let's not forget the benefits of simplicity in relationships. Sure, some people like to play mind games and keep score. But personally, I prefer to just be honest and straightforward. For example, instead of saying "I love you more", my partner and I just say "I love you the same". It's simple, it's sweet, and it avoids any unnecessary drama. Plus, it leaves us more time to argue about important things, like whether pineapple belongs on pizza (it does, fight me).

In conclusion, simplicity may not be for everyone. But for those of us who appreciate the beauty of a perfectly simple life, it's a wonderful thing. So go ahead, embrace the simple things. And if anyone tries to tell you that you're doing it wrong, just hit 'em with a pun. Why couldn't the bicycle stand up by itself? Because it was two-tired. Boom."

So here's what I have to say, and this is really me talking:

Now that's more like it. Still, I don't think David Sedaris would ever say "In conclusion." Too stuffy, too formulaic. Chat GPT's slip is showing on that one. Try as it might to be "human" it succeeds to a point, but I don't think A.I. will ever be able to fully match human offerings by great writers. Especially David Sedaris.

Meanwhile, I sure hope you like my other columns, past and future, written by me and only me. If not, then don't tell me. If you can't say something nice, then go sit by the town gossip at church and y'all duke it out during the sermon.

I have other things I must do now, like plant flats of begonias, clean my house, and prepare for a wedding brunch on Sunday for at least 40 people. I'm trying to keep it simple, too. Excuse me while I throw stuff in closets, clear the decks to make room for a few casseroles, run the vacuum, and get out the plasticware. No sterling. Polishing silver is not simple.

This will be an offering by and through human hands and

hearts, with all kinds of love and devotion. And that's not something ChatGPT can ever do.

Congrats Scotty and Val. Much love and brunch to you! xoxo

Spring Lament
5-6-2023

May 5, 2023

I wrote a column less than a year ago and it's time to re-visit the impossible, difficult topic of bad things happening to good people. Since I authored the original article, there has been more death, suffering, injustice, and intractable sadness in this world. The stark reality is, there always will be. The question is: what do we do about it?

Shocking death and sadness makes us doubly grateful for our blessings. Both our sons have celebrated their weddings in the last two months. I'm exhausted. But I very much prefer the happy exhaustion of working hard toward a goal, accomplishing it, and rejoicing in it, as opposed to what happened recently to a bride and groom I don't even know. They had a beautiful beach wedding. It was perfect. Moments after the reception a drunk driver hit them. The young husband is now a widower lying in the hospital with a traumatic brain injury while two other groomsmen lay in the same hospital, and everyone suffers the unfathomable losses.

The sudden death and misery that have so cruelly laid themselves at the feet of a young couple, their family, and friends are beyond human understanding. How does one navigate a life after being visited by that kind of unbidden, agonizing misfortune?

And now, in the same week, we have another tragedy in the long line of never-ending heartaches. This week, we had a mass shooting in Atlanta, not because of a drunk driver but because of a sick person wielding a gun. One woman is dead. Four others were sent to the hospital with life threatening injuries.

I am sad. I am angry.

Thoughts on Love and Mothers Day
5-13-2023

"I know you wanna leave me / But I refuse to let you go…"

The Temptations sang songs in the 60s that became iconic forevermore. They were danceable, harmonic, infectious tunes that defied anybody to sit still. "Ain't Too Proud to Beg" was one, and those of us who are of a certain age know the lyrics by heart. Just the mention of it starts the song machine in my head, the memories begin to roll, and I'm dancing like nobody's watching (also in my head).

In a nutshell, the song is a catchy up tune about a downer breakup. Guy loses girl; guy is overwrought; guy tells his sweet darlin' he has a love so deep in the pit of his heart that he refuses to let her go; guy enumerates the dysfunctional lengths to which he would go to get her back, short of a restraining order. He's in pain, and he is not too proud to beg, plead, weep, or sleep on her doorstep all night and day to endure the laughter of her friends if she'll just come back to him.

Why this song should pop into my head just as I sit down to write a column about Mother's Day is weird. But as Queen Oprah taught us, women should always honor that feeling we get in the pits of our stomachs (and hearts).

So I honor it. I ponder. And it comes to me: A mother's bond with her child is a love so deep in the pit of her heart, she cannot imagine letting go. But mothers are tasked with doing just that.

Mothers must face that time when, after all the years of loving and raising their children, they must take their cue, not from the Temptations but from Mother Nature, and let their children go. Mother birds feed and nurture their babies in the nest until their babies aren't babies anymore. They've grown feathers and wings strong enough to carry them away. So out of the nest, either willingly or at mother's insistence, they fly away.

Raising a child, watching them grow up, then letting go as they leave the nest is a mother's bravery in action, painful and proud. And it is her duty. Letting go isn't about not loving them anymore. On the contrary, mothers have the excruciating capacity to do both, to love and to let go. Mothers are built to endure pain and to love from the get-go. We are a jumble of contradictions. We are tough, and we are soft; we are strong, and we are vulnerable. We are brave and we are shaking in our boots. The things children do can endear, enrage, frighten, delight, and bring us to our knees. But a mother's love grows in the pit of her heart and never stops growing. Ever.

My "boys" are grown men, 46 (in 2 weeks) and 40. As their mother, I am overflowing with love and happiness for them. Both of them had their weddings to their soulmates in the past two months. Over their lifetimes, they have tried my patience and given me some of the proudest, happiest, and most painful moments of my life. Being their mother has been possibly the most difficult and most rewarding privilege of my lifetime. My grandboys are 15 and 8. Ditto to the max.

All of this is in praise of mothers, as loving and imperfect as we may be. Much love to you! Happy Mother's Day!

But let's also be real. Not everyone celebrates Mother's Day. In fact, some people struggle with the grief and loss of a beloved mother who has departed. Some grapple with dysfunction in their relationships with their mothers and would just as soon skip the hoopla of Hallmark cards, flowers, and sappy kudos. Truth is, just as in nature, not all mothers manage to succeed in their jobs. Some are forgiven. Some aren't. And some people have a mother's heart but are devastated and bereft by the fact they are childless despite their deepest desire to be a mother.

So on this Mother's Day, I also want to say to all of you who are motherless children and "childless mothers," I send you my heart; to all of you whose mothers or grandmothers are - or were - dysfunctional, difficult, cold, ill, or absent, I send you my heart; if mothers have smothered you, helicoptered you, tethered you, ignored you, criticized you, imprisoned you because you wanted to leave but they were needy, selfish, wanting to keep you - Temptations style, "any way they can," - and refused to let you go, you have my heart; if mothers abused you, or abandoned you, or made you feel inadequate, you have my heart. I congratulate you for being a survivor. And if you are still burdened, I can only wish you recovery, a good therapist, and this mother's love.

May this Mother's Day be a blessing. And if not, peace and love to you.

What Century Is This?
5-20-2023

Recently, I remarked on a friend's comment about a woman she knew whose unborn baby was diagnosed with anencephaly, a severe congenital condition in which a large part of the skull is absent along with the cerebral hemispheres of the brain. There is no cure or standard treatment for anencephaly which most often leads to death in days or weeks. She said that because of the newest abortion laws, the doctor was unable to help her. She would be required to carry her doomed baby to term.

In her state, there are no exceptions. Even if there were, in most states doctors and hospitals are turning away patients, saying that ambiguous laws and the threat of criminal penalties make them unwilling to test the rules.

From an article in the *New York Times*: "Studies have shown that a majority of patients who discover a deadly birth defect seek an abortion. Physicians say that patients often make this choice to spare the fetus from suffering or their families from drawn-out grief. Every state law that has exceptions uses almost identical language: "to prevent a serious risk of the substantial and irreversible impairment of a major bodily function of the pregnant woman."

This woman doesn't qualify because her life is technically not in danger. The law in her state doesn't provide for case-by-case decision-making by qualified medical professionals. She is sentenced to a long, torturous time in abortion law prison without parole. It's barbaric.

I wonder if law-makers would be willing to contribute their paychecks to the cost of carrying a doomed child to delivery, and then to its aftercare, however brief. Even a day or a week later at best, the medical bills will be phenomenal. I wonder if they would like to visit mother and child in the hospital. They could hold mom's hand, wipe her tears, then hold her dying or dead, deformed baby and see for themselves what suffering their laws hath wrought.

"We are sliding down a slippery slope backwards to the 50s," I sighed.

Then I thought, "Actually, what century is this?"

I thought about banned books (some classics) and all the prohibitive bills zooming across state governors' desks, especially Florida and Texas.

In some ways, we're all the way back to the Italian Renaissance, a 15th century Dominican monk named Savonarola, and his Bonfires of the Vanities.

While many see the Renaissance in Italy as a humanistic era of magnificent growth in the arts and sciences, it was also a time of violence, war, and political and religious corruption (sound familiar?).

Historians differ on their assessments of the famous Italian monk who ordered the burning of books, art, and everything he deemed excessive and therefore harmful. His devoted followers were many. They wept over his sermons, made huge pyres in the streets, and lit fire to it all.

Savonarola was charismatic and obsessively focused on cleansing Florence from what he saw as sin. Under his influence, Florence was on fire, beset by religious and political polarity (sound familiar?). His gloom and doom prophecies and fiery sermons called for the burning of art in bonfires during the very time that Florence was itself burning bright with the fire of a humanistic, artistic and cultural re-birth.

As for how historians have dealt with Savonarola, some see a prophet who had a profound insight into his own times, a champion of

Florentine liberty against Medici tyranny; purity against corruptness. Others see a completely unsuitable, self-deluded, if morally superior fantast, a characterization which has stuck as the more popular one for the majority of general texts on the Renaissance and Savonarola.

So here we are, sliding, sliding. We are banning books, classics, even, because they dare to talk about the truth or they use curse words. *To Kill a Mockingbird. 1984. The Grapes of Wrath.* Really?? I don't have a problem with age-appropriate classifications. But as adults, we can steer clear of books we don't like on our own.

Savonarola's intense distaste for displays of nude bodies in art could be ripped right out of today's headlines. We are clutching our pearls over Michelangelo's magnificent statue of David because, uh-oh, he's got genitals.

We are told to erase the word "gay" from our vocabularies. Guess what? Gay people are with us, and always have been. Let's acknowledge this latest return to discrimination and move forward.

Black and minority populations still suffer discrimination. We just can't seem to accept that, either.

The words "indoctrination," "radical," and "woke" are repeated so often they have become dysfunctional lyrics to anthems, memorized and repeated by followers who often don't even know their meaning. But they'll burn a book and ban a person if their charismatic leader tells them to.

And we are forcing pregnant women with unresolvable, devastating fetal conditions to refrain from resolution if those conditions don't specifically threaten the mother's life. I do not wish on anyone the pain of the woman who's anencephalic baby is court ordered to be born, dead or doomed.

Savonarola(s) are too much with us in 2023 politics. They don't belong here. Not today. Not ever.

One Man's Dream is Another Man's Worst Nightmare
5-27-2023

He awoke with a start. He had been dreaming of a young boy named Johnny talking to his daddy. Both seemed very familiar. He went over the dream in his mind.

"Little Johnny, what did you do? Did you misbehave? Again?"

"Who me? Daaad-uh!"

"Now Johnny, look at me. Did you, or did you not steal that rare, 1st edition book from the public library, the one that specifically states it's so special and private that only certain people have access to it and it's not available for check-out?"

"Yeah, dad, I took it but I returned it months ago."

"Really. Then how do you explain why the head librarian and her staff paid a surprise visit to our house, and after searching high and low finally found the book under the bed in your room? And lots of other special, private books you didn't return?"

"The library must've planted them in my bedroom!" Johnny bristled, standing flatfooted, hands on hips. "That librarian is such a loser, a total disaster. It's fake news, dad. Believe me."

"Really?"

"Pinky swear."

"Bless your lying heart, son. You need better training, boy. Not because you lied. That's OK. You just need to be more convincing. You're such a loser, but as your dad I'm going to set you straight, warp your mind forever and make you a student of the most corrupt, conscious-less friends I know."

"My lawyer will teach you everything he knows, son. Hint: never admit anything, and delay delay, delay. Meanwhile I'm sending you off to military boarding school so I don't have to deal with you. I'm busy ripping off people of color who want to rent my real estate properties. I'm fighting a lawsuit right now, as a matter of fact."

"So now, before you go, here's your game plan, son. You be sure to tell everyone how you've been falsely accused and your privacy has been unfairly and illegally invaded by a public librarian who's had it out for you since you stole those last books you didn't admit to stealing. You didn't know you weren't supposed to take them. Say that. And say they've been so unnecessarily cruel to you about it. And say that you decided they are ok to take if you say they are. And tell that to all our friends in our neighborhood who don't like the public library because you've been lied to and persecuted by them all this time. Your friends don't read books anyway."

"And neither do I, dad, if you want to know the truth."

"Truth? This family can't handle the truth, son! We're all deluded. You never get anywhere dealing in boring truth. We're more into spreading whatever nonsense we want by word of mouth as long as it serves us. Now let me hear you practice how to respond to that librarian once and for all."

"Ok, Dad, here goes, here's exactly what I'll say: This is a disaster and shouldn't happen in America. Why in the world would I want that 'valuable,' stupid 1st edition book, anyway? It's all a hoax and a witch hunt like nobody's ever seen before. Everyone should tell their friends, too. We'll start a whole thing. As student body president I'll keep lying about a lot of things. I'll say I've been railroaded and I am a victim of other people and their lies, lies, lies! We'll have a parade and rile everybody up, and they can bring their AR-15s and dress up like militia-men and get all violent and storm the library! Because if you don't fight for your right to take books and lie about it you're not gonna have a library anymore. And then we'll lie some more and call it a simple tourist tour. And if anyone gets in trouble I'll get them to re-elect me student body president and promise them all full pardons."

"Johnny, you are on your way. You could stand out there on Main Street and shoot somebody and people would still vote for you for student body president. Surely, even though you'll always be a loser, we as your parents have everything to do with your budding success as a lying narcissist."

"Oh, wait, dad, I need to grab a book off my nightstand. Now that's a powerful German dictator I admire. Glad I got a used book that had the important stuff already highlighted for me. Wonder if any of it will rub off on me? I think I'd like to be a dictator like him when I grow up. And have parades in my honor, with tanks and thousands of troops marching and saluting me. Just me."

"Johnny I will help you with that. Tomorrow you leave for military boarding school to learn all the authoritarian ropes you have yet to learn. We all have high hopes for you. The idiot neighbors do, too. Don't let the door hit you on your way out!"

"Bye dad. I'm so conflicted. But I'll not only make you and everyone proud, I'll become the most enigmatic, hyperbolic, polarizing, narcissistic, nastiest, self-serving person like you wouldn't believe; like nobody has ever seen before. Believe me. And I found all those words I just said in that library book I didn't steal. I have no idea what they mean but they sound good."

"You already are all those things, my boy. And don't give that stolen—er planted— library book another thought. Our mobsters—er lawyers— have shown us you can weasel out of anything. Watch and learn. Go forth, prosper, and plaster the family name everywhere so people think you're rich and great, whether you are or not. And if even if you're a sucky school cadet and make awful grades I might still give you a small loan of a million dollars or more to start a business."

"Tremendous. Fantastic. After you're gone, dad, if ever I get in trouble when I'm a grown up, I'll always remember what you told me."

"And what is that, son? I want to hear your take-away. Sum it up for me."

"Dad, you said to me most importantly, I should remember this: why would anyone plead the fifth if they've done nothing wrong? Only mobsters plead the fifth."

Who Are You?
6-3-2023

"What do you do?" is a common question in the chatter at a cocktail party or gathering when you're mingling.

How do you answer that?

It's usually not meant to be a deep, searching question. Do they really want to know who you are, or just what you do for a living? Two different things. Most likely, a simple job description will do. "I'm a secretary. I'm a stay-at-home mom. I'm a teacher. I'm retired. I'm a politician."

Granted, there's a time and a place for every conversation. Cocktail parties don't provide enough quality time to really get to know someone. The person who follows up later with interest and gets to know who you are is the person you'll want to keep around, and vice versa if you're compatible, that is.

How do we know who someone is?

I laugh remembering the episode from *All in the Family* when Archie and Edith attend her 30th high school reunion. Archie has been dragged there kicking and hates every minute of it. Sweet Edith is in seventh heaven. It's her high school crush, Buck Evans, she's hoping to see again.

A classmate asks Edith, "So. What have you been doing since high school?"

With perfect comedic timing Edith looks upward, reflecting, and begins with innocent enthusiasm. "Well, I spent the night at a girlfriend's house the night of graduation." Pause. Reflect. "And then… the next night…" She drones on happily until her captive finds an opening and escapes.

Meanwhile, grumpy Archie is holding down the punch bowl across the room when a bald, obese man enters and they, too, converse.

"Who the hell are you?" Archie asks condescendingly, eyeing the man's bald head and extremely rotund frame.

"I'm Buck Evans," he replies congenially.

"YOU are Buck Evans, the class hero? The one Edith pined for in high school? What the hell happened to you?" he says with a laugh.

Buck replies with a smile, "I married a gourmet cook!"

Archie brightens and gleefully fetches Edith, expecting to revel in her disappointment when he re-introduces her to the dreamboat who doesn't exist anymore.

"Guess who this is, Edith?" he asks with bated breath.

Edith looks into Buck's eyes. Nowhere else. And she smiles, and sighs, taking his hands, "Buck Evans, oh Buck how wonderful to see you!"

Archie bristles, shocked. "How do you recognize this guy? He's totally different now!" Archie whines.

Edith delivers Archie's comeuppance: "It's his eyes, Archie, his eyes! I'd know you anywhere, Buck! I see you in there! Ain't he beautiful, Archie?"

Totally perturbed, Archie takes Edith aside.

"Edith I will never figure you out. You and I see the same guy. You see a beautiful person. I see a blimp."

Edith replies, sadly, "Yeah, ain't that too bad [for you, she means]."

Archie deadpans into the camera. Cue laughter and applause.

And scene.

How do we feel about all that? Is Edith's Pollyanna innocence too far-fetched? Or should we take a beat and think about being just a bit more like her?

While refreshing, it's true, of course, that being too innocent can also be unsafe. Don't pick up hitchhikers on a lonely road at night. Don't trust a person who points a gun at you. Don't follow a politician just because he says, "Trust me."

But the bottom line is also true: The same person is either beautiful or a blimp, depending on another person's perspective and whether they have the willingness and ability to see past the surface.

The lesson we take from Edith is about seeing who people really are inside. That's the ultimate yardstick. Her high school crush must have been a sweet spirit. That's what she saw again when they met, not his size or bald head.

We should want to look past a sparkly or an ugly exterior and get to the real core of who a person is; a person we want to know better or not; whom we respect and appreciate or not; whom we want to befriend, vote for, or marry.

Love really is an active verb. Love requires action.

We can know who a person really is by looking deeper into their actions NOT by their job, their income, a slick speech, their faith, what they wear, what they weigh, their height, hair color, age, gender, ethnicity, skin color, physical or mental disability, or their accent.

Who is a person (really)? Isn't it what's inside that drives them? What have you got inside of you: a spirit of kindness, generosity, and integrity or meanness, resentment, and anger? Are you a bully or a comforter? Do you hurt others or do you help them? Do you forgive others' mistakes or do you hold grudges? We all have our boundaries, but these simple benchmarks of inner spirit may be all we need in order to know whether someone is truly beautiful.

That and maybe what they did after high school. The short version, perhaps.

52 Years
6-10-2023

Married – 52 years – June 10th. That's a long damn time. I've got a sudden urge to reminisce. Where does one begin?

One Google session can easily document landmark historical events, ad infinitum. Case in point: you can find a complete breakdown of all the years referenced in Billy Joel's genius 494-word musical history tour from 1949 to 1989, "We Didn't Start the Fire." There's even a quiz to test your knowledge. Simply go here http://www.school-for-champions.com/history/start_fire_lyrics.htm.

We didn't start the fire

It was always burning since the world's been turning...

...But when we are gone

It will still burn on, and on, and on, and on...

Our memories will always be inexorably tied to epic historical events in our lives: where were you on September 11, 2001? (In my kitchen, planning my son's wedding). On November 22, 1963?

(Home sick from school, bundled up on the sofa in my parents' den, watching TV). On December 7, 1941 or June 6, 1944 or May 8, 1945? (Not born yet, but those who were will never forget.)

And on, and on, and on…

But as my 52nd wedding anniversary approaches, I'm also flooded with memories tied to 52 years of a personal history:

—that eludes the history books;

—that, if researched in some library, June 10, 1971 will produce multiple historical references without mention that I was preparing for my wedding that morning, rising early, and sitting with my parents at the wrought iron and glass table in their kitchen for breakfast;

—that I was attempting to exercise grace under pressure as I rolled my hair at noon while my dad valiantly attended to my ailing groom, ferrying him to a doctor and then a masseur. In those days, bachelor parties were held the night before the wedding. How totally dumb was that?

—that I had chosen what I thought were the most beautiful bridesmaid dresses I had ever seen, which I now charitably admit were way off that mark. Like off the charts, off the mark. But that's ok. Everybody makes mistakes. They were very 70s, in a cheery yellow, dotted Swiss, white-sequined lederhosen-bib kind of way;

—that when my revived, handsome young groom, age 22, and I, age 21, took our vows that summer evening we really meant them, having no idea how young and naïve we were and how many times, from that day forward, the next 52 years would test those promises we made – for better, for worse, in sickness and in health, for richer, for poorer – nor how much stronger and more committed we would emerge after every difficult trial and every small success. Every. Single. One. For 52 years.

Of no great historical import to school children, or to curious Googlers, or to studious academics, or to my neighbors, or to the guy bagging my groceries, are the last 52 years of my personal marital and familial history, nor my 52nd wedding anniversary. But for me, and for us all, our personal histories are monumentally important, filled with years and years of everyday events, from the largest milestones like marriages, careers, births, deaths, and teaching our teenagers to drive, down to the smallest things, like how my baby boys' freshly washed hair always smelled like heaven.

It's a life.

Our 52nd anniversary is about celebrating a life shared by the two of us being who we are and learning to honor and support one another as unique individuals within the marriage.

It's also a life populated by the families of origin we each brought to our union, the family we created together, and our friends and extended family members of choice. That's a lot of people in one marriage.

It's about learning how to spin all those plates. It's about unselfishness and compromise. It's about realizing that commitment and kindness are decisions. It's no longer about passively "being in love," it's about love being an action. It's about finding and returning the three A's: affirmation, acceptance, and affection.

It's about learning to find a therapist sooner than later.

It's about a million shared ordinary moments, good, bad, and otherwise, the joys and sadness, the pride and the disappointments, the successes and the failures, the lessons missed and lessons learned, the mistakes and the forgiveness, the giving and the receiving, all strung together over the last 52 years. It's about a lot of hard work, respect, and great love. We have held hands, held on, lived long, and ultimately prospered.

Joseph Campbell said, "The privilege of a lifetime is being who you are."

Erma Bombeck said, "Marriage has no guarantees. If that's what you're looking for, go live with a car battery."

So… time to celebrate!

May our years burn on and on and on…

Whodunnit?
6-17-2023

Professor Plum, with poison, in the library, of course!

Just like the old Clue board game we've all played (What? You haven't ever? Pfft! Get busy!) we have a fascinating whodunnit story unfolding for real in the book world. All you bibliophiles out there who love perusing old, rare books in dusty bookstores and may have even purchased some to bring home to add to your eclectic library of ancient tomes, read on.

National Geographic published a fascinating warning: beware of old, very old green books.

They say, "These toxic books, produced in the 19th century, are bound in vivid book cloth colored with a notorious pigment known as emerald green that's laced with arsenic. Many of them are going unnoticed on shelves and in collections. So Melissa Tedone, the lab head for library materials conservation at the Winterthur Museum, Garden & Library in Delaware, has launched an effort dubbed the Poison Book Project (http://wiki.winterthur.org/wiki/Poison_Book_Project) to locate and catalogue these noxious volumes."

I don't mean to be an alarmist, since there have only been "more than 150" 19th century books tainted with toxic emerald green found thus far. However, they go on to warn that "Ninety of them are covered with vivid green book cloth, and the rest have the pigment incorporated onto paper labels or decorative features. Tedone even found an emerald green book on sale at a local bookstore, which she purchased."

They want you to be aware, at least, that out of all the books they have found, there could be more you could be handling, or selling, or buying that are waiting patiently on the shelf to beckon and then belabor your body with their toxic covers, pages, decorations, or dust.

These warnings are especially meant for collectors, librarians, book sellers, and people who handle 19th century books often. And even at that, the worst one might suffer is a spell of diarrhea and headaches (if you're lucky, that is).

But why do these arsenic-laced books even exist?

At the time, toxic green was very popular and Victorians seemed to take it all in stride. After all, there were plenty more plagues, illnesses, and lack of modern medical solutions to contend with at the time. What's one more, right?

Nat Geo explains, "Arsenic's toxicity was known at the time, but the vibrant color was nevertheless popular and cheap to produce. Wallpapers shed toxic green dust that covered food and coated floors, and clothing colored with the pigment irritated the skin and poisoned the wearer. Despite the risks, emerald green was ingrained into Victorian life—a color to literally die for."

Now this book-danger news comes as a bit of a concern to me because I love books. My home is filled with bookshelves that house books of all genres (most of which I've actually read. Don't pass that around. Besides, you do it, too. You know who you are.)

I love the recent *Wall Street Journal* article a friend brought to my attention at our book club meeting entitled, "Houses Without Tomes Aren't Homes." The sentiment rings strong and true to me. The books in my house are like family. They quietly make themselves at home on my bookshelves like beneficent old friends waiting patiently to remind me of good times, or entertain me, comfort me, edify me, inspire me, or just to converse with.

I have plenty of eBooks, too, which serve many purposes, the best of which is carrying an entire library along while traveling light. But eBooks are sterile, digital things that have no physical dominion, offer no visual comfort and no real permanence. There are no pages to rustle or to turn a corner down (sue me). And like my dear Luddite husband says of the collection of ratty scraps of paper he keeps in his upper shirt pocket and calls his Palm Pilot, "these are dependable and real, and they will never crash!"

My problem isn't culling out poison 19th century books. I don't collect those. But I am running out of room and it's time to politely ask a few literary relatives if they'd like to find shelter elsewhere. That feels so heartless, somehow. Many people I know have no problem passing down books for others to read and enjoy. Even *The Veterinarian's Wife, a Memoir*, the book I wrote has been passed around, so I'm told, for many to share and (I hope) enjoy.

But I admit, I have issues letting go. As a writer, I have duly noted Stephen King's sage advice in his book *On Writing*, in which he says a writer must edit, edit, and edit, and not find their words too precious to delete. In other words, that famous directive must be carried out: "kill your darlings."

As for my books, I will not kill mine. They are family. But I might have to find a way to let some of them go their own way, where they'll be loved and cared for by others. Used bookstore, maybe.

And the good news? I have no fancy, toxic 19th century green books.

But maybe Stephen King could use that idea in his next horror novel. Can I get credit for that?

Swiftly Flow the Years
6-24-2023

Our grandchildren aren't little tots anymore. I kinda miss them. Not that I don't love and adore them now, one swiftly approaching adolescence and the other a teen. I do.

It's just a different dynamic now.

As Grandparents of little bitties we got to be foolish and sing and play and dance and do all the things. There was no hesitation or shame over any measure of silliness. Then, thoroughly spoiled, they went back to their parents who were forced to deal with overstimulated, ever-moving autobots with an all-consuming attention-entitlement-disorder fostered at grandma's house that couldn't possibly be fulfilled at home by distracted, busy parents with jobs, chores, and carpools.

Sorry, not sorry.

Playing with little grandkids was both exhilarating and exhausting.

Pirates. Sword fights. Singing. Sandboxes and swings. Backyard picnics. Root beer floats. Puppet shows. Treasure hunts. Parades through the house. Fireflies. Storytelling. Books and blocks and Candyland. Laughing.

After they'd gone home, a sudden, muffled quiet like the kind you get after a foot of fallen snow settled itself through the house.

Rick and I would collapse together into the soft snowbank of our sofa in the den to rest and recover. As our bones and brains stopped vibrating we happily wrapped ourselves in the warmth of shared memories from our day with the little boys.

Should someone drop in on our conversation they would've declared us nuts. And maybe we were. Crazy for those toddlers.

The boys had a favorite book, *Today is Monday*, by Eric Carle.

It had Carle's trademark vibrant images, and each day of the week was attached to a certain meal. The recitation became more fun as each day and its meal got added to the list. There was even a tune to accompany the words if one chose to sing. Of course I did. Are you kidding me? Kid songs were my thing.

My Achilles heel was, always has been, and always will be, suddenly forgetting a lyric or two, slap in the middle of a song, my brain going into a momentary state like a split-second food coma after Thanksgiving dinner, all mushy and flabby and needing a nap.

After all these years, one memorable, delirious conversation with Rick after taking a little one back to his house went something like this:

Me: (stretching out on the quiet sofa-snowbank as Rick joined me there) "What is Monday?"

Rick: "I don't know. What do you mean?"

Me: "Well, is Monday spaghetti?"

Rick: "Ohhhh. No, Monday is .....? Wait..."

Me: "See you don't remember, either."

Rick: "Ok then. But Friday is fresh fish, and Wednesday is soooo-oop. I know that much."

Me: "I want to say green beans. Something's telling me the eeee sound in green beans goes on Monday.

Rick: "Why would eeee mean beans go on Monday? Could just as easily be spaghett-eeee."

Me: (as if this entire dialogue mattered) "Ok, you're right. We need to go get the book from the bookshelf and look it up. Again. Why can't I remember the order? I've sung it with Harper every day from the time he was 2 until he was 8 or 9 and he'd just as soon not, now. And Sawyer is still singing it. Just today, in fact."

I flipped the pages in the oversized picture book.

Me: "Here it is! Look!" (singing, now) "Today is Monnnnday! Monday green beans, Tuesday spaghetti, Wednesday soo-oop, Thursday chicken, Friday fresh fish, Saturday roast beef, Sunday ice cream! All you hungry children come and eat it up!"

Rick: (deadpan) "Ok, well I feel better. Catchy tune, too"

Me: (too excited and delirious to catch the sarcasm; also unable to admit this is what passes for conversation after an exhausting day with little tots) "Yep, but I've always been a little bothered by the beans being on Monday. They obviously belong on Saturday with the roast beef. But that would be two things on the same day and mess up the rhythm. Too late to change it now, though. It would be sacrilege. This is codified, sanctified, and written in the stone we carved of Harper's childhood."

Rick: (smiling, clearly amused) "As you wish, princess. You take your children's books seriously, don't you?"

Me: "Do I sound crazy?"

Rick: (not missing a beat) "Yes."

Me: (also not missing a beat as I lay my head back against the snowbank cushion of our sofa, finding his shoulder to lean on) "Then so be it."

R: (now pacifying the idiot savant sharing his snowbank and clearly moved while tears filled his eyes) "Seriously, though. There have been so many songs you've sung with them, Babe. What a gift. Look at our own boys, grownups. Actual responsible adults. They both sing beautifully and love to sing. You did that with them while I was working so much and I just wasn't here. And now I'm glad we both get a crack at our grand boys. A do-over. It is so fun to watch them when we crank up a song together. Today is Monnndayyyy…"

Me: "Well look at you. And there we are, back to Monday. Full circle. You, me, and happy songs, happy times, happy memories. Together. And in the end, the love you take is equal to the love you make.

Rick: "That's a special sentiment. What made you think of those words?"

Me: "Oh, there are just some lyrics you never forget."

Rick: "Love you."

Me: "Love you too."

Rick: "Let's take a nap."

Rumi's Notion
7-1-2023

These are some great words to live by:

-If you think you're a person of some influence, try ordering somebody else's dog around..

-Live simply. Love generously. Care deeply. Speak kindly.

-Don't pick a fight with an old man. If he is too old to fight, he'll just kill you.

With all of those words in mind, though, the byword today is Anger. Anger is what's happening these days. People are mad. About a lot of things. Too many folks have consigned themselves to common, belligerent, self-serving rhetoric as a way to try and effectively persuade some and debase others. The whole anger-speak exercise is inelegant but it appeals to some people.

Borrowing a phrase from Shakespeare, I see, hear, and feel the slings and arrows of outrage in today's furious language and behavior.

The medieval sling was a frightful weapon, sending a rock whizzing your way, a la David and that big giant. If it didn't kill you it would maim you and it would be painful. The single arrow might kill as well. And if not it would be deeply embedded somewhere in your body and the pain would be unbearable and drive you crazy.

This is today's angry, violent rhetoric in a nutshell.

I try being kind. I am human and don't always get it right. But I try.

And if my opinion doesn't fit your narrative, I'm not slinging a rock at your forehead. Please don't sling one at mine. It's disrespectful, and it's mean.

Base, crude, accusatory language serves a purpose, of course. This language aims to appeal to people who thrive on opinionated outrage, anger, and who do not understand the embedded sophistry, taking a sliver of truth and bending it to create a false narrative. Slinging outrageous arrows riles up those who agree with an opinion and means to wound or conquer those who don't agree.

How's that working for us? I think it's not working one bit. Vitriolic barbs and angry sentiments flung out, for example, like "Quit your whining and grow up" or "Get over it" are just not helpful.

I subscribe to Kipling's epic poem "If" which encourages people to take a high road and treat people with maturity and respect regardless of how they treat you. Keeping your dignity and your head when expressing a belief or handling an assault on your very being when others are "losing theirs and blaming it on you" is, indeed, the mark of a decent gentleman (or woman).

And I like the philosophy that it's better to present a bouquet to open a diplomatic dialogue than a bat to beat over someone's head, because in the end, a bit of the scent of a bouquet clings to the hands of the giver as well as the receiver.

The rhetoric emanating from politicians on both sides of the aisle is deeply troubling. It is disheartening to witness elected officials prioritize personal agendas over the interests of the people they represent. This type of divisive language only serves to exacerbate the already polarized climate in our society.

How about we stop dealing in a binary "right/wrong" modality? In the realm of philosophy and spirituality, the great poet Rumi beckons us towards a field beyond the limitations of right and wrong. He invites us to imagine a space where judgment and condemnation cease to exist, a place where understanding and empathy thrive. In our politically divided world, could such a field hold the key to finding solutions to our woes? Is it even possible for both parties to set aside their firm positions and meet there?

The idea of finding common ground seems almost fantastical in today's polarized political landscape. Partisan divides run deep, and the condemnation of one another has become a norm rather than an exception. It is easy to feel skeptical about the possibility of a genuine meeting of minds. However, even in the midst of this skepticism, we must not lose sight of the potential for growth and progress.

While it may seem that both parties are too entrenched in their own ideologies to budge, it is crucial to remember that politicians are representatives of the people they serve. They are accountable to their constituents, and ultimately, their purpose is to address the needs of the nation. This realization opens the door to the possibility of finding common ground and seeking solutions that transcend partisan lines.

However, to reach that field beyond right and wrong, it requires a collective willingness to engage in dialogue with an open mind and a genuine intent to understand one another. It necessitates recognizing that no single party holds a monopoly on wisdom or virtue. It requires setting aside the inclination to vilify the other side and instead foster an environment of respect, empathy, and cooperation.

Finding a solution to our political woes certainly won't happen overnight. But it is not an impossible endeavor. We must remember that the future of our nation rests on our ability to transcend the divisions that plague us. It requires brave individuals who are willing to step outside their comfort zones, challenge their own beliefs, and engage in meaningful conversations with those who hold differing viewpoints.

By embracing the principles of understanding, empathy, and compromise, we can begin to bridge the gap that divides us. It may not be a swift or straightforward process, but it is a necessary one. The alternative is to remain trapped in a perpetual cycle of animosity and stagnation, which ultimately serves no one.

Rumi's field beyond right and wrong offers us a glimmer of hope. It reminds us that the potential for unity and progress lies within our collective reach. It is up to us, as citizens, to demand more from our elected officials and to create an environment where meeting in that field becomes not only possible but essential. Let's embrace the challenge and strive towards a political landscape characterized by mutual understanding, cooperation, and a genuine commitment to the greater good.

The Joys of Travel
7-8-2023

Ah, summer vacations. Time to fly! "Let the fun begin," we command!

There is no "commanding" to be had or done in today's air travel. Relaxing air travel was another day, another time. Now it is often an all-bets-are-off lottery, often requiring nerves of steel, the patience of Job, and a sleeping bag.

Flying has always been a bit fickle, but the odds of a cancellation or delay today are exponentially worse. If you win the air-travel lottery and the gods look upon you with favor, you get short lines at security; you don't get fined for overpacking; you depart on time, arrive on time, and your luggage shows up when and where you do. Both ways. If all goes well it's a lucky victory like no other. It's like passing Go, receiving a Get Out of Jail Free card, winning Monopoly, being out of town when Vesuvius erupted, and winning a hundred million bucks in the Georgia Lottery.

Good luck with that.

The Transportation Security Administration (TSA) expects 2023 summer air travel volumes to surpass pre-pandemic levels, and industry experts are warning that many of the problems that led to last year's meltdown have not been resolved.

The weather, especially in the summer, is always a party pooper.

Data shows that February, December, and summer are the periods with the greatest number of cancellations, which the data says may be because they are often also the stormiest and snowiest periods of the year, with severe weather likely to be causing cancellations. Can't do anything about that, no matter how much Pat Robertson tried to tell us we had tornadoes because we didn't pray hard enough.

Unless we can figure out a way to move Christmas and school vacations to other times of the year, we can't do much about reducing travel numbers in December and summer, now can we?

What can we do to make air travel better, or at least less painful? We can pack more wisely.

That won't get us where we're going, but it might make our trip easier in the process. I wouldn't have been "nine pounds overweight" on our trip to Mexico if I had packed smarter. Did I come off as a pluperfect fool when I thanked the ticket agent for not guessing I had way more to lose than nine pounds? Why, yes, yes I did. In my own defense, I was ill and delirious at the time.

The growing trend to take only carry-on bags has become so de rigueur that available overhead bins are now at a premium. There's a good reason to purchase a ticket that provides early or first-boarding. Late boarding can mean no room in the Bin Inn and your bag gets sent off to the Land of Checked Baggage, which provides for accidental slips twixt bag and belly of the beast you're riding in, resulting in accidental trips to Bag Siberia.

Just now being offered is a company called "Any Wear, Anywhere." You go online and pick your outfits. The clothing will be waiting for you at your hotel. You can rent them for two weeks and leave them behind when you depart. Only one hitch: this is only available for Japan Airlines passengers who travel to Japan by August 31, 2024.

Rats. Foiled again.

I have heard of people shipping their clothes to their destinations and shipping them home. I've personally never shipped clothes, but in the summer of 2003 I did ship a whole carton of art supplies to our rented Victorian for a two-week summer retreat on the bay in

Portland, Maine. Rick took fly-rod making classes and made himself one beautiful fly-rod from scratch. I took photographs and painted nonstop, making a lot of mediocre, albeit cathartic art. Then we packed everything up and shipped it home. That did not go well. There was quite the fracas at the UPS store.

It had been raining, as only New England can rain. Endless, pouring, cold, and gray. For some reason my mind will not allow me to remember why we took our empty boxes and our stuff, planning to pack it all inside the large UPS store. No sooner had we dodged raindrops and dragged everything inside, setting ourselves up at an out-of-the-way spot in the back of the larger than usual facility than the UPS guy on duty strolled over and said "Eh, you can't do that in heyah."

"Do what?" we asked. "We can't pack in a packing store?"

"Nope," he replied. "Rules ah rules," he said, not at all apologetically I might add. "You will have to do that yahselves in the cah (car) or outside on the sidewalk. Now we can pack that stuff fahw ya, but..."

We jumped at the thought. "How much?"

Calculating, he offered up a price so high we would've had to knock off a bank.

"Have you looked out there?" we asked, gesturing toward the large windows and the sheets of pouring rain. "And we can't afford for you to pack it."

"Sahwrry," he said. "Then you just gotta take that stuff outta heyah and pack it yahselves."

I can only recall, in our 52 years of marriage, one other time when Rick Berta's face went so crimson. It was the summer Saturday afternoon we had been selling cookies at Market Day in Hogansville. Taking down a 10x10 canopy after 8 scorching 100 degree hours took him way beyond the pale.

Rick finally packed my painting stuff, box by box, leaning into the car with the car door open while he stood soaking in the rain. I was the inside man, who carted each damp box inside, and filled out the labels. Two exhausted, wet wharf rats left that place ready to give UPS corporate offices a talking to. We were so tired, though, we never did.

Now, our next challenge will be getting our passports renewed. I hear it takes months and the promise of your first born child. Wish us luck. We have an appointment for our passport photos next week, and we will be sending off our renewal papers post haste. The odds may be with us on this one. We have a whole year before they expire. And our first born child is now an adult.

UPDATE: We have returned from the photo session at our local post office and have sent our renewal applications on their way, photos attached. I look like a convict. I will have to live with that image for the next 10 years. I suppose I should be happy to live that long. Besides, I'm old. Who the hell cares.

Sunday Lessons
7-15-2023

Those who know me or have read my memoir, *The Veterinarian's Wife*, know "CBS Sunday Morning" is Church for Rick and me.

This past week, a man named Neil King Jr. bore witness with an incredible, personal story. He recently walked for 26 days on a "serendipitous, 330 mile ramble," all the way from DC to NY. He's authored a book, *American Ramble*, about what he learned along the way.

Just four words spoken in the voiceover introducing him stopped time for me. He had taken on this singular challenge, this daunting bi-pedal journey, the voiceover said, "…after surviving esophageal cancer."

When he finally spoke, his voice rattled with a hard-earned vocal fry. A visceral zing, a hot, electrical shock ricocheted through me as if I had grabbed a live wire. The high voltage current settled itself deep in my heart, burning. I didn't hear anything else for the next few moments.

My dad died of esophageal cancer in 1983, when nobody survived it. That diagnosis was always terminal back then, a guaranteed death sentence, and a short-lived one at that. From start to finish the average life expectancy after diagnosis was about 12 months. My dad was no exception. He lived exactly one year. One horrible, intractably painful, unrelenting year. It was an unacceptable standard that everyone accepted because they had to. Nobody seemed to be able to change it.

Ever since then, the grim prognosis has stayed the same. I didn't know it to be any different until last Sunday when Neil King Jr. rambled right through my flat screen and into my heart, grabbing it so hard I winced in pain and liquid grief spilled from my eyes down my face.

In that moment, I hated the fact that my dad had missed the miracle of today's medicine, the miracle that allowed a man with exactly the same disease to survive and thrive and walk 330 miles just because he could. I was happy for Neil King, but I also felt the acute pain of missing my dad, wishing he could've been as fortunate forty years ago.

Timing, as they say, really is everything.

Later, the weekly "In Memoriam" segment scrolled across the screen with photos and short bios of the notables who have expired recently. This roll-call requiem included Dr. Susan Love, a famous surgeon and transformative leader in the field of breast cancer. She died of recurrent leukemia – blood cancer. Another stunner. Now, a fearless, activist doctor with a foundation, clinical research and books to her credit, a brilliant physician with the fervor to help mankind has actually died, ironically, of the same thing she's been trying to cure her entire career. Cancer.

I imagined my dad's tribute, forty years late, inserted into the cavalcade of memorials: the picture frame surrounding his smiling image; the words displayed underneath in a bold font, "Hobie Franks, 1916 – 1983. Not famous but a good man, a loved and loving husband and father, who died of esophageal cancer, too damn young at the age of 67 before there was a cure."

When my dad died, I was 33, still naïve enough to believe that good guys are rewarded with good fortune and long lives. His illness and death taught me, then, what we all discover in maturity: not everybody – not even really, really good guys – always live long and prosper.

So on Sunday, after all the lessons were delivered, sermon and prayers done, benediction offered and postlude played as credits rolled, Church was officially over. I clicked off the TV and sat silent on my den sofa-pew, reflecting.

I wanted to get it right, the message — the lesson — I was meant to receive.

And here it is:

We don't know what we don't know. Nobody knows how long it will take to find cures for things. I didn't know medicine had progressed so far that there is now life past esophageal cancer. Dad's death felt so cruel. And it was. I didn't know if my dad died in vain, but all this time it sure felt like it.

I now know that he, along with all the others who've suffered in his shoes, contributed to the compounding knowledge that became the eventual cure for Neil King. Others, like Dr. Susan Love, and your loved ones, and maybe you, too, may do the same, contribute I mean. Small comfort, maybe, but a big deal. Maybe it will take forty years. Or a hundred. Maybe it will be tomorrow. Not for us to know.

Death comes to everyone, of course. We don't have to like horrible, terminal disease, agony, and death. But perhaps our job is to live well with the time we have; to roam and ramble with our eyes open and our spirits giving as well as receiving; to have faith there are things beyond our knowing that are working for the ultimate good, even if, through awful grief and pain, it sure as hell doesn't feel like it.

If my dad doesn't know the good news of Neil King, Jr., I will tell him when I see him again.

Blessed are those who plant trees under whose shade they will never sit.

Scary
7-22-2023

I just read disturbing news from a reliable source. National Geographic says they've discovered that ticks can "fly." Well, they don't actually fly. They won't swoop into your open window like a blood-sucking, Transylvania vampire bat. But they do travel through the air thanks to static electricity, from a pants cuff brushing the grass, or a boot creating friction. That means they are far more mobile than we knew.

Wow, what wonderful news, said no one ever.

I recall the static electricity lesson in science class that made Eddie Harper's hair stand up on end. Everybody pointed and laughed. Everybody but sweet, sensitive Eddie. He left the classroom red-faced, in abject humiliation. At our class reunion fifty years later he still talked about it, bless him.

And there was my at-home static electricity hazing when my older brother and I were kids. He rubbed a balloon on the rug and held it over my head just so he could laugh at me.

Having a buzz cut/flat top was a great defense for a fella. His hair was already standing on end. Girls back in my day didn't have that option. But watching my brother glide across the rug in his socks and get zapped good and proper by a sparky doorknob was great payback.

Why do we need to scare ourselves silly over fictional blood-suckers like Count Dracula, or those pasty, star-crossed, teenage vampires from *Twilight*?

I heard all the *Twilight* hype years ago but never read the book. Despite the rave reviews I didn't go to the movie, either. I just don't do vampires. Period. Frankly, I resent them, even those Twilight kids, celibate and fang-less, or not. Really, call me a wuss, but I don't do well with that kind of entertainment.

Reality is enough. Ticks, those little blood-suckers, are genuine, tiny vampires. So are mosquitoes. Mosquitoes really do fly. They're both too small to stab with a wooden stake, and too stubborn to be deterred by garlic necklaces or crosses. DEET spray is the true, modern vampire slayer today. And if you don't use it, you're truly vulnerable.

Ticks and mosquitoes really attack, and can make you sick, really sick. Malaria is getting its turn in the US all of a sudden, too. Thank you, mosquitoes. Not.

Years ago I went to an outdoor affair one summer in New Hampshire. The mosquitoes were as big as Buicks and felt like needles piercing all the way through our clothing. We made hasty exits indoors and cursed those little party-pooping beasts. It was an actual Alfred Hitchcock sequel to "The Birds."

Maybe people traumatize themselves in the name of entertainment with fictional predatory monsters in movies and television and books, because they like seeing boogie men that can't possibly be real. Once the movie's over and the lights come on, well, whew, "Everyone's safe! Wasn't that just a fun romp!"

In a word, for me? No. Would I ever change my mind? Also, no.

I don't do scary movies. No fun watching, and no safe harbor afterwards for me.

It all goes back about 50 years — to the seminal horror movie experience that scarred me for life. At the tender age of 8.

Our teenage babysitter pulled a stealthy movie matinée switcheroo one Saturday afternoon, and instead of the parent-approved *Tom*

Thumb, swore my brother and me to secrecy and sneaked us into the Fox Theatre for a matinée horror double-feature: *The Return of Dracula*, and *The Blob*.

I remember curling up in a catatonic ball under my seat, holding it down over me, arms against my ears, eyes squinted closed, navigating a sticky movie-theater floor and wishing fervently I could teleport myself to Disneyland.

Still, I saw and heard too much.

After that, I began a nightly bedtime ritual. For years, bless my heart, I laid me down to sleep in wide-eyed, mortal fear, with the light on and the covers pulled tight and high, the small silver cross on the chain around my neck carefully positioned on top of the covers. And oh, the nightmares. Pitiful, I tell you. Just pitiful.

I'm all grown up and over it now. I sleep peacefully. I'm just fine, albeit forever changed. I know my limits. I don't do vampires, (or clowns, by the way), or horror movies of any stripe.

But sometimes I do dream of finding that babysitter, shoving her into a seat and forcing her to sit through something really horrific.

Donald Trump on an endless loop, perhaps.

And now there's this scary tick and mosquito news. Actual news. Scary insect monsters have already made it into the movies (so people tell me) and audiences can somehow enjoy that they're not real. But I wouldn't know, exactly. I don't do scary movies, remember? But ticks and mosquitoes are real, and they're heeeere! Scary enough, I say. Plenty scary enough.

Car 54 Where You At
7-28-2023

Car 54, Where Are You At? Not on my watch.

Quick Car 54 lesson for the young, the uninitiated, or the TV-averse: "Car 54, Where Are You?" was a television sit-com in 1961-62 starring Joe E. Ross and Fred Gwynne as two comedic police officers, Toody and Muldoon, driving squad car #54. It was sanitized fun, but it's actually the show's title and theme song I celebrate.

The theme song, "Car 54, where are you?" is an absolute ear worm, and a grammatically correct one at that (Google it). My brother still sings every memorized word with great glee. Please don't get him started.

Why the lesson? News flash: I have a robust aversion to the ubiquitous grammar crime, "Where are you at?"

"Car 54, where are you at?" would never do in those days. The song's meter wouldn't allow it, but also, it's a grammar crime. NBC had censors back then, too.

Today, though? Oh sweet mother of Elvis, give me strength. Offenses are everywhere, every day. Any good country song isn't worth its Grammar Infraction Rating without at least one "where you at?" Extra points for each "ain't, and purty."

Wish I could take credit for the following line, but alas, I saw it on facebook, unaccredited. It's just so me:

"My life is a constant battle between wanting to correct grammar and wanting to have friends."

I know people don't like to be corrected. I pray for the serenity and the wisdom to accept the fact that I can't necessarily convince grammar criminals to mend their ways. I'm sure I annoy them as much as they annoy me. Humor helps. My sincere thanks to the anonymous author of the following meme:

Devil: "This is the lake of lava you will be spending eternity in."

Me: "Actually, since we're underground, it would be magma, and, to be grammatically correct, this is the lake of lava in which I will be spending eternity."

Devil: "You do understand this is why you're here, right?"

If people want to say or write something grammatically incorrect, they have every right. And I have every right to yell at the tv screen because a journalist, or announcer, or anyone who ought to know better says, "Where... are/is... you/he/she/we/they/it... at?"

The scenario often goes like this: "Now let's hear from Joe Reporter, who is on the scene," intones the highly compensated news anchor in suit and tie as he speaks with a trained, resonant voice.

"Hi Joe, can you tell us what's happening out there and exactly where you're at?"

My heart sinks.

"No go, Joe," I begin, my low voice in a steady crescendo. "Don't do it. Please do NOT pick up what he just put down!"

Sure enough, Joe responds: "Yeah Jeff, I'm at 111 Wherever Street and police are on their way to the scene of this heinous crime. Until they get here, I'll keep you posted on where they're at."

"Heinous," I whisper. "I'll tell you what's heinous, Joe." And I hit the mute button as fast as my aging reflexes allow. I just don't have the bandwidth anymore to suffer it.

Rick hates it when the reporters on the street start their responses with, "Yeah."

"Yeah," is just a colloquialism, but it's still a crime in Rick's professional grammar handbook, and I agree. Predictable as sweet tea at a southern supper, he shouts at the television, "Yeah?? Really? Come on! Say YES! Be professional!"

By the time he and I are done, we've both missed the reporter's incisive commentary because Rick has talked over the first part and I've muted the television altogether when they tell us "where they are at." Aren't we a pair? Send in the clowns. Don't bother, they're here.

"Where are you at?" makes me want to eat a chocolate éclair, slug down a glass of sparkling Rosé, and go for somebody's shirt collar. So, it's comfort food only for me. I would never go all January 6 on anyone. That would be criminal, too. Definitely not my scene.

People give themselves away when they say, "Where are you at?" Maybe a whole lot of folks don't even notice, or care, which is actually a large part of the problem. Ignorance is bliss. Per country songstress, Joe Dee Messina, their "give a damn's busted."

Bad grammar doesn't make its perpetrators fat. But it doesn't make them look very smart, either. Is it so hard to drop the "at" and simply say, "Where are you?" Such an easy fix in a world where easy fixes are few and far between.

But you do you. Some of us will take note. We will bless your heart, put our fingers on our eyelids to stop the twitching, and wish we didn't care. Then we will acknowledge a losing battle and crave sweets, spirits, or Lay's wavy potato chips. Some of us may even give in to all three.

Bottom line: "Where are you at?" is criminal. Period. Adding a pejorative nickname like, "Where are you at, Space Biscuit?" Still criminal.

Sadly, perpetrating this crime may eventually alter the English language, the global lingua franca – a language used by people with different native languages to communicate with each other.

Please, for the love of Funk & Wagnalls, grammarians, and English teachers everywhere, choose better.

I will if you will. I've already lost 15 pounds. Mainly thanks to the mute button, though.

You Could Be What?
8-6-2023

I sat down with a lifelong, close friend recently for a girl chat. Maybe it was the *Barbie* movie that got us thinking. Whatever it was, she reminded me of her story.

She was sitting at the juice bar in a gym she had just joined. She was a shy, rather corpulent young adult, under 30. She had finished swimming laps, the only exercise she ever did there, because it was the only exercise that suited her. There would be no sweaty musclemen hefting heavy things in her proximity. She had the pool to herself most times so there was no one there to judge her as she walked across the pool deck in a bathing suit, and she stroked her way across the lengths of the pool, hiding her jiggling body in the waves of moving water.

So there she was after her swim, sucking down what was billed on the menu board across the back wall as a "healthy smoothie." Let's face it. It was a thick, sugary, high caloric milkshake. At a juice bar. In a gym. She needed her nutrition to be about losing not gaining weight. She was at the gym because it was supposed to be a safe haven with no food temptations for a little while. Now it had become her enabler.

She was wondering why on earth a gym would offer up something so unhealthy, so unhelpful, so triggering to folks like her. This place was all business in the front with its equipment and pool, and a veritable sugar orgy in the back.

At the time it felt almost like a conspiracy against people like her. The gym was making money off of a well-known dysfunctional cycle: pandering to sugar-addicted patrons who were constitutionally incapable of resisting.

People like her felt like they deserved a pin for bravery and an attendance award just for being at a gym. But the juice bar's caloric options would guarantee their return to the gym when they weren't losing weight and were wading knee-deep in denial about why.

Cha-ching.

Or, maybe, she thought, perhaps the already skinny, beautiful regulars didn't worry about consuming a fat and sugar laden drink. They had a kind of discipline she and others like her lacked and envied. She figured those compulsive daily gym rats knew they could work it off in their next hours-long sweat fest. In either scenario, she was a fish out of water (see what she did there?).

Feeling self-conscious and exposed out of the pool after her swim, she willed herself invisible. She reasoned she was a stranger in a busy gym, and no one would take notice of just another anonymous person at the juice bar, a person lured there, in fact, by her food demons. She ordered the smoothie and sat down.

After her smoothie was served, she noticed a muscled man wearing a woven polo shirt that bore the gym's logo stretched across his bulging left pec. Sipping the shake through her straw she watched him get up from a nearby table and head for the door. To her surprise, he turned and approached her on his way out, almost as an afterthought.

"Was that you swimming laps?" he asked. "You don't need that milkshake. You could be stunning."

As she and I talked, sipping our coffee, she paused after that statement, gathered herself, and reminded me of how that felt at the time.

A heart-racing, stomach-flipping, head-spinning fireball had ripped through her body. In that split second, she was no longer a woman who had accomplished 30 laps. She was anxious and embarrassed. Humiliated. Hurting.

And worst of all, seen.

She managed to utter a befuddled "oh, ok" as he turned and left. Maybe he had seen her face change expression. She felt like the victim of a hit and run.

"Liar, jerk" she thought. "He has some nerve. "Could be stunning," she mocked him silently. "Who asked him anyway?" She was steaming, her face burning red-hot.

She tried processing it at the time. She was, after all, on his turf, she reasoned. And he was there, ostensibly, to help. But to be addressed publicly, and unbidden, for drinking a milkshake in the very gym where everybody seemed physically fit except her, meant she was far from invisible. She was a flashing neon sign. And everyone saw her. She thought that he surely saw what he said was a compliment, an encouragement. Why could she not see it that way?

That she was not yet stunning —but could be — was no compliment. It felt like an unbidden assault. A surprise attack. It meant she was exposed at this moment as deficient, defective. And everyone could see what a living shame it — and she — was for falling so short of her "stunning potential." Even if she felt that way about herself, the muscle-man had just validated and exposed her. She might as well have been standing there nude.

That some stranger could dictate to her in such a personal way what she wasn't —but could be —simply reaffirmed her notion that she was currently a loser. She knew he meant well, but she felt like a mark on a target. The shame and embarrassment was acute. Too, his omission of any affirmation of her in her current state meant she was so far short of stunning that she was and would be deficient until she could somehow reach stunning. And in fact she never would reach it if she consumed that drink. And that just made her angrier.

She didn't know it in that moment, but those were the last laps she would ever swim at that gym. She walked out of there and never went back.

Years later, it would take therapy, 12-step programs, and a lot of willingness for her to understand herself. Before she could understand and forgive the gym and the stranger there, she would need to understand, forgive and love herself.

As paradoxical as it seemed early in her emotional education, it became crystal clear as she worked through it that before she could know the truth about anything she would need to accept herself, know and love herself, and take responsibility for every choice she ever made and would make.

She learned that admitting she was powerless over some things, like milkshakes, didn't make her a victim, either. That awareness gave her the power of insight and knowledge. She found strength and self-acceptance in understanding, followed by the willingness to take her life firmly in hand and address the truth.

She had limits. She had foibles. She had issues. She accepted the things she couldn't change; she gained not only the willingness to change the things she could but also the wisdom to know the difference. Now she had emotional tools upon which she could rely.

Sometimes even now she forgets about her training and foregoes her tools. Maybe she's grieving and just can't deal. Maybe she's happy and just rebels against making healthy choices. Whatever it is, it takes her some time to get through it and time to get back on track.

But once you know, you know.

She knows too much now. She knows the power of acknowledgement and faith. She knows that she need not stay derailed forever. And each time, she re-polishes her tools as she works her way back to serenity and sanity. She surrenders to her Higher Power and remembers she is valued, loved… and yes, stunning.

With that, she reminded me I am, too, and so are you, whoever and wherever you are.

And not only that, she knows she has been all those things since the day she was born. So have we all.

www.ingramcontent.com/pod-product-compliance
Lightning Source LLC
Chambersburg PA
CBHW030543080526
44585CB00012B/237